CURRENT CONTROVERSIES IN MENTAL HEALTH AND ADDICTIONS: AN EXPERT'S ANTHOLOGY

LLOYD SEDERER, M.D.
Columbia University

cognella® | ACADEMIC PUBLISHING

Bassim Hamadeh, CEO and Publisher
Kassie Graves, Director of Acquisitions
Jamie Giganti, Senior Managing Editor
Miguel Macias, Senior Graphic Designer
Kassie Graves, Acquisitions Editor
Claire Benson, Project Editor
Elizabeth Rowe, Licensing Coordinator
Christian Berk, Associate Editor
Kat Ragudos, Interior Designer

ISBN: 978-1-5165-5693-9

cognella® | ACADEMIC PUBLISHING

CONTENTS

AUTHOR'S NOTE

Cancer has been called the "Emperor of all Maladies." But its pride of place is eclipsed by mental and addictive disorders, which should be called the Zeus of all maladies. Their ubiquity, suffering, burden, and social and financial costs are the measures that demonstrate their painful hegemony in the world of chronic diseases.

Mental health and substance use disorders are now also more in the mainstream of public and media attention. Often this is because of sensational or horrific events (like mass murders), celebrity gossip, or the reporting of their losses to these conditions, or the plight of our veterans. Yet, as meaningful and prominent as all of these are, they do not convey how terribly common these conditions are, or the massive impact of mental disorders, including addictions, on personal and family suffering, individual and collective social and financial burdens, and the losses of societal contribution at school, work, and the economy that result from untreated mental and addictive disorders.

An estimated 20% of adults in the US experience a mental illness each year that impairs their functioning. That is in excess of 40 million people. Yet, fewer than 40% receive any form of treatment, and when it comes to the frequent and potentially disabling condition of depression, less than one in five affected people receive anything that meets the standard of "minimally acceptable care."

For substance use, an estimated 21 million people annually, ages 12 and older, have a Substance Use Disorder in this country. Nearly 8 million people have both a mental and substance use disorder. Here the gap between need and service provision is even more gaping: Fewer than one in ten people with a substance use disorder receive *any* treatment. Overdose deaths from opioids now exceed motor vehicle accidents in this country. The tragic irony is that both mental and addictive disorders are highly treatable, now more than ever as evidence-based treatments and more comprehensive care are being delivered by clinicians and clinics. Effectiveness studies indicate that treatment for mental conditions match the results achieved in general medical care for a variety of chronic illnesses like heart and lung diseases, diabetes, and cancer.

The death toll from suicide in the US is over 42,000 people year; it is the only preventable major cause of death that has been going up for years. Suicide deaths globally are estimated to be a staggering 800,000 each year.

These are chilling statistics, but they are abstractions. Think of people you know and love who have been affected. Think of their families. Think of their friends and co-worker. Here, the realities are grave and palpable. Their stories are too often heartbreaking.

In short, there is clearly a lot of work to be done. And you are the future of our fields. We will need your dedication, knowledge, innovation, and hard work in clinical and administrative settings to close the gap between what we know and what patients actually receive when in clinical care. Delivering what needs to be done to increase access and improve the lives of people affected, and managing services well to prudently employ resources to better save lives and even save dollars are essential elements in the work ahead.

But as Andre Gide said, "One doesn't discover new lands without consenting to lose sight of the shore for a very long time." That means that you will have to stretch, leave your comfort zones, and rise to the clinical and public health challenges we all face. I hope some of the readings here, the ideas offered, will help you in your journey.

Lloyd I. Sederer, MD

PS: Many of the articles reprinted below do not have links embedded to the additional material that was supplied in the actual publication. However, the citation to the original material that appears atop all the individual articles can take you to them, where these additional links will be accessible.

OPENING COMMENTS

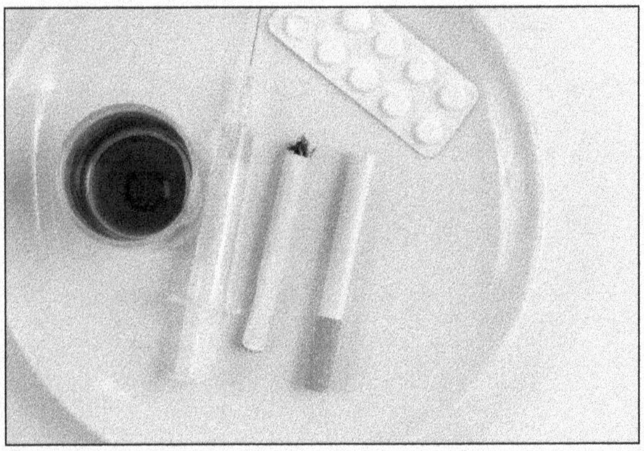

VARIETIES OF DRUGS

I believe that the use and abuse of, and the dependence on psychoactive substances is one of a handful of the most pressing social issues we face, in this and many other countries—up there with climate change, immigration, hunger, and terrorism.

In this section, I compile opinion pieces, blogs, and movie and TV reviews I have written for the general public dating back a half-dozen years or so. Some of the older pieces seem as timely as the newer ones. But they all seek to understand what the primary drivers of psychoactive drug use are, what the consequences are, and how a society and its health care system can better address the epidemic of drug use and abuse. Each article has a short annotation by me, noted by LIS, at its outset.

Articles from *The Huffington Post* are reprinted in their entirety. Articles from U.S. News & World Report have a link to them, with an annotation by me describing each one and their relevance. Other pieces are reprinted with permission, and are also annotated.

Each article can stand alone or be read with others for information and discussion.

I hope you enjoy them and use them well.

'NOT FOR HUMAN CONSUMPTION' — SYNTHETIC PSYCHOACTIVE DRUGS

Lloyd Sederer, "'Not for Human Consumption' -- Synthentic Psychoactive Drugs," The Huffington Post, ~4.

LIS: Synthetic psychoactive drugs are dominating emergency rooms and newspaper headlines as their availability, affordability and popularity grows, especially among youth as well as impoverished and mentally compromised individuals. This article identifies the next generation of synthetic drugs, particularly those that mimic marijuana and amphetamines, in the pipeline. The future is not looking so good.

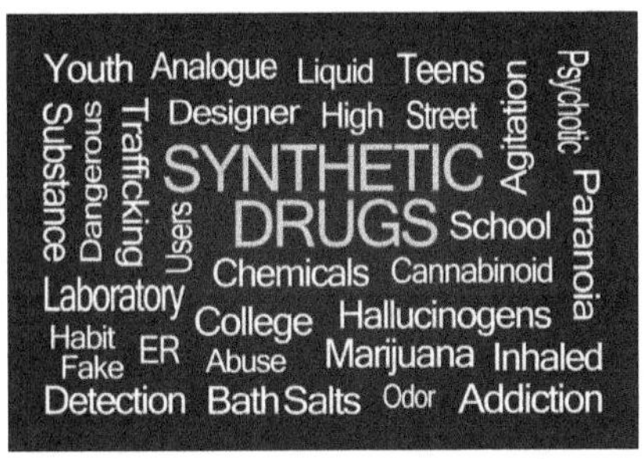

SYNTHETIC DRUGS

We have heard a lot about K2 (Spice, Black Mamba and other quaint names), the synthetic "marijuana" that has been ravaging people and cities. And about Ecstasy and other illegal stimulants that are club drugs as well as students' and "mothers' little helpers" (expression thanks to The Rolling Stones). The use and abuse of synthetic, illicit drugs has become a public health crisis that is not going away, and in fact it may become more serious.

New York City, in 2015, saw thousands of emergency visits for toxic reactions to synthetic marijuana alone (The Not-So-Nice Spice). These visits, as well as emergency calls to poison control centers, finally diminished after a major police and public health mobilization with raids on key distribution sites enabled by governmental executive orders, which shut down the major manufacturer and local suppliers.

The next generation of illegally synthesized and distributed drugs with powerful effects on the human mind (and body) is in the pipeline. New production of synthetics has ratcheted up to replace last year's drugs, in response to public health bans and criminal consequences.

Researchers recently reported in the Journal of Drug and Alcohol Dependence (1) an abundance of what they termed "novel psychoactive substances" (NPS); "novel" seems a euphemism for these newly synthesized and highly toxic drugs en route to sales and consumption, in this country and abroad. The researchers identified over 400 compounds, with 255 of them newly synthesized; their data was from the 2012–2014 European Union (EU) Early Warning System (EWS).

With perhaps tragic irony many of these novel drugs are labelled "Not For Human Consumption." They are promoted as "herbal highs" and "plant food," and sold online, in head shops, bodegas, truck stops, and from drug dealers. Another recent survey reported that near to 3 million youth in the EU, about 5 percent of those ages 15–24 had consumed NPS (2). The novel psychoactive substances span many classes of drugs but the great predominance are compounds meant to mimic marijuana and stimulants. We will focus on those two groups here.

SYNTHETIC CANNABIMIMETICS

In fact, two thirds of the novel psychoactives are "synthetic cannabimimetics"—literally "mimics" of cannabis, or marijuana. The manufacture of these drugs, most recently K2 and the like, dates back about 10 years when sold as alternatives to marijuana. The actual NPS are chemicals cooked up in fly by night labs, sprayed onto herbs, dried and packaged for sale. A good deal of their production is going on in China and Russia. Unlike marijuana, they are far more potent and last longer in the body, cheaper, promoted as "natural," and "legal" (until they are illegal, at which time they are replaced by yet another mimetic). Especially vulnerable to sale and use are people living in poverty, those with mental and addictive disorders, and youth—all of whom seek cheap, accessible and potent products. The NPS marketing, including trendy names, colorful packages, and ostensible low risk of criminal prosecution, make them truly dangerous to the public health.

The synthetic cannabimimetics already available have shown a host of serious adverse effects, as NYC and many other cities have seen. These include acute toxic symptoms such as high blood pressure and rapid pulse, nausea and vomiting, profound somnolence to the point of being unresponsive, panicky feelings, aggressive actions, disorientation, psychosis and seizures. Kidney damage has been seen, which can lead to long term renal disease. Fatalities have also been reported. These types of reactions are apt to be more severe with the new drugs because of their greater potency and duration of action, as well as their potential to interact with prescribed and non-prescribed other drugs a person may take.

SYNTHETIC CATHINONES

The illegally synthesized cathinones are a great variety of amphetamine-like drugs. Some of their early versions, also dating back almost 10 years, were sold as alternatives to pharmaceutical psychostimulants (like Ritalin, Dexedrine and Adderall). MDMA (Ecstasy or Molly) and Bath Salts add to the list of synthetic cathinones—as have other drugs more recently with street names such as Ocean Breath, Fire Ball, Sextasy, which are sold to replace or pretend to be Ecstasy.

These compounds act primarily on the noradrenaline and dopamine brain receptors (with some effect as well on serotonin). This mode of action explains their euphoric and excitatory effects, as well as their capacity to raise blood pressure and heart rate (including palpitations), sweating, insomnia, muscle twitching, dizziness, grinding of teeth, and nausea and vomiting. Paranoia, hallucinations, and agitation have been reported, and can result in emergency room visits and hospital stays. Cathinones are known to be toxic to the liver as well.

DRUGS ARE BIG BUSINESS

The EU reports on the plentitude of NPS, and the financial windfalls they represent in Europe and the US, can only predict more illegal activity ahead. That means, as well, grave medical and social consequences from the glut of new drugs we may soon see.

Most countries, including the United States, have employed a variety of legal actions to forestall the production and distribution of synthetic drugs of abuse. Raids on labs and points of sale can make a difference but only in a limited way and transiently so, since many of the labs are abroad and the points of sale can change on a moment's notice. Moreover, the drug manufacturers stay a step ahead of the law by introducing a minor modification in the drug's chemical structure, adding a fluoride ion for example, and thus becoming "legal" again, until authorities declare the latest product illegal.

In other words, supply-side efforts to control drugs have proven very limited, over decades.

Demand-side efforts, aimed at reducing consumer demand have generally emphasized public service announcements and education in schools aimed to make drugs appear aversive. We know, from anti-tobacco campaigns, that the most effective ads are those that are the most gory and distasteful (e.g., those showing dying people or those who cannot breathe or have a tracheostomy). Getting people to watch those, particularly youth, is a challenge. Peer influences in schools are generally more effective than adults or didactic exhortations.

Perhaps the strongest evidence to date for the effectiveness of demand-side approaches is in treatment. Estimates are that for every $1 spent in treatment that $10 is saved in societal costs. Treatment, however, must be comprehensive and continuous, not just a reliance on one approach or a short-sighted view that addiction is a temporary condition.

There seems to be a growing interest in fighting drug trafficking by destroying the profits of the manufacturers and distributers. The UK Editor for The Economist, Tom Wainwright, who spent years as a correspondent covering the cartels in Mexico and Latin America, describes how this might be done in his new book, Narco-Nomics, which I reviewed. In the US, four states and The District of Columbia already have made recreational marijuana legal and many more have introduced medical marijuana. We need to see, over the next few years, if legalization cuts deeply into the pocketbooks of illicit drug manufacturers, especially those selling marijuana and synthetic cannabimimetics.

The conventional "war on drugs" has failed repeatedly, cost a fortune and has unjustly targeted the poor and people of color. To better face a future with more illegal drug importation and distribution we need new ideas, new approaches to protect the public health. Perhaps at least one approach should derive from the admonition, "it's the economy, stupid."

REFERENCES

1. Zawilska, JB, Andrzejczak, D: Next generation of novel psychoactive substances on the horizon—A complex problem to face, Drug and Alcohol Dependence, 157 (2015) 1–17
2. Corazza, O, et al: "Spice, Kryptonite, Black Mamba: an overview of brand names and marketing strategies of novel psychoactive substances on the web, J. Psychoactive Drugs 2014, 46, 287–294.

WHY ARE PSYCHOACTIVE DRUGS SO POPULAR?

LIS: People take psychoactive drugs, always have, for a reason, a purpose. These are substances that, at least at first, help alleviate psychic and physical pain, isolation and loneliness, or simply offer a transient departure from the mundane and the repetitious. Understanding their purpose(s), in each person and collectively in a society, is an essential first step to offering alternatives or combating their potentially destructive effects.

Now that we, by and large, are blaming people less for having addictions we can get a better glimpse into the popularity of the substances these individuals chose.

There has been a long and cruel history that has regarded addiction—to alcohol or drugs—as a weakness of character. Right on the heels of that erroneous and harmful characterization follow many personal and social disgraces and punishments. Individuals are ostracized, shamed, jailed, and often denied many societal benefits including housing, education, employment, safety, food, health care and comfort.

But addiction is not only another complex and confounding brain disorder it is a means by which individuals achieve definitive and demonstrable changes in their brains. These alterations in neurotransmitters and brain circuits are experienced in ways as varied as relief of pain, pleasure, calm, composure and stamina—depending on the agent used and its effect on any given individual.

People use psychoactive substances for a purpose. They often select among alcohol, tobacco, opioids, stimulants, marijuana, tranquilizers, and psychedelic agents according to the affects these agents produce. People with addictions imbibe, swallow, inhale, snort, and/or inject not because they are weak but because they have a brain problem, an illness, that these drugs help alleviate, at least at first. The view that people with addictions have greater brain responsivity to substances and that impels them to abuse these drugs has been disputed. In fact, for many, their brain reward pathways are less responsive to drug intake than those who are not suffering addiction http://www.drugabuse.gov/videos/dr-nora-volkow-addiction-disease-free-will).

Tobacco (nicotine) can relax tension and helps with cognitive focus. Alcohol calms and promotes socialization (it also is a pain killer, an analgesic). Opioids do many things well known to historians of science dating back millennia, including pain relief (in civilians and soldiers), enabling of stamina, escape from psychic agonies and abysmal circumstances, and even ameliorating melancholia. Stimulants enable us to deny our need for sleep while elevating our mood and confidence; in the short run they can enhance focus and productivity. Marijuana can take a person on a buoyant high and is an effective analgesic for some forms of chronic pain and debility. Tranquilizers, at first Valium and Librium, were introduced to offer a "non-addicting" alternative to barbiturates; now a host of their successor agents provide rather prompt relief from anxiety by both relieving its mental distress and its bodily tensions. Psychedelic agents, like psilocybin, ayahuasca and LSD, produce a sense of wonder that we often leave behind in childhood.

I do not mean to glamorize these drugs. Instead, I seek to stress the nature of their attraction to us humans with our panoply of sufferings and desires. If we can appreciate the utility of drugs we can develop new strategies to combat them that may be more successful than the failed efforts to control their production and distribution (http://www.usnews.com/opinion/blogs/policy-dose/articles/2016-04-19/substance-use-treatment-works-better-than-any-war-on-drugs).

For example, psilocybin has been researched for many years at The Imperial Medical College (London) as well as at Johns Hopkins, NYU and Stanford. Initially, it was to assist terminally ill patients who were suffering emotionally from the imminence of their death. Now, work is underway for its use in treating addictions, as well as for depression and obsessive-compulsive disorder (Michael Pollan, The New Yorker, http://www.newyorker.com/magazine/2015/02/09/trip-treatment) (1).

For example, a recent medical journal report and accompanying editorial (2,3) discussed the use of opioids for the many cases of depression that do not respond to conventional treatment with medications and therapy. An Op-ed in the New York Times by Dr. Anna Fels added their potential in treating Borderline Personality Disorder, which produces chaotic and self-destructive relationships and behaviors (4). These reports identified a synthetic opioid introduced into this country over a decade ago, buprenorphine (called Suboxone when combined with an opioid blocker to help prevent diversion, abuse and overdose), as a possible treatment that we have now, not one that awaits discovery. All urged caution as well as exploration.

Alternative measures to reduce pain are not confined to chemicals, though most alternatives would also likely act on the brain's chemicals and circuits in ways that resemble ingested drugs. One particularly promising, and ancient, approach is Mindfulness (and Mindfulness Meditation), which, for example, was studied and shown to be effective in people with chronic low back pain (5). Other researchers, using imaging techniques, determined that Mindfulness induced pain reduction was associated with parts of the brain that control thinking and emotional regulation. When these researchers administered naloxone, which blocks our internal opioid response, to the study participants the meditation still worked, suggesting that it was doing the job of pain relief in our brain in a different way (5).

Our species is quite extraordinary in its capacities for thinking, emotion, awareness, empathy, adaptiveness, mastery and resilience. But we are merely human: we have our pains and pleasures, our griefs and discontents, and our mental and additive disorders. These are not apt to simply vanish or suddenly abate from further efforts to try (futilely) to "say no" or control access to them. Solutions to our psychic and physical ails need to start by recognizing that people are driven to get what they need, often at any cost. That understanding can be the gateway to seeing an end to addiction as we have known it.

REFERENCES

1. Novel psychopharmacological therapies for psychiatric disorders: psilocybin and MDMA: Mithoefer, MC, Grob, CS, Brewerton, TD, Lancet Psychiatry 2016; 3: 481–88
2. Opioid modulation with buprenorphine/samidorphan as adjunctive treatment for inadequate response to antidepressants, Fava, M, Memisoglu, A, et al, Am J Psychiatry, 2016: 173:499–508
3. An Opioid for Depression? Kosten, TR, Am J Psychiatry, 173:5, May 2016
4. Can Opioids Treat Depression, Fels, A, NYT, Sunday Review, June 5, 2016, p10
5. As Opioid Prescribing Guidelines Tighten, Mindfulness Meditation Holds Promise for Pain Relief, Jacob, JA, JAMA, Medical News & Perspectives, May 20, 2016.

BETTER LIVING THROUGH PSYCHEDELIC CHEMISTRY? LSD, PSILOCYBIN AND KETAMINE IN THE HEADLINES

LIS: Whether you consider psychedelic drug use to open the doors of perception or to shut down the "default network" in the brain (see below), substances like LSD, psilocybin, ayuasca and ketamine offer recreational, therapeutic and mind-expanding opportunities. These are psychoactive substances that open closed doors and for some open the mind and the heart.

> "Taking LSD was a profound experience, one of the most important things in my life. LSD shows you that there's another side to the coin, and you can't remember it when it wears off, but you know it. It reinforced my sense of what was important—creating great things instead of making money, putting things back into the stream of history and of human consciousness as much as I could."—Steve Jobs

MAGIC MUSHROOMS

The Centre for Neuropsychopharmacology at the Imperial College in London recently reported a study of 20 healthy volunteers who received LSD, not on a blotter but administered IV, on one occasion and a placebo on a second occasion. The pharmaceutical quality LSD produced "robust psychological effects"—as we would imagine (the placebo did not)—not just right away but notably two weeks after the drug was taken: The study reported increased optimism and openness two weeks after taking LSD. While the acute effects (at the time the drug was administered) included psychotic-like thinking (e.g., paranoia and delusions), these did not persist, and curiously the subjects did not report distress but rather were apt to describe a positive mood and even a "blissful" experience

LSD exerts its neurochemical effects on our brain's serotonin system. One particular serotonin receptor, 2A, seems to be central to its effects because if it is blocked by an antagonist specific to this receptor site the psychedelic effects of psilocybin (another drug that amplifies serotonin action in the brain) do not occur.

The London research subjects were screened to exclude people under 21 years of age, with histories of mental and substance use disorders themselves (or in their families), having a significant general medical condition, or being pregnant. But that does not exclude a lot of people who might consider taking LSD. The authors, incidentally, are not new to the science of psychedelics and in seeking routes to change our reality in beneficial ways. More about this shortly.

LSD is not the only mind-altering agent that has been making headlines.

Another is psilocybin, or "magic mushrooms," which has been used at Johns Hopkins and New York University (as well as by the Imperial College) for the treatment of anxiety in cancer patients. Researchers at UCLA have also done pilot work using psilocybin for smoking addiction. Over 500 administrations of psilocybin at Hopkins and NYU have not produced any serious negative side effects. Some wonder about its beneficial effects on addictions other than smoking as well as its utility in treating people with clinical depression.

Still another agent is Ketamine, which has had considerable media attention for its rapid treatment of resistant depression. It has long been approved by the FDA as an anesthetic agent for surgery. Ketamine has also been shown to have prompt effects in diminishing the symptoms of obsessive-compulsive disorder (OCD), a seriously emotionally painful and functionally impairing condition. The problem here is that it generally does the job for a week, then the effects disappear calling for weekly administration if it is to provide ongoing help. Ketamine does not act through the serotonin system; instead, its action is by the glutamate receptor (seldom discussed despite its ubiquity in the brain). Ketamine has been used as a club drug, often called Special K, because of its euphoric effects. Ketamine is different from the club drug Ecstasy, or MDMA, which is a highly addictive, stimulant-like drug.

What is fascinating about the research on psychedelic drugs is the conceptual thinking scientists have offered—beyond what receptor site the drug may impact.

American author Tom Wolfe wrote: We're shut off from our own world. Primitive man once experienced the rich and sparkling flood of the senses fully. Children experience it for a few months-until "normal" training, conditioning, close the doors on this other world, usually for good. Somehow, the drugs opened these ancient doors. And through them modern man may at last go, and rediscover his divine birthright ..."

Neuroscientists, including Washington University professor Marcus Raichle and others, tend to be less poetic than Tom Wolfe. They have proposed what is called the default-mode network. I recently watched my 4-year-old nephew run around excitedly, full of wonder at the world around him. He was joyous—at least until he got too tired and then he was a pretty unhappy camper. But soon, as he ages, inescapably for his sake and that of civilization, he will be drained of this wonder by the default-mode network. We need this layer of brain tissue, which develops as childhood proceeds, to exert an inhibitory effect on our emotions and impulses. Otherwise, we would be at the mercy of predators and never get to school or work on time. The default-mode network has been likened to an "orchestra conductor" or "corporate executive" in the brain that manages our mental state and enables us to function in the real world.

What the psychedelic drugs appear to do, supported by functional MRI studies, is to transiently shut down the default network, allowing us to enter a world freer of constraint and control and one redolent with wonder. Bliss, some call it. Remarkably, as well, the effect of disabling the default network can be enduring. Research subjects, not only Steve Jobs, report that their overly controlled states of mind, including those with addiction or OCD or even those of use whose doors of perception may simply be too closed, are more flexible, open and even happier after using psychedelic agents. Excessive control seems to have its limits.

Hunter Thompson, the founder of gonzo journalism and the author of Fear and Loathing in Las Vegas (and other audacious works) commented: "As for LSD, I highly recommend it. We had a fine, wild weekend and no trouble at all. The feeling it produces is hard to describe. 'Intensity' is a fair word for it ... just sit in the living room and turn on the music—after the kids have gone to bed. But never take it in uncomfortable or socially tense situations. And don't have anybody around whom you don't like."

I am not recommending finding a local drug dealer or knocking on the door of your neighborhood university brain researcher to get some LSD, psilocybin or Ketamine. But like many others, I am hoping that what we learn from these drugs might open new pathways to treat some very disabling mental and additive conditions, enable some of us to quiet our fears when ill with cancer or close to passing, and possibly add a touch more creativity and flexibility to our world.

THE FIVE SIGNS, FLOTUS, POTUS, ROCK & ROLL AND BRIAN WILSON

LIS: When the President and First Lady of the United States and Brian Wilson (the famed musician and composer of the Beach Boys) team up to make a difference that's something to pay attention to. Their cause, here, is to promote the "5 Signs" that anyone can know to be able to tell if a friend or loved one is suffering emotionally and may need help. There is a route to 'Good Vibrations' for those in distress.

> "Not feeling like u?"
>
> "Feeling agitated?"
>
> "r u withdrawn?"
>
> "Caring for yourself?"
>
> "Feeling hopeless?"

These are Five Signs that may indicate that someone you know is suffering emotionally and may need help. Each has an emoticon that depicts the sign. They all can be understood and can serve as a bridge to reaching out to someone in trouble.

First Lady Michelle Obama (FLOTUS) and President Obama (POTUS) each have spoken out with their support of The Campaign to Change Direction (www.ChangeDirection.org). The 5 emoticons for these signs can be viewed at their website.

FLOTUS's letter (shown here in full) states " ... individuals across our country and around the world will have the opportunity to learn more about the 'Five Signs' of emotional suffering and engage with this important campaign."

POTUS, at the National Convention for Veterans of Foreign Wars, adds his unequivocal support for recognizing the signs of mental distress and being able to respond to those who are suffering—pick up video at 28:20 to hear the President speak about the 5 Signs). And the numbers of people with mental problems, and their families, are legion, as both the Obamas recognize from the unending news of suicides, violent acts, and human and economic costs from untreated mental conditions in this country.

At first I thought, oh, another campaign, that's a good thing but we have many of those. But then I discovered what's different about The Campaign to Change Direction.

First, it amplifies the work of 150 organizations (to date, and growing). Each participating organization signs on to spread the Five Signs to their specific audiences and constituency. Partners include The National Alliance on Mental Illness (NAMI), Justice for Vets, Easter Seals, the Federal Substance Abuse and Mental Health Services Administration, The American Foundation for Suicide Prevention, Bell Canada, The National Council on Behavioral Health, Active Minds, The JED Foundation, The National Association of Drug Court Professionals, The American Red Cross, The American Psychiatric Foundation, The American Academy of Child and Adolescent Psychiatry, The American Psychological Association, Aetna, and many others. The idea is to accelerate change through collective impact. The Campaign's goal is to reach 30 million people in 5 years; they reached 15 million in six months. That's collective impact.

Second, the Campaign capitalizes on the good will and generosity of notables. Having the President and First Lady is no small start. Another supporter is Brian Wilson (and his wife Melinda) whose fame dates back to the extraordinary success of The Beach Boys, where he not only sang falsetto but wrote and arranged much of their breakthrough music (Not So Good Vibrations: 'Love & Mercy'—The Brian Wilson/Beach Boy Movie). Mr. Wilson has been vocal about his problems with mental illness and addiction, and his road to recovery. He will perform in concert outside of D.C. on November 4, with the proceeds to benefit Give An Hour (a national non-profit organization that provides free mental health services to our men and women in the military and veterans' communities). Give An Hour, now 10 years old, is the backbone organization of the Campaign To Change Direction; both are the creations of Barbara Van Dahlen, PhD.

I had a chance to speak with Brian and Melinda Wilson about the film, Love and Mercy (which starred John Cusack and Paul Dano, as the older and younger Brian, Paul Giamatti, and was directed by Bill Pohlad) and about the Five Signs Campaign to change the culture that surrounds mental disorders.

Mr. Wilson remarked that his creativity had an "upside extension" from his use of hallucinogenic drugs. But he was quick to add that the price to be paid, for him, was that it " ... leaves you with hallucinations." The story in Love & Mercy, according to both Brian and Melinda, was an accurate rendering of his musical life, mental illness, and battle to recover (including the exploitation he experienced at the hands of an unscrupulous psychologist who later lost his license and had a restraining order preventing him from approaching Mr. Wilson). Mr. Wilson wants the film and the Campaign to encourage others to speak about mental illness, how treatment is available, and how there is hope for those affected—" … they are not doomed".

As a psychiatrist, I asked Mr. Wilson what he thought about another class of drugs, namely psychiatric medications. Was he on them? Yes, for depression, anxiety and sleep problems. Did they help? Yes, the newer medications have fewer side effects, he added. Did he think they limited his creativity today? No, but he thought he was receiving "mild" doses that helped and did not mute his mind. Seems like he now has the good treatment that eluded him early in his illness.

Changing human attitudes about anything is hard; we all resist change, especially if we don't understand what is happening or feel helpless to do anything about it. Campaigns that foster understanding and offer clear and simple ways to act are among our best hope. They can spread the word that mental illnesses (including the addictions) are prevalent, not the product of weak character, and that recovery is possible when hope combines with loving support, good treatment, hard work, and the tincture of time. That's a song worth singing.

HOW DOCTORS THINK: ADDICTION, NEUROSCIENCE AND YOUR TREATMENT PLAN

LIS: Because of the complexity and doggedness of substance use disorders there is no "treatment size" that fits all. Moreover, reliance on one form of intervention (whether it be 12-Step or medication) does not appreciate the multiple points of therapeutic opportunity offered by our current knowledge of brain circuits and cognitive neuroscience. A good treatment plan needs to be comprehensive and understandable to patient and family. Here's why ...

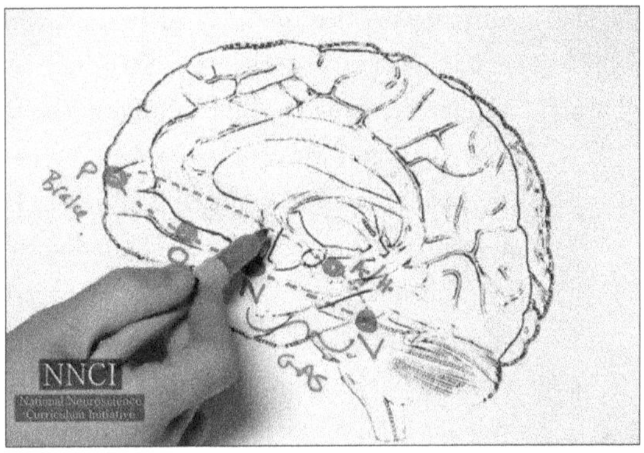

HUMAN BRAIN

Ever wonder how a (good) doctor comes up with her/his recommendations for treatment? What the critical thinking underlying the suggestions might be?

As an example, we can look at a comprehensive treatment plan for drug and alcohol addiction (forthcoming posts will look at other conditions, like depression, bipolar disorder and schizophrenia).

A premise I hold to is that comprehensive care should be a standard to aspire to as a patient, family member or clinician. Individual, proven treatments for a condition tend to augment one another (1 + 1 = >2) thereby providing a more robust response. An overreliance on one form of treatment (e.g., medications or therapy or 12-step alone), with the exception of other recognized approaches, often reflects a bias or limitation on the part of the clinician (or system of care) and seldom is in the ill person's interest.

A Substance Use Disorder (SUD) is defined as: the overuse or dependence on a drug with adverse effects on that person's physical and mental health, as well as negative consequences on others. The use of the substance, whether it is cocaine, Percodan, heroin, alcohol, marijuana or other drugs, persists despite clear and serious problems with family, work and personal relationships. Legal problems also tend to accrue.

Two related fields of science have substantially informed the treatment of a SUD—which includes alcohol and legal and illicit drugs. These are the fields of biological and cognitive neuroscience. An understanding of the brain, still perhaps the most complex organ and system we know of, has grown vastly in recent decades. We understand far better the parts of the brain, their respective functions, their neurochemistry and circuitry, as well as how to impact them. We are far from claiming mastery of the central nervous system but that need not keep us from acting on what we know. Knowledge is what a good doctor brings to an encounter with a patient, and which should illuminate the opportunities for effective intervention.

As an example, let's consider those who are dependent upon heroin or narcotic analgesics (like Oxycontin, Percodan, and Methadone). An epidemic of their use has ravaged the U.S., accounting for more deaths than motor vehicle accidents and homicides. 12-step programs (AA, NA) have been the mainstay of intervention for SUD but today represent only one of a number of tools that can help. Comprehensive care calls for more than reliance on a 12-step program. That's where neuroscience comes in. Your doctor can offer more than AA or NA alone.

Instead of approaching addiction as a laundry list of signs and symptoms, aka conventional diagnosis, a doctor can now consider the underlying brain mechanisms driving the self-destructive behavior.

This link (https://youtu.be/qqnpkycitx0) will take you to a psychiatric resident explaining how the brain works when addicted (it also mentions an anxiety disorder but that is extra). He uses the following drawing of the brain to describe how a treatment plan emerges from an understanding of the brain. The video is 15 minutes; the last six minutes focus on a treatment plan for a person with a narcotic addiction.

What this doctor understands—how he thinks in developing recommendations for a patient—is that the brain has a reward circuit that powerfully drives our behaviors. Of course, the brain is more complex but this is information for a patient and family, not a neuroscientist, and it is actionable.

Two sections of the brain (marked V & N above, the ventral tegmental area and the nucleus accumbens) signal a source of pleasure (instrumental to survival of the species—as are food and sex) by delivering a spike of dopamine. This is like an accelerator pedal. With addiction, that spike is from a narcotic not everyday life, hence the idea of how an addiction highjacks our brain from its normal sources of pleasure or reward.

The circuit then continues to the section marked O (orbital frontal cortex), which is instrumental to human drive and motivation. This region is then pumped up by the dopamine spike and gets us going, namely wanting more. It drives us to repeat the experience, even if it is a handful of narcotic pills or a needle in our arm.

But it is the P (the prefrontal cortex), where judgment and reasoning reside, that can operate to control the drive, to put some brakes on the accelerator pedal now going at a very high RPM, so to speak.

Finally, there are the A/H (amygdala and hippocampus), which are regions of the brain that store the memory of what is so rewarding. They also register what is salient to the reward; these are the cues associated with the source. Remember, Pavlov's dogs salivated, over time, to the bell not to the food, which is known as a conditioned response. It is the reward that drives us to repeat the behavior—to survive or simply to enjoy life. But the cues offer opportunities for intervention.

In a brain addicted to narcotics this circuit of five regions is pirated because opioids (heroin and synthetic narcotics like Oxycontin and other synthetic analgesics) directly boost dopamine in the V & N sections of the brain. This triggers the circuit to powerfully fire and drives a person to seek repetitive sources of the pleasure. However, that source is not love, or food, or altruism in this case, it is finding more narcotics to ingest.

Here is where the doctor can construct a comprehensive treatment plan that targets components of the circuit, and additively increases the patient's likelihood of success:

—A number of medications are now available (Medication Assisted Treatment of Addiction, or MAT) that either block the effect of the narcotic in the V & N regions (like naltrexone) or control its release to less intense levels (like buprenorphine—or methadone). The doctor may suggest MAT as one part of the plan.

—Motivation to resist desire to re-experience the spike—the O region—can be enhanced by Motivational Interviewing (MI) a brief technique that has been used in addiction for many years, and is now popular in helping people with any number of problem behaviors (e.g., overeating, tobacco use and gambling).

—The section of our brain which labors to have us use good judgment, the P region, can be substantially helped by a variety of interventions, including NA/AA, family psychoeducation and support, and promoting coping skills (like surrounding yourself with people who are not addicts, eating and sleeping well, and stress reduction practices like yoga and slow breathing).

—Finally, the A/H regions can also be impacted, especially the H region. Environmental triggers can drive cravings and relapse; these include the sight of a needle or pill, contact with other addicts or dealers, commercials about pain relief, even reports of the OD death of Philip Seymour Hoffman. Cognitive Behavioral Treatment (CBT) can be very effective in enabling a person with a SUD to avoid or have a reduced response to a trigger.

A comprehensive plan for a person with a narcotic addiction would, therefore, (with the doctor employing Motivational Interviewing) offer the patient, and supportive loved ones, a plan that included MAT, 12-step recovery, family psychoeducation, CBT, and a number of wellness activities like yoga (and yogic breathing), meditation, exercise, nutritional food, as well as the company of those dedicated to life, not addiction. This is more than a menu of services, it is recommending effective action along a variety of critical brain and behavior pathways.

If I, or a loved one, had an addiction, I would want a doctor who thinks this way. A doctor who comprehends the complexity of addiction, its neuroscience underpinnings, and the variety of treatments and self-care that, when done together, can save a person, and their family, from the catastrophic effects of untreated addiction.

Is there an argument that can be made against comprehensive treatment of this sort? Not that I know of. But it does require an informed doctor who recognizes the power of attacking tough problems in a variety of ways that augment one another. It also requires a doctor who talks with, engages, her/his patient to help them help themselves. And, of course, it takes an informed patient, family, and public to expect no less.

My thanks to Dr. Melissa Arbuckle for her groundbreaking work in teaching neuroscience.

ADDICTION: THE EQUAL OPPORTUNITY THREAT TO LIFE

LIS: Addiction is the leading cause of preventable death in the U.S.A. In this article, we follow the story of a privileged young woman, Christina Huffington (daughter of Huffington Post Editor-in-Chief and media spokesperson Arianna Huffington), as she enters a life of substance abuse at age 12, progresses from alcohol to cocaine, and finds her way into recovery. She is one of those who did not succumb to their addiction.

Addiction spares no one because of age, gender, race, privilege or social status. In a pair of interviews in Glamour magazine (September 2013) and the Today show, Christina Huffington, the 24-year-old daughter of the editor-in-chief of The Huffington Post and prominent spokesperson, Arianna Huffington, told the all-too-familiar story of the progression of the disease of addiction until she was living on the knife's edge of life.

Addiction is a disease. Addiction is not recreational drug use or risky behaviors (like adolescent binge drinking or buying drugs on the street). It is characterized by alcohol and/or drug abuse (compulsive use despite clear harm to relationships, work and physical health) and dependence (where the body experiences withdrawal when blood levels of a substance drop).

Addiction is the leading cause of preventable death in the U.S., which is why, in addition to its being blind to who you are, it is the equal opportunity threat to life. Of the approximately 2.5 million deaths in 2009 in the U.S., nearly 600,000 deaths were attributable to tobacco, alcohol or other drugs. The costs of addiction to government, (not to mention families, businesses and communities, exceed $468 billion annually. Yet, and this may be even more difficult to believe, only one in 10 people with addiction report receiving any treatment—at all.

For Christina Huffington, her road to addiction began at age 12, with surreptitious use of alcohol. By the time she began boarding at an eastern prep school, she was drinking compulsively and showing, in her words, binge eating—another compulsive behavior that led to admission to a eating disorder program and return to LA and being closer to home. Then, at age 16, came that moment that people with addiction so frequently describe: that experience of using a substance and feeling like they had never before, a feeling that seemed to demand repeating, and repeating, and repeating.

Cocaine became her "drug of choice," an expression in the addiction community that portrays the one drug that an addict prefers more than any other. She denied having a problem (another feature of the disease early on) and stopped after she was caught at home. But she did not stop being an addict, she stopped using—for the moment. She worked hard at school, getting into Yale, and was clean for three years until she took the next snort. It was if not a moment had passed; she was again as compulsive, and secretive, a user as she had been. That feature of going from zero to 60 right away is also characteristic of the disease of addiction. Everything else gives way to using. She developed tolerance (where increasing doses are needed to get the same high) and a host of physical problems from her daily drug abuse. She got scared and told her mother. That is the first step in recovery: admitting you have a problem.

The next step was rehab, the beginning of a journey in recovery where it is not the drug a person faces but who they are, and what it is about them they use the drug to bear or run from. Rehab also begins a process of turning to others for support, and not only to stay sober—though that is essential. Many people in recovery, though not all, follow the 12-step approach familiar to many from AA, NA (Narcotics Anonymous), and Alanon. Rehab begins a process of learning to live a drug-free life, one where love, work and purpose serve as the natural highs we all need. For sure, the first time in rehab is not the one that works for many people. It can take a number of tries at being clean and sober, at living a life of recovery, before the process takes hold. Experienced clinicians know not to give up hope even though it can be very hard to predict when recovery will really kick in; people with addiction, and their families, need to know this as well to stay the course, to not abandon hope, to persist and be there when a person wants to try again.

What we don't want to see or admit, we do not confront. Within a family and within our culture, tackling addiction starts with detecting it. Simple screening tests for alcohol, drugs and tobacco exist and can be made standard practice throughout medical care (and in educational and counseling settings). SBIRT—Screening, Brief Intervention and Referral for Treatment—is a recognized, proven and even reimbursed medical procedure that awaits general use despite the consequences we suffer from not using it.

There are many paths for people to take to addiction recovery. No one size fits all. For some, 12-step programs are lifesaving. Others benefit from medications that aid in remaining drug free (called medication assisted treatment, or MAT) coupled with psychotherapy. We all, not just addicts, need to surround ourselves with people who want to support our wellbeing, and assiduously avoid people who want to exploit and otherwise take advantage of us.

Addiction is America's most neglected disease. Bravo to Christina Huffington and her family for speaking out, for baring their struggle, and for offering hope to so many others.

THE 'WAR' ON DRUGS

LIS: We cannot wage a war against what is not an actual enemy. Yet that fool's errand has been dominant in the USA (and many other countries) for almost one hundred years. All that prohibition achieved was to create the enduring and prosperous institution known as the Mafia. We continue to expend vast amounts of money and resources on crop destruction, border interdiction, police "buy and bust", etc. on this 'war' despite the evidence it does not work. Moreover, criminalization of drugs has been a major method of discriminating against people of color, who disproportionately populate our jails and prisons. Drugs are what people with addictions use—they are not armies at the gate. Consider what else can be done …

WAR ON DRUGS

Can we wage war with something that is not an actual enemy, not a sovereign power or an uprising within a nation? If indeed the metaphor of war is liberally applied, as it has been to campaigns against a variety of ills, can those wars be won?

As the United States convenes its political conventions, and September marks National Alcohol and Drug Addiction Recovery Month, we have an opportunity to consider what has been called the "war on drugs." We have also witnessed the "war on poverty" and the "war on cancer," among other ails. The history of these efforts bears attention so let's take a short look at each, starting with poverty, then cancer and finally drugs.

In 1964, President Lyndon Johnson, in his first State of the Union address, called for an "all-out war on human poverty." It was part of his vision for a "great society." President Ronald Reagan, also using the grand moment of a State of the Union address, pronounced that the war had failed, saying "My friends, some years ago, the federal government declared war on poverty, and poverty won." But it took President William Clinton to reframe the problem in 1996 when he claimed the legislation passed by his administration would "end ... welfare as we know it"—principally through personal responsibility and work opportunities (more or less the name of the legislation he passed). In other words, if there was something that figuratively could be considered a war on poverty, we had lost, according to both political parties, and it was time to find not only another metaphor but also a better approach.

The "war on cancer" dates back to President Richard Nixon, who in 1971 signed the National Cancer Act that sought to find a cure for cancer. We have not won this "war" either, if indeed we can consider this effort a war. Certainly huge sums of money have funded research to end cancer. While some cancers now can be cured and others have more effective treatments that allow people to survive longer, the fact remains that after 40 years cancer remains a huge public health problem in this country and throughout the world. Sadly, we have not seen a significant decrease in the overall population death rate from cancer since the "war" began—though there has been notable progress with greater survival rates in recent decades, especially for children's leukemia and cancers of the lung, prostate and colon (in men) and breast and colon (in women), in part due to earlier detection and more targeted treatments.

It was President Nixon who first used the metaphor "the war on drugs." A combination of prohibiting drug use in the United States and military intervention in other countries, he asserted, would destroy the illegal drug trade. But notable global leaders, including Kofi Annan, former presidents of Brazil and Columbia, the prime minister of Greece, Paul Volcker, and prominent writers and policy experts, issued a report in 2011 that pronounced that "the global war on drugs has failed."

The casualties of this "war" are great. Since President Nixon declared war, the incarceration rate in the United States has increased over 400 percent, resulting in this country having the highest incarceration rate in the world. By 1994, the "war" led to one million Americans arrested each year for drugs; about one in four arrests then were for marijuana possession; more recently marijuana was the charge in half of all drug-related arrests in this country. Many states implemented "Three Strike" laws in the 1990s that mandated very long sentences. By 2008, 1.5 million Americans were arrested annually for drugs, and one in three incarcerated. There is ample evidence that our prisons are filled with people of color; African-Americans are sentenced to state prisons 13 times more frequently than are Caucasians. Former prisoners are denied access to public housing (and other benefits) and stigmatized in hiring, thereby making the road back all the more steep.

President Barack Obama, however, in 2009, claimed that the term "war on drugs" was not useful and would not be used by his administration. The White House Office of National Drug Control Policy

(ONDCP) declared, in 2011, that "drug addiction is a disease that can be successfully prevented and treated," and that "making drugs more available … will make it harder to keep our communities healthy and safe."

The proposition underlying war is that there is an external enemy (or collection of enemies) outside our borders, or a civil uprising (such as the U.S. Civil War and countless examples abroad) threatening the future of a nation. This is where the war metaphor applied to drugs, poverty and cancer seems to fail us from the very start. War was declared on these human problems without the conditions to win; these "wars" seem to have met the fate that has been said of many wars, namely that they last until politicians and generals run out of money, or interest.

Drugs are what people with addictions use—they are not armies at the gate. Addiction is "self-induced changes in neurotransmission that result in problem behavior." There is no external enemy but instead the powerful convergence of biology and social circumstance, the interplay of nature and nurture, which produces addictions (which span alcohol, drugs, and a variety of compulsive behaviors like gambling, video games and some sexual disorders).

Can we put an end to addictions, or at least greatly reduce their prevalence and burden? This seems the core question after we move beyond the metaphor of war. I believe we can incrementally achieve a society not consumed by addictions. Not by war, but by public health and community strengthening efforts.

There are public health approaches to controlling addictions. These are very different from criminal justice efforts that lock up drug users, or engage in interdiction at our borders, or crop destruction abroad. Instead, public health focuses on prevention, early intervention and effective treatment.

Drug courts are a growing alternative to incarceration for drug possession. They allow offenders to obtain treatment instead of doing prison time. Many states have drug courts, but not enough of them (the same can be said of mental health courts).

Prevention can be delivered through public education campaigns, and by fostering strong families and school programs that give youths alternatives to drugs. Prevention is also achieved by limiting access to drugs (and alcohol), but not by their prohibition (we tried that once in the United States and by the time it was ended the consumption of alcohol was greater than before it began). Limiting access is accomplished by regulation (not necessarily legalization) and what is called "price sensitivity" (the more a substance costs the less it is used, which is particularly effective with adolescents).

Science may add to our ability to limit drug (and alcohol) abuse by helping us to better understand the pleasure (reward) circuits in human brains (especially the neurotransmitter dopamine), and to develop compounds that enable those people with brains that seek substances to better achieve satisfaction in relationships, work and play; or by helping us discover and advance other interventions (including natural substances or altering the brain with yoga, meditation or other ways of producing calming brain patterns).

Early intervention means detecting addictive behaviors early and initiating help as soon as possible. Screening for alcohol and drugs is apt to become standard practice in primary care settings because that is where it is most apt to be discovered, insurance payment now possible for doing so, and where motivational techniques can help those who screen positive reduce their intake or seek treatment.

For those who already have developed the disease of addiction, we know that treatment can work—and that there are many roads to recovery. These include 12-step programs (like AA and Narcotics Anonymous), medications that can reduce craving and assist with maintaining sobriety, recovery treatment programs, and a host of nutritional and non-Western approaches. The evidence is very strong that the longer a person stays in treatment the more likely he or she is to succeed. Greater emphasis (and funding) for treatment, rather than interdiction and prisons, is more likely to reduce the impact of addiction on our society.

Perhaps the greatest challenge, and one that does not comport with "war," may lie in the strengthening and revitalization of families and communities. Neighborhoods that have been scourged by poverty, crime and improbable exit from the "'hood" are breeding grounds for addiction. The prospect of a life with work, purpose and dignity, with the hope that has inspired centuries of classes of people to move beyond the limits of their current realities, may be the most difficult yet the most powerful anodyne to addiction that exists. When war can be put aside, real and metaphorical war, we stand to find better ways (and more money) to change communities, to give youth and adults opportunities to succeed, and to fashion a life where addiction will be seen as the enemy of success, rather than as a comforting friend.

ADDICTION: HELP YOU CAN GET BEYOND 12-STEP AND CONVENTIONAL WESTERN MEDICATIONS

LIS: This article is an introduction to a Huffington Post series on addictions. The series considers not just 12-step programs and the prescription of medications. It also touches on alternative and non-conventional recovery paths for people with compulsive and addictive behaviors, often called "complementary and alternative medicine" (CAM). Addiction is hugely prevalent, and profoundly undiagnosed and inadequately treated. In the USA only one in ten youth and adults receive treatment that could lead to recovery.

> "Every form of addiction is bad, no matter whether the narcotic be alcohol, morphine or idealism."
>
> —C.G. Jung
>
> "When you can stop you don't want to, and when you want to stop, you can't ..."
>
> —Luke Davies

The concept of addiction has evolved from its ancient roots in alcohol and drug dependencies to what now has been aptly called " ... self-induced changes in neurotransmission that result in problem behavior." (Milkman, H.) What continues to astound so many is that these ruinous, compulsive behaviors persist despite their obvious—at least to others—painful consequences. Quite amazingly, the addict in the throes of addiction may be most blind of all to the losses he or she incurs in love, health, work and everyday life—that is, until recovery begins.

Because there is magic in naming, old habits can die hard about what we call an addiction. "And Rumpelstiltsken was his name ... " said the imprisoned queen, and by uttering his name she freed herself and her child and destroyed that greedy creature. Even great wizards and witches of Harry Potter fame trembled at the name of Voldemort! Addiction too is a name (and thus a concept) with great power and one that needs changing: It is time for its updating. Addiction is more than alcohol and drugs. Addiction is a complex phenomenon with expression in a multitude of compulsive behaviors. Addiction is also the end point of the convergence of a ménage of brain, behavior and social forces. Addiction today needs to be considered anew, and so should be its remedies.

The director of the National Institute on Drug Abuse, Dr. Nora Volkow, writes that there is good evidence for non-substance-induced addictions. Dr. Volkow wrote the brain is:

" … composed of a finite number of circuits for … rewarding desirable experiences … So it is almost by necessity that we'll find significant overlaps in the circuits that mediate various forms of compulsive behaviors. We have yet to work out the details and the all important differences, but it stands to reason that there will be many manifestations of what we can call diseases of addiction. Thus, addiction to sex, gambling, alcohol, illicit drugs, shopping, video games, etc. all result from some degree of dysfunction in the ability of the brain to properly process what is salient, accurately predict and value reward, and inhibit emotional reactivity or deleterious behavior."

Dr. Volkow was speaking to the ubiquitous presence of compulsive behaviors that we see all around us. She was talking about the pleasures that compel so many of us to act in ways we know are destructive to our lives (and to those we love) yet which we cannot seem to resist. We witness these unbridled behaviors in gambling, sexual promiscuity and porn, overeating, drug and alcohol abuse, "shop til you drop" and video games, to name a few.

Recovery from addiction traditionally has been the domain of 12-step programs, dating back to Dr. Bob and AA. More recently, recovery has been aided by a variety of Western medications that diminish craving and reduce painful withdrawal symptoms and thereby help control drug and alcohol abuse. The first one used on a large scale was methadone; more recently, doctors are using buprenorphine and naltraxone. But as we learn more about the brain and its reward centers, new methods of controlling addictive behaviors are emerging.

In this series we will consider a variety of interventions beyond 12-step and medications. We will examine alternative and non-conventional recovery paths for people with compulsive and addictive behaviors. These have been called "complementary and alternative medicine" (CAM)—but the term "medicine" seems too narrow, and we will go beyond medicine but not beyond what evidence and experience suggests can be helpful.

Addiction is a dark life, full of misery for the addict and all who love and support him or her. For those scores of millions of Americans and hundreds of millions of individuals world-wide who suffer the consequences of unchecked compulsive behaviors, there is hope; there are alternatives.

Life need not continue to be dark: "One must wait until the evening to see how splendid the day has been." (Sophocles) By reviewing a variety of approaches to addiction beyond 12-step and Western conventional medications, we hope to offer readers prospects for changing how their day shall end.

ADDICTION: AMERICA'S MOST NEGLECTED DISEASE

LIS: This HuffPost summarizes an exceptional report on the addictions released by The National Center on Addiction and Substance Abuse at Columbia University (CASA Columbia). The Report considers legal and illicit drugs, alcohol, and tobacco. It discusses prevalence, cost, and lost opportunities to close the "science to practice" gap and thus make a difference in the countless people affected, their families and their communities.

The National Center on Addiction and Substance Abuse at Columbia University (CASA Columbia) released a report on addictions today that is remarkably comprehensive and even more remarkably honest in portraying the virtually utter failure to identify and effectively treat addiction in the U.S.

The report, titled "Addiction Medicine: Closing the Gap Between Science and Practice," starts with the premise that addiction is a disease. Addiction is not recreational drug use or risky behaviors (like adolescent binge drinking or buying drugs on the street). They focus on abuse and dependence on alcohol, legal and illicit drugs, and tobacco. While the authors recognize a group of addictive/compulsive behaviors, they are not covered in this report.

CASA Columbia is a renowned research center on addiction. For the past five years it brought together a team of addiction, public health and judicial experts, universities, medical centers, and other mainstream officials under the direction of Drew E. Altman, Ph.D., president and chief executive officer of the Kaiser Family Foundation, to study and survey the field of addiction in order to give us a landscape report of such precision and breadth. Scientific literature was reviewed, extensive surveys were conducted (throughout the U.S. and an in-depth survey in New York State), leading researchers and experts were interviewed, focus groups were held, and state and federal licensing, certification and accreditation rules and regulations were examined. Care was taken to hold to high standards of analysis and evidence. In short, this is one tome we ignore at our own peril.

Their definition of addiction is alcohol and drug (including tobacco) abuse (compulsive use despite clear harm to relationships, work and physical health) and dependence (where the body experiences withdrawal when blood levels of a substance drop).

Their definition of treatment is that of psychological and social therapies (like motivational interviewing/motivational enhancement therapy, cognitive behavioral therapy—CBT—provided individually and in groups, the often highly-effective but controversial contingency management approaches that reward abstinence, and family therapies) and medications used to treat additions (like naltrexone, nicotine replacement and buprenorphine—see here and here). They do not include detoxification (typically repetitive, expensive, and often medically-unnecessary interventions that are generally ineffective in promoting recovery), peer—and religious-based counseling, emergency room and prison/jail services. Don't bother to pick up this 573-page report (more than half of which is appendices and references) if you believe addiction is a failure of will, a form of moral turpitude, or habits where people should "just get over it" (though some future campaign should try to change your mind).

The consequences of untreated addiction, and its predecessor risky alcohol and drug use, are chilling. The report concludes that:

> "Risky substance use and addiction constitute the largest preventable public health problems and the leading causes of preventable death (emphasis mine) in the U.S. Of the nearly 2.5 million deaths in 2009, an estimated minimum of 578,819 were attributable to tobacco, alcohol or other drugs."

The report also estimates the costs of addiction and risky substance use behaviors to government coffers alone to exceed $468 billion annually. Yet, and here is the most important finding of all, only one in 10 people with addiction to alcohol and/or drugs report receiving any treatment—at all. Can you imagine that measure of neglect were the conditions heart or lung disease, cancer(s), asthma, diabetes, tuberculosis, or stroke and other diseases of the brain?

Tobacco use is the leading preventable cause of death and disability in this country. But the catastrophic effects of addiction do not stop there: The report considers car crashes, where 40 percent of fatalities involve someone under the influence; the five-fold increase in prescription drug overdose deaths since 1990, where OD fatalities exceed traffic accidents; increased risk of heart and lung diseases, cancer and sexually-transmitted diseases; and parental substance abuse, which increases the risk of their children performing poorly in school and developing conduct and trauma disorders, asthma, ADHD, depression and, of course, addiction itself. Family dysfunction warrants particular notation, since addiction produces financial and legal problems (property and violent crimes) and increases domestic violence, child abuse, unplanned pregnancies, and motor vehicle accidents.

The report is exhaustive in the ways it considers legal and illicit drugs, alcohol, and tobacco. Each section is clear, compelling and exceptionally well-supported with tables and references. A thorough analysis of why we are at this deeply troubling state of neglect examines how addiction has been systematically omitted from medical care, how treatment providers are terribly undertrained to deliver a range of proven treatments, how treatment programs are not sufficiently held accountable for delivering evidence-based practices, and how private insurance payers have eluded the provision of adequate benefits and defaulted payment to the public sector. But what we need to know far beyond the inescapable evidence of how big and bad the problems are is what can be done?

The opening recommendation is a page out of every good textbook of public health. Start by detecting a problem that is—by inattention or aversion—kept out of sight. We do not deal with what we do not confront. More than 80 million people (!) in this country ages 12 and older abusively engage in substance use without meeting criteria for addiction (defined above) and represent an exceptional opportunity to intervene early and effectively, yet this is not happening. Simple screening tests for alcohol, drugs and tobacco exist and can be made standard practice throughout medical care (and in educational and counseling settings). SBIRT—Screening, Brief Intervention and Referral for Treatment—is a recognized, proven and even reimbursed medical procedure that awaits general use despite the consequences of not using it.

The report offers a set of treatment recommendations and asserts importantly that comprehensive treatment (combining psychosocial and pharmacological interventions) is generally better than reliance on one approach alone. There is an abundance of information on treatment, beginning with stabilization of the disease and continuing on to acute care with therapy and medications. The authors provide critically-important and urgently-needed information about how chronic disease management techniques extant throughout medicine today need to be applied to addiction. Nutrition and exercise are woven into the treatment approaches. AA, NA, SMART and other longstanding and effective recovery programs find their way into the report as "support services," revealing its particularly medical and judicial framework.

One finding that may pertain to readers of this post, or people they know, is that public attitudes about the causes of addiction " ... are out of sync with the science." Their survey work reveals that one-third of Americans still regard addiction as a " ... lack of willpower or self-control." We can be our own worst enemy, and local and national efforts to change minds and hearts are needed.

Further recommendations are framed as major sections on how to close the science-to-practice gap (to make happen in everyday practice what we know from science that works): commencing a national public education campaign, mandating program adherence to proven practices, establishing quality improvement tools and procedures to steadily and progressively improve program performance, insurance reform, and organizing federal oversight into one agency on addiction.

There is so much more in the report that this summary cannot cover. Among the findings readers may also want to take guidance from are on special populations (from youth to the elderly, and including veterans, pregnant women and those with co-occurring medical and mental health disorders), on parity legislation and the do-or-die role of funding prevention and services, and on education and practice standards. The report serves both as a call to action and an encyclopedic warehouse of information.

The CASA Columbia report's strengths are its veracity, clarity and credibility, the last based on the excellent science they summarize and the caliber of the report's authors. A shortcoming is that it was developed by experts in medicine, addictions, public health and jurisprudence; as a result, it does not report on the emerging and abundantly-used field of complementary and alternative approaches to addiction "treatment" (such as yoga and acupuncture) nor dedicate much report real estate to 12-step and related recovery models. Nor does the report consider how making legal substances more expensive and more difficult to get could be used as means of controlling youth drinking and other compulsive habits, though CASA Columbia did consider these interventions last year in a report on adolescent substance abuse (see here and here).

Practitioners, policy makers, educators and responsible citizens should more than consider "Addiction Medicine: Closing the Gap Between Science and Practice." It needs to become an agenda for action. Not doing so will mean that this country would have decided to continue to neglect its most prevalent, destructive and costly of diseases.

CASINOS FOR KIDS

LIS: You've likely been to these "casinos for kids"—as a younger person yourself, or with family and friends. They just aren't called that. But what such gaming centers offer, and how they offer their seductions, makes them indistinguishable from casinos. What's more, they begin to change the brains of vulnerable youth, and set some onto the path of compulsive behaviors that we call addiction.

You can hear the sounds of excitement from afar—before you see the vast well of games and the legions of children (and adults) swarming around the scores of hyperbolic machines with brilliant flashing lights and swelling sounds that rival modern atonal music. You have arrived at a casino for kids.

Of course, they are not called casinos. I am not sure what they are called—and it doesn't matter. It's what they deliver—not what they are named—that counts. Look around. Is there a window? A clock? A rectangular wall? Nope. You are in a rounded cocoon without boundaries of any sort that might ground the visitor in reality. A number of business franchises have made these settings ubiquitous and highly successful, in this and other countries.

Addiction traditionally was defined as "a chronic, relapsing disease characterized by compulsive drug seeking and abuse and by long-lasting changes in the brain" (National Institute of Drug Abuse, http://www.drugabuse.gov/). Scientists have come to understand addiction as not confined to alcohol and drugs. Broader definitions of what produces addiction are necessary to account for the variety of compulsive behaviors in youth and adults that, like drug and alcohol abuse, persist despite harmful consequences. While gambling certainly occurs without compulsiveness or harm, just as drinking does, both carry the risk of addiction. Some predictable percentage of people who use or gamble will escalate to the uncontrolled behaviors that cause profound distress and disruption in their lives as well as that of their families and communities. The need to manage these addictive behaviors has produced not only AA (Alcoholics Anonymous) and NA (Narcotics Anonymous) but also GA (Gamblers Anonymous—http://www.gamblersanonymous.org/qna.html).

The Director of the National Institute on Drug Abuse, Dr. Nora Volkow, has written that there is good evidence for non-substance induced addictions. Dr. Volkow wrote the brain is:

" … composed of a finite number of circuits for … rewarding desirable experiences … So it is almost by necessity that we'll find significant overlaps in the circuits that mediate various forms of compulsive behaviors. We have yet to work out the details and the all important differences, but it stands to reason that there will be many manifestations of what we can call diseases of addiction. Thus, addiction to sex, gambling, alcohol, illicit drugs, shopping, video games, etc. all result from some degree of dysfunction in the ability of the brain to properly process what is salient, accurately predict and value reward, and inhibit emotional reactivity or deleterious behavior."

In casinos for kids, in addition to the games there are drinks and food everywhere you turn: high-sugar and high-fat foods, including huge glasses of sugary beverages, nachos and potato skins in which cheese and bacon swim, sour cream like it was running water, and chicken and buffalo wings as plentiful as kudzu. These foods fuel the brain and body for the high intensity, electronic world of video games (and the few retro toss-the-ball games embedded among the digital delights). These are foods that antecede (and later accompany) the nicotine and alcohol that youth will graduate to further stimulate the reward centers of the brain.

There is also the paper gaming tickets of varying values in casinos for kids. Youth and adult players buy these at a gazebo located at the very center of the well of machines so there is never far to walk to convert paper money for valueless paper that lets you play. The tickets are paper versions of gambling chips, of course. There is a store at the rear where wads of tickets can be exchanged for stuffed toys of every color in the rainbow. The machines are programmed to let some win, some of the time, just like in any casino. But make no mistake: The house always wins.

Brilliant, I thought. The gaming (gambling) industry has developed and propagated youth gaming centers, gambling prep schools if you will, which can serve as gateways to adult casinos and breeding grounds for compulsive gambling. I'll bet that the rates of compulsive gambling and video game addiction will increase in the years to come. In fact, I'll give you odds.

PRESCRIPTION DRUG ABUSE: THE NEW KILLER ON THE BLOCK

LIS: More people die of drug overdoses than of motor vehicle accidents each year in the USA. Drug control that involves police-like interventions of finding bad guys and locking them up doesn't work. Public health approaches stand a far better chance of reducing abuse, saving lives and even saving money. This article outlines a variety of public health and clinical approaches to stemming the drug epidemic that has seized our country.

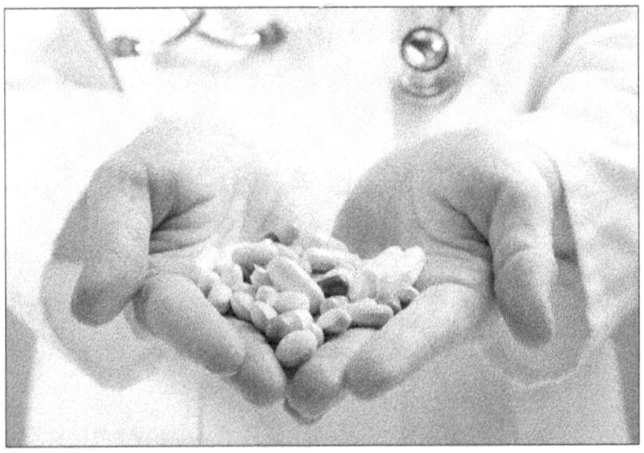

TAKING MEDICINE

Every 14 minutes a person dies of a drug overdose in the United States. This means more than 35,000 deaths every year, exceeding motor vehicle crashes, homicides and suicides!

The director of the White House Office of National Drug Control Policy (ONDCP), R. Gil Kerlikowske, a former police and justice official, has called the illegal use of prescription drugs, especially narcotic medications in pill form, the nation's "fastest-growing drug problem." What once dominated the world of overdoses in the U.S., namely heroin, has been eclipsed by the prescription painkillers (see below). These drugs are termed opioid analgesics, referring to substances produced from the opium poppy or manufactured synthetically with the same pain killing effects on the human brain (analgesic means lack of pain).

Where are the drugs coming from? More than 70 percent of those who have abused prescription narcotics got them from a friend's or relative's prescription. In other words, the supplier is no stranger. And the problem starts early: A 2009 national survey done by The Substance Abuse and Mental Health Services Administration (a federal agency) demonstrated that 1 in 3 youth ages 12 and older began their path to drug abuse by using prescription drugs for non-medical purposes, namely to get high. Teens now report, according to a report by the National Center on Addiction and Substance Abuse at Columbia University, that it is easier to get prescription drugs than beer.

In 2009, hydrocodone (Vicodin™ and generic equivalents) was the most prescribed prescription drug in the U.S.—twice that of the second most prescribed drug, Lipitor™. Sales of opioids have increased more than six-fold since 1997, as reported by the Drug Enforcement Administration of the US Department of Justice.

We've learned through experience in drug control that police-like interventions of finding bad guys and locking them up doesn't work. Public health approaches stand a far better chance of reducing abuse, saving lives and even saving money. While no single approach works for the diversity of problems that drive this epidemic, there are a number that have proven effective in states that have implemented them, and that have gathered the support of the Centers for Disease Control and Prevention (CDC) and the ONDCP. Some of these involve you.

FOR YOU AND YOUR FAMILY

Getting rid of unused medications: This involves drop boxes, conveniently located so that families can dispose of medications they no longer need, including opioids. Most people do not know what to do with medications they are no longer using and are concerned about flushing them down the toilet. Drop boxes are a simple solution.

A medicine cabinet inventory: This simple form helps individuals and families keep track of medications they have in the home. If you watch your liquor cabinet you surely should watch your medication cabinet. If you keep an inventory you can tell if pills are missing and, if so, this is an opportunity to talk to your children or other family members about prescription drug abuse. It is an alert that you need to protect your family members from gaining access to dangerous medications.

FOR PROFESSIONALS AND GOVERNMENT AGENCIES

Prescription Monitoring Programs: These are programs run by states in which pharmacies supply the state with information on who is prescribing what medications to which patients in what doses. This may sound like surveillance—and it is. Thirty-three states, including New York, have a prescription monitoring program (PMP) where pharmacies are required to send data to state health departments about controlled substance prescriptions (which include opioids—and tranquilizers and sedatives as well). This allows state health departments and drug control agencies to pinpoint their education and intervention efforts at doctors and clinics.

Official Prescription Form: Many states now use special prescription pads that are numbered and very difficult to forge. These are so effective that a blank prescription itself has a significant street value, not just the pills themselves.

Educational Resources for Professionals: Doctors and other medical professionals benefit from bulletins, guidelines and training programs (see the work of the NYS agency for alcohol and substance abuse—www.oasas.ny.gov—including its Opiates and Addiction Medication Workbook and Guide for Acute Pain Management for Patients Receiving Maintenance Methadone or Buprenorphine Therapy). More work is needed to better educate doctors about how people with chronic pain are best prescribed analgesics in ways that appreciate their suffering while also offering other means of reducing pain than just high doses of narcotics.

Narcan™: This medication is an antidote, given by injection, which immediately reverses the respiratory depression that is typically the cause of death in narcotic overdose deaths. It can be given easily by any bystander. Narcan™ is used as a part of an overall drug abuse strategy called "harm reduction," where instead of "just saying no" there is a recognition that it is important to keep people alive until they themselves can avail themselves of treatment and successfully say no to drugs.

These are a few of the strategies in use and in need of more widespread implementation. The work ahead is not about keeping pain medications from patients in need. It is about good medicine and public health: identifying who needs opioid medications for pain and other disorders, establishing the best practices to meet the needs of these individuals, discovering the service gaps between what people need and what they are getting and promulgating best practices to close this gap (called the "science to practice gap") and monitoring who is doing what needs to be done and intervening in a variety of ways, from education to enforcement, with those who can do better.

Doing all this is hard work. It takes a partnership among patients, families, doctors, clinics, professional associations and government agencies. It takes good communication and sophisticated tracking of what works for whom. It takes ongoing dedication to a needed cause. When those elements of a campaign to reduce opioid abuse and overdose death are in place we will save a lot of lives.

BROWNIES YOUR MOTHER NEVER MADE: FDA ISSUES WARNING

LIS: The creativity of drug dealers seems to know no end. In this post, I discuss how brownies, not those sold in legal dispensaries in Colorado (for example), are being laced with melatonin—in doses uncertain and quality even more so. These are not your mother's brownies!

The Food and Drug Administration has issued a warning letter to Baked World, a Memphis, Tenn., company marketing brownies laced with melatonin. The FDA notified this company that their product, first called "Lazy Cakes" then renamed "Lazy Larry," is in violation of the law for its production of brownies with this food additive while representing the brownie as just a brownie, and not something that contains a food additive, namely melatonin.

Melatonin is a naturally occurring compound that the FDA described as " … a neurohormone that is used for medicinal purposes, primarily as a sleep aid in the treatment of sleep-related disorders." Their letter went on to say:

"You should take prompt action to correct this violation and prevent its future recurrence. Failure to do so may result in enforcement action without further notice."

Clearly, the FDA is not happy with this company's loading brownies with melatonin and not even saying so.

For good reason. Melatonin has side effects that include nightmares and sleepwalking, daytime sleepiness and confusion, and headaches. It also can interact with medications taken commonly, like birth control pills, anti-coagulants and drugs used to treat diabetes and suppress immunity (taken for conditions like rheumatoid arthritis, colitis and lupus). And who knows what doses of melatonin a person might ingest from a "Lazy Cake" or "Lazy Larry"?

Melatonin can be a helpful supplement, used thoughtfully, with careful dosing and mindfulness of its side effects and interactions with medications. The issue is not melatonin, it is slipping it into a brownie that lures youth into yet another promised state of mental alteration and makes no mention of how.

These are not your mother's brownies. Let your kids and friends know about these "lazy" products. You might want to remind them that old-fashioned brownies are really good with milk or coffee—and are a lot safer.

'BATH SALTS' AREN'T WHAT THEY USED TO BE

LIS: 'Bath Salts' are stimulants, cooked up in underground labs that don't even come close to resembling those in "Breaking Bad". They are sold on the internet, at head shops, convenience stores and even some gas stations. Bath Salts are taken by mouth and sometimes inhaled or even injected. A public education and clinical information campaign needs to help keep these unsafe drugs out of the bodies of our children, our friends, and our neighbors.

Remember when bath salts were what you put in hot water before you lowered yourself into a bath so you could have a wonderful soak? Well I suppose you can still get these, but sales of another form of 'bath salts' are reaching new records—and bringing grave health hazards. While news of their popularity (and risk) has circulated for some time, there is very disturbing information just out.

The Centers for Disease Control and Prevention (The CDC) has released the first report on 35 patients who appeared in Michigan Emergency Departments (EDs) from mid-November 2010 until the end of March 2011. One of the people who ingested the 'bath salts' was already dead upon arrival at the ED. The others suffered from severe agitation, rapid heart rate, high blood pressure, paranoia and other psychotic symptoms including hallucinations and delusions (ideas contrary to reality and not responsive to efforts to correct them with reality). Some of these patients were violent. Half of those who came to the EDs required hospitalization, half of those were admitted to the intensive care unit. Sixteen of the cases had pre-existing mental health or substance abuse problems.

'Bath Salts' are stimulants, cooked up in underground labs. They are sold on the internet, at head shops, convenience stores and even some gas stations. The packages typically contain methylenedioxypyrovalerone (MPDV), mephedrone and pyrovalerone, all amphetamine-like in their action. The drugs are taken by mouth and sometimes inhaled or even injected. Needless to say, the last two routes of administration are associated with the worst reactions. While stimulants are controlled drugs, the labs often produce variations of existing drugs to avoid regulation.

Bags of 'bath salt' sometimes have written on them "Not Intended for Human Consumption." New York State's Health Commissioner, Dr. Nirav Shah, banned their distribution. Several states have proposed legislation, as has happened federally, to prohibit these substances, but the law is a slow tool in a rapidly moving market. These substances are also marketed as 'plant food' and 'pond water cleaner', and in many other ways to elude detection and control. In other words, it will be the same word of mouth that has driven their consumption that is needed to control it.

Speak to your friends. Talk to your children. Doctors, mental health and addiction counselors warn your patients. Let them know: The bath you take with 'bath salts' is dangerous and at the deep end of the toxic pool.

MEDICATION FOR ALCOHOLISM: ALTERNATIVES TO ABSTINENCE

LIS: The primary agents available today that are changing the treatment of alcoholism are naloxone (Narcan™, Depade™, ReVia™ and Vivitrol™). Vivitrol lasts for a month and is given IM. Topimarate (Topamax™) and Acamprosate (Campral™) have also been reported to show some utility though recent reports cast some doubt about their effectiveness. If I had a relative with repeated relapses into drinking, I would want that person on Vivitrol (in addition to a comprehensive psychosocial program). More details about these medications, and how to introduce them into general practice (including primary care), are in this post.

Alcoholism comes in many forms. There is binge drinking, all so common among young adults; alcohol dependence, when the body reacts to reductions in blood alcohol levels with misery and sometimes (dangerous) withdrawal; and chronic alcoholism when this drug, which in moderate amounts is known to protect our health, is heavily ingested over many years and irrevocably destroys brain tissue and body organs like the liver, kidneys and heart.

Alcoholism is the third leading cause of preventable disease and death, after smoking and obesity. Each year over 80,000 people die of its complications and countless more suffer and create heartache and economic hardship for their families, communities and countries. There are many paths to recovery from alcoholism—the most familiar being simple abstinence (foregoing any consumption on your own) and abstinence aided by 12-step programs (AA is the most well-known). While these paths deserve the respect they have earned there is one path that has not gained the recognition it merits; as a consequence too many people, and their families, go without the help that could lead to a better life with less of the ravages of this disease.

In recent years we have seen the use of a number of medications that have been scientifically shown to work. These medications, especially when added to counseling, significantly improve a person's chances of getting and staying sober. Yet medications are remarkably underutilized. Here we have an example where the pharmaceutical industry has not swayed how doctors prescribe or patients' consume their products.

Why are medications not commonly used in light of the ubiquity of alcoholism and its consequences? To begin with knowledge of these effective medications seems to not have been spread widely as it has with antidepressants, tranquilizers, asthma inhalers, statins and erectile enhancers. Moral views of alcoholism have been slow to die, as well, despite decades of evidence that it is a brain disease not a character weakness or failure of will. More troubling are the legions of old school alcohol counselors who may insist that any drug is a drug to be avoided (perhaps because they themselves gained recovery by abstinence and recovery programs before the advent of these agents) and often disdain a path assisted by medications, even if it might be more effective for some people.

Disulfiram (Antabuse™), where someone chooses to take a medication they know will make them horribly sick if they imbibe, has been around for ages. But that is not what we are talking about here. Instead we need to consider several medications that work by affecting specific brain centers related to pleasure, distress and mood, all which drive our behaviors. The primary agents available today changing the treatment of alcoholism are naloxone (Narcan™, Depade™, ReVia™ and Vivitrol™—the last works for a month and is given IM) and topimarate (Topamax™). Acamprosate (Campral™) showed good success in early studies but recent reports cast some doubt about its effectiveness though it bears mentioning.

Each of these agents works a bit differently. Which one to use is informed by whether someone has early manifestations of the disease or has progressed to dependence or chronic alcoholism. What you need to know is that these medications exist—not necessarily which one (just as you need to know there are antibiotics for infection but not which one you need). One of these medications may help you or your loved one. naloxoneacts in the brain to reduce the pleasure and reinforcement produced by a drink; the effect is that a person is less apt to want to drink. Topiramate, a medication in use for seizure disorders, appears to reduce the craving for alcohol. Acamprosate is thought to work by reducing the symptoms of going dry, including anxiety and insomnia, features of withdrawal which can last for months. These are important interventions for people with the disease of alcoholism to consider, just as antidepressants are for serious depression, antihypertensives are for high blood pressure and statins are for high cholesterol.

But no pill is a magic bullet. Medications need to be combined with counseling. A type of counseling now proven to work is a brief (several sessions for some people more for others—with ongoing monitoring and support) intervention focused on improving a person's motivation to get and stay sober. This form of counseling is termed motivational enhancement therapy (MET). Remarkably, MET is readily learned and can be practiced by primary care physicians, psychiatrists and other mental health professionals, substance use counselors and even emergency room medical staff. This means that many people can be effectively served (though not all) by medication and brief motivational counseling in general medical and mental health settings thereby greatly expanding access for those who have not turned (or may not) to traditional alcohol rehab programs. That is big news.

One word about depression and alcoholism, also now well-studied. People who show both conditions, and they commonly co-occur, do better when an antidepressant (e.g., a selective serotonin agent like sertraline {Zoloft™) is combined with one of the medications mentioned above, particularly naloxone. Medications combined with motivational enhancement and psychotherapy for depression is the optimal treatment plan when depression and alcoholism coexist.

Where can we start to advance the use of these effective medications? We can start by making screening for alcohol problems standard practice in primary care and mental health practices. We can start by using a simple screening tool, like the CAGE or AUDIT (both very brief questionnaires completed by the patient while in the waiting room that produce a score which can uncover the presence of the disease to the doctor). You can Google these screens, which are readily available at no cost on the Internet. Your doctor (or a trained clinician) then pursues the findings of the screen by asking a series of questions about drinking that can confirm the diagnosis, sometimes with various lab tests that may show the effects of the disease on the body. Screening and systematic questioning by a clinician for alcoholism is no different from screening for high blood pressure, diabetes or high cholesterol. Screening and treating these other medical conditions is now standard practice in primary care. Screening and brief intervention for alcoholism need to become standard practice as well—in primary care as well as mental health settings.

When screening becomes standard practice for a disease, so does the delivery of its treatment. Physicians and other professionals learn to treat a condition when it is detected by a screening test and their examination makes the diagnosis. The treatment for alcoholism, a disease found so commonly in every type of medical and mental health setting, can be highly effective. It's time to get beyond ignorance of these medications, over moral judgments and now dated practice patterns to give people what they need, namely more effective and broader access to treatments for a condition that wreaks havoc with their lives and ours.

ALCOHOL ENERGY DRINKS: THERE'S MORE YOU SHOULD KNOW

LIS: When this post was written, Caffeinated Alcoholic Beverages (CABs) had become exceptionally popular, to the detriment of too many youth who were appearing in Emergency Departments around this country and the world. The use of these substances continues. They are a combination of alcohol and an energizing soft drink with lots of caffeine, sugar and other stimulants (like guarana, taurine and ginseng)—sort of a toned down version of speed mixed with the disinhibiting effects of alcohol. CAB drinkers are also three times more likely to binge, putting them at additional risk of overdose death seen too commonly in youth drinkers.

Alcohol energy drinks are a combination of alcohol and an energizing soft drink with lots of caffeine, sugar and other stimulants (like guarana, taurine and ginseng). Sort of a toned down version of speed mixed with the disinhibiting effects of alcohol.

These drinks, often called Caffeinated Alcoholic Beverages (CABs), have become exceptionally popular, to the detriment of too many youth, who are now appearing in Emergency Departments around this country and the world. According to the U.S. Federal Centers for Disease Control and Prevention (CDC), there are about 25 brands of CABs; the leading two experienced a 67-fold sales increase from 2002 (when marketing started doing its job) until 2008.

Not only do these drinks have mega doses of caffeine (two to seven times that of a Coke or Pepsi), and other stimulant additives, the amount of alcohol can be twice or more than that of a bottle of beer; beer is 4 to 5 percent alcohol while the CABs may have up to 12 percent. Dehydration from the diuretic effects of caffeine and alcohol make the impact on the brain of both drugs even greater. The stimulants in the beverage can mask the effects of alcohol so the drinker does not feel as tired or woozy and can believe he or she is fine to drive. Judgment is significantly impaired and alcohol poisoning (overdose) or risky or aggressive sexual behaviors can result.

CAB drinkers are three times more likely to binge drink. Binge drinking (five or more drinks at a setting for a man and four or more for a woman—usually within two hours) is associated with 40,000 deaths in this country and is especially prevalent among young people. Some colleges have banned CABs from their campuses. Alcohol abuse is the gateway to prescription drug abuse, the fastest growing form of drug abuse in the United States.

A public education campaign has begun about the dangers of CABs. Did you know what is in them or the health and safety problems they present? Are you watching out for your friends or children so that they don't drink and drive when loaded with a CAB? Or that one CAB can be the equivalent of several beers, and then some? Families and friends can deliver a message of concern and protection—if you don't who will? Doctors, nurses and other health professionals who come in contact with youth should not be shy about asking questions and giving information; the white coat still carries quite a bit of authority. Colleges and universities can make CABs a primary health issue on their campuses.

The mounting use and ill effects of these drinks led the New York State Department of Health and the New York State Office of Alcohol and Substance Abuse to issue two advisories (see links below)—one for professionals and one for those imbibing themselves (or others with influence). These advisories offer important additional details about what can be done about the wave of CABs hitting the shores of communities everywhere.

ADDITIONAL RESOURCES

http://nyhealth.gov/community/youth/development/docs/2010-12-02_oasas_doh_cab_health_advisory.pdf

http://nyhealth.gov/community/youth/development/docs/2010-12-02_oasas_doh_material_cabs_for_colleges.pdf

A NEW TREATMENT FOR NARCOTIC ADDICTION

LIS: While not so new anymore, the use of buprenorphine in the US remains far below the need presented by the prevalence of opioid dependent people. Unlike methadone, which is only distributed (for addiction) at Methadone Maintenance Programs (MMPs) where a person must go every day, give a urine sample to test for other drugs and be observed by staff to swallow the usually red-pink colored liquid, 'Bupe' is picked up at a pharmacy with a doctor's prescription (which can be for up to a month). While considerably more expensive per pill than methadone, buprenorphine does not involve the ongoing costs of a MMP, and many users who do not want methadone or a MMP need an alternative. In France, in the year after its introduction some time ago OD deaths from opioids decreased by 85%. Recent Federal Health & Human Services (HHS) regulations and the CARA legislation of 2016 will allow buprenorphine prescribers to carry larger caseloads to help meet the demand for this medication.

Americans are Puritans when it comes to dealing with drug addiction. They get their spines all straight and spout righteous claims like "just say no" or "why coddle an addict?" How much more proof do we need before the rational presides over irrational? How long before those that promote punishment realize this is a disease that needs treatment? Before those with addictions get what we know can help?

Stuart was not what you would expect in an addict. He was a white, suburban, middle class teenager who played sports, had an intact family, friends and good grades. After college, he began his own business and was soon making a six figure annual income. But the process of addiction had begun: there is an expression, man takes the drug, drug takes the drug, drug takes the man. In college it was the club scene, with alcohol, pot and club drugs like ecstasy and ketamine. But they lost their appeal. Then there was the "game changer"—that moment I have heard many a time from people who become drug dependent—when he tried Vicodin™ and Percodan™. Stuart described to me that when the opiate in the pill started to course through his blood to his brain that he felt a sense of well-being, of " ... being complete ... this is how life should feel ... something was missing and it wasn't anymore." Man takes the drug.

It was not long before Stuart was on to OxyContin™ as he began to chase the feeling that got him hooked in the first place. He needed this stronger pill—and lots more of them—even grinding them up and sniffing them to achieve the same effect because his body was becoming tolerant of the opiates. Drug takes the drug.

When he didn't feed his habit he began to experience withdrawal—another consequence of addictive substances when not having a drug provokes a lot of really uncomfortable feelings in the body and mind. He was spending $100/day on pills and his business suffered the same neglect as just about everything else in his life. For Stuart it was then only another small step to heroin—first sniffing then shooting. That doubled the cost to $200/day and his life collapsed about him. The drug takes the man.

Stuart's mother told me she first went through denial of his addiction, even though she saw the obvious signs of avoiding everyone, losing weight, being abrupt, wearing long sleeve shirts in hot weather. Then she said she blamed herself: she should have handled things at home differently. She covered up for Stuart, tried to pick up the pieces of his strewn life. But then she too discovered that denial and blame don't work. She started to attend Alanon meetings and ask herself how she needed to be different with Stuart for herself and for him. That worked.

This story has a good ending. Stuart now has marked over three years without any drugs, unless you count buprenorphine ("bupe") which he takes every day. He is back working, earning good money and rebuilding relationships that were battered by drug abuse. You too probably have never heard of buprenorphine, or its brand name Suboxone™. Burprenorphine is a prescribed medication that became available, with harsh limits on how it could be prescribed, in 2002 in the US. Yet it was the first truly novel (and safer) treatment for narcotic addiction—for heroin as well as narcotic pain pills—since methadone was introduced in the early 1960s. From a public health viewpoint, when bupe was introduced in Europe and Australia many years earlier it reduced overdose deaths dramatically (by over 80 percent in France). Three people, on average, were dying of narcotic overdoses in NYC every day in 2002. This seemed like a treatment that NYC needed and it was my job, as its mental health commissioner at the time, to set about trying to introduce bupe to the City.

Buprenorphine works differently and is distributed differently than methadone, or heroin. As a person takes more methadone (and heroin and narcotic pain pills), their breathing is increasingly slowed until eventually they stop altogether. This how death occurs in these types of overdoses. With bupe, there is a "ceiling" effect, so taking more does not get a person higher, nor does it slow the breathing. This means buprenorphine is far less likely to be abused, and to cause preventable fatalities.

It is also available in a very different way. Methadone is only distributed (for addiction) at "Methadone Maintenance Programs (MMPs)' where a person must go every day, give a urine sample to test for other drugs, and be observed by staff to swallow the usually red-pink colored liquid. MMPs often become crime zones in their communities as drugs and stolen goods are bartered in the blocks that surround the site. Bupe is picked up at a pharmacy with a doctor's prescription (which can be for up to a month). It tends not to produce the nodding that methadone does; with a clearer mind a person is more able to function and work.

Stuart was clear about bupe: "It is not a cure for drug addiction. It is a pill, a medication that allowed me to do the work of recovery." He mentioned that early on, when he relapsed (the rule, not the exception with drug addiction—so be patient) he went to a respected Rehab Program that wanted him to stop the medication; they were old fashioned and thought that taking any kind of drug, even a prescription medication, was not the "right" way to do recovery (this is called the abstinent treatment model). He and his doctor protested, saying he would do better on it than off. Their prediction has proven true. Even (some) rehab programs have a thing against bupe. Stuart said:

Recovery takes dedication, you have to make it happen. I learned a lot from 12-step programs like AA from my psychiatrist, and from my family who have been so supportive—even when I was trouble. I knew I had to get back to work, that work is part of recovery. I don't want to take this medication forever, but it's a lot better than being an addict.

The use of buprenorphine throughout the USA has been slow in its growth despite the most recent National Household Survey on Drug Abuse (NHSDA) estimating 2.9 million lifetime heroin users and over 600,000 who used this drug in the past year. Heroin use is growing in young people. And this is just heroin: estimates of narcotic pain pill abuse and dependence are higher and growing faster. Why has buprenorphine use been so limited when those who could benefit are so many?

First, doctors have not been prescribing it: Federal rules require that doctors must take an eight hour course and pass a test to be allowed to use it—the only medication in this country with that requirement; and many doctors are biased against addiction, not wanting "addicts" in their offices, as if they weren't there already. Second, the methadone "industry," a nationwide largely for-profit group of providers, makes a lot more money from MMPs than they would from bupe. Their business interests are squarely contrary to the provision of buprenorphine, which in other countries is being used far more than methadone by a long shot. Third, there has been far too little public education and information, reflecting Puritan views that Americans don't promote addictive drugs, even if they are prescribed and work.

The consequence of not providing this treatment is that many people who could be helped are not. We are not only shunning people with the disease of addiction we not helping ourselves. Untreated narcotic addiction means crime to support habits, greater incidence of HIV/AIDS and hepatitis, and havoc in the lives of those affected, their families and their communities despite having a treatment that enables people, like Stuart, to work, rejoin their families and rebuild their lives. The National Household Survey alerts us to how many more people there are who may benefit from this sort of new treatment.

To find a physician or program that provides buprenorphine go to the National Institute on Mental Health agency site: http://buprenorphine.samhsa.gov/bwns_locator/

PROBLEM DRINKING

LIS: Someone is injured in an alcohol related crash on average every minute—500,000 people each year in the USA—and one third of MVAs are associated with intoxication. Crime, including domestic violence and rape, is frequently perpetrated under the influence. We have proven public health and education as well as clinical strategies for reducing alcohol use and abuse. But the gap from what we know to what we do remains vast. This post identifies a number of evidence-based interventions that await the will and determination to implement.

MEN IN PUB

How many times have you seen on TV or read in the paper of a DUI (driving under the influence) to later find out this person has offended before? Someone is killed every 22 minutes in the USA from an alcohol related crash. Someone is injured in an alcohol related crash on average every minute—500,000 people each year in the USA—and one third of MVAs are associated with intoxication. Yet, we are more active about the health impact of passive smoking than we are about the (passive) victims of drunk driving. But DUIs are only a small part of the consequences of problem drinking.

Crime, including domestic violence and rape, is frequently perpetrated under the influence. Rates of sexually transmitted diseases such as HIV/AIDS, syphilis and gonorrhea, escalate when alcoholic disinhibition is at work. Pregnant women with problem drinking are at higher risk to deliver babies with fetal alcohol syndrome and a host of developmental delays and disabilities. Eighty percent of fire and drowning accidents involve heavy drinking. Alcoholism produces brain atrophy, peripheral nerve disorders, liver disease and pancreatitis, among other health problems. Sure, we have all read that a glass of wine promotes a healthy heart. But three glasses of wine or a six pack actually increases risk of hypertension, diabetes, even breast cancer.

Estimates of the criminal and health impacts of problem drinking are surely underestimated since often the diagnosis is not made, or disguised in order to protect someone or get insurance companies to pay for medical care in emergency rooms, hospitals and doctors' offices. What's more, we don't measure the cost, in terms of suffering, lost productivity and other costs, to family members—nor the often tragic consequences to those injured by cars and crimes as a result of alcohol abuse. Still, global studies (such as by the World Health Organization) attribute alcohol to have about 5% of the global burden of disease and injury (2004). In this country, the cost of alcohol related problems is $186 billion each year.

But this testy problem is not without proven strategies for improvement. What works from a public health point of view is making alcohol less available and more expensive; banning alcohol advertising; and lowering the legal levels of alcohol while driving—and regularly stopping drivers (sobriety checkpoints). When France and Sweden restricted alcohol advertising it was challenged by the European Commission and the challenge failed. You may want to know that there is little evidence of the effectiveness from media campaigns such as "responsible drinking" (though alcohol manufacturers like to use this method), nor of marketing limitations that are self-imposed by the alcohol industry. Designated driver campaigns when studied have not shown effectiveness.

At the individual person level, researchers have demonstrated we have an effective means of identifying and intervening with people with problem drinking through a simple query by a doctor, nurse or other health professional when a patient comes for a medical visit. Called SBIRT (Screening Brief Intervention and Referral for Treatment) this is done by talking about drinking (counseling) and has shown remarkable impact. The simple, first step (screening) in SBIRT asks three questions: 1) On any day in the last month, have you ever had more than 4 drinks (men) or more than 3 drinks (women)?; 2) Think about your typical week, on average, how many days per week do you drink alcohol?; and 3) On a typical drinking day, how many drinks do you have? Responses above specified levels have the clinician provide brief counseling and referral if the person is ready.

Unhealthy drinking goes down dramatically, just like smoking, when people hear from their doctors that drinking a lot is unhealthy, that their doctors are concerned about the potential of drinking on their health, and they are given opportunities to consider and take action.

Results from a nation-wide SBIRT study of more than 600,000 patients showed nearly 40% of heavy drinkers cut down or stopped drinking six months after screening and brief counseling. A study in a large urban hospital found that brief alcohol counseling of injured patients reduced re-injury and re-hospitalization by about 50%. Medical procedure codes now exist so primary care doctors can bill for SBIRT. In other words, we have a simple, low burden, effective means of helping large numbers of problem drinkers. Studies of mandatory treatment, in fact, show far less robust effects than SBIRT (though this could represent differences in the severity of the problem).

Problem drinking is all too common. Solutions are clear and proven. But their use is rare. The safety, health and economic costs of problem drinking are legion. We can make a difference and we are hardly paying attention.

SO, YOUR CHILD IS GOING OFF TO COLLEGE ... DRINKING, DRUGS, DEPRESSION AND DEALING WITH COLLEGES AND UNIVERSITIES

LIS: The three things that tell you your child is having trouble are: academic difficulties, her reporting she is "not fitting in", and any call or contact from the school. This article was picked up by National Public Radio because of its interest to countless parents across the country. It contains a set of detailed QUESTIONS AND ANSWERS for parents and other caregivers. Take a look, you might find these of use.

This article is co-written with Henry Chung, MD.

One half of mental illnesses appear by the age of 14 and two thirds by the age of 24. These are the years when youth leave home for college or go on to university. In other words, mental illnesses, including alcohol and drug abuse, are the conditions that arise and may affect your child as he takes on the developmental steps of leaving home to go off to school. In fact, an important study of the mental health of college students by Dr. Carlos Blanco of Columbia University reported that almost 1in 2 college aged individuals had a mental disorder in the past year.

The most common conditions are alcohol and drug problems with 25 % of college youth (18–24) impacted. Remarkably, this is greater than the presence of a mood disorder (depressive or bipolar disorders) which was 11% and anxiety disorders (panic, social anxiety, phobic and generalized anxiety disorders) which were 12%. Importantly, less than 25% of those youth with a mental disorder sought treatment in the year prior to their identification in this survey; far more youth with mood and anxiety disorders in college sought treatment (34% and 16% respectively) than those with alcohol or drug disorders (only 5%).

As your child heads off to school there are a set of questions you may have and would like answered. These may be the questions that you have.

Q: What are the more common mental health conditions that strike when students go off to school? Why is that?

A: Mood and anxiety disorders are the most common. These conditions come on in adolescents and those in the college years. Social anxiety disorder is particularly prominent, and not a condition many think about.

Co-morbidity (the presence of more than one disorder at the same time) is highly prevalent—especially depression and anxiety. Some 60% of those youth with a social anxiety disorder will develop depression by the time they are in their 20s.

Depression is very common, and associated with suicidal thinking and behavior. Often youth come to college with a depressive condition that may or may not have been detected or treated. So, often they arrive at school already ill with this condition or develop a first depressive episode at the college.

Attention Deficit Hyperactivity Disorder (ADHD) is another common condition. This condition is often previously diagnosed and students (and their families) want assistance maintaining prescribed medications or receiving special accommodations for the condition.

Alcohol abuse and drug taking are unfortunately quite common challenges at colleges and universities. But many students do not see it as a problem, and don't seek help for these behaviors. There is a 1 item screening tool endorsed by the National Institute on Alcohol Abuse and Alcoholism (NIAAA—http://www.niaaa.nih.gov/) that show how many times a student in the past year has had 5 or more drinks in one sitting, 4 or more drinks if a female. If the answer is yes a more extensive evaluation is in order.

Interestingly, when depression is identified in students they are generally relieved, even grateful, to have the problem detected and their troubles explained; but when schools identify alcohol or drug abuse in students the response is often "what's the big deal?" Clinicians may need to develop specific interviewing skills to help students overcome their dismissal of these problems—which are endangering their health and safety and compromising their school performance.

"Why now"? First, there is the biology of mental health disorders, which are common and emerge in this age group. A family history will often reveal which students are especially at risk for mental and substance use disorders. But there is something about going off to school that may be less about separation and more about a natural desire of youth to be independent. Those already with mental health problems, like depression or anxiety, often envision going to college as a "new phase of life". If they were on medications they often think "I can stop the meds, I can do it". Sometimes they tell their doctor at home and sometimes they don't. They have a good summer, go off to school, stop taking medications and by mid-semester they relapse. That's when they appear for help.

An underlying vulnerability combined with the stress of leaving home and facing the developmental challenges of living on one's own. These are heightened by the academic and social demands of school. Sexual exploration and the emotionally destabilizing effects of alcohol and drugs add to the risk for youth in college. In other words, quite a cauldron of ingredients for developing or worsening mental health problems.

Another problem, fortunately more talked about today than in the past, is the presence of sexual assault—in females principally but in males as well. This includes sexual abuse, rape and unwanted touching. Sexual assault in school also reawakens past traumas for some as their experience at school kindles an underlying history and vulnerability. The American College Health Association has a brochure entitled "Sexual Violence: What Everyone Should Know"—for a nominal price from their website http://www.acha.org. The psychological consequences of assault include anxiety (PTSD and other dissociative disorders) and depressive disorders as well as alcohol and drug problems.

Q: How can parents know a child is in trouble? What would they look for? How should they behave?

A: First, be attentive but don't be hovering.

What a parent should do starts before the child goes off to school. This is a conversation, that doesn't happen nearly often enough, where a parent finds the moment to talk about both the academic and health aspects of going to school. A parent needs to say "I care about your health, not only your grades." The conversation ought to cover the main health areas of significant concern for students, which are sexually transmitted diseases (STDs), alcohol and drugs, and depression. You child may say or think " … mom/dad, you'll never understand" (or look at you like you are suddenly speaking Latin—but don't be put off. A parent can say " … I have read that 55–60% of students report stress, and that it affects their lives and their grades." And add " … Going to school can be wonderful but I know things happen to lots of kids, so I want you to know not only that I know these are common problems but that I am here for you if they occur."

The three things that tell you your child is having trouble are: academic difficulties, her reporting she is "not fitting in", and any call or contact from the school.

Once a child is off to school the first signs of trouble are typically academic performance. Yet many students minimize the problem and a parent is not apt to get a report from their child about grades. There are school agreements a student can sign that allow parents access to their transcript and grades—but these can be revoked by a student at any time, as can permission to know anything about medical problems or treatments. In fact, even when these agreements exist many schools first check with the student even when the agreement is in place saying "we have it but do you want us to use it?" So, open communication with your child is always the best route to follow.

Most students are on their family's medical plan, even though schools also offer insurance plans. Parents can discover that their child has used medical benefits from the EOB (explanation of benefits), the insurance form we all receive in the mail after using medical services, which are sometimes identified in language we can understand. Medications may also be covered by the family medical plan and on the EOB.

Some youth bring up the stress of school by saying something along the lines of "I'm just not fitting in. A parent can say that indeed she heard that at orientation (or somewhere) that stress is one of the most common experiences new students have. A parent can ask "how do you think you can connect? Are there things on the school website or around the campus that offer opportunities, since you are likely among many feeling the same thing?" This may help make their distress feel not so strange and at the same time encourages autonomy to act. Some youth may welcome contact with a counselor. For them, you can suggest turning to the health center or an academic adviser. But always say, "Call me—there are some things I know you will want to keep private. I am always here for you."

The third sign is any contact from the school. Any. This is a warning sign a parent should not blow off. It may be the school calling to report dormitory or other conduct violations. There may be episodes of drinking that exceed the school's rules. Whatever it is—take it as a sign that there is trouble because schools are very reluctant to call. A threshold has been reached and the school is telling you something is the matter.

Finally, and this is not really a sign, but something parents need to know: you as a parent can call if you have reason to be concerned. Families may see or hear something that the school may not. A parent can call the Dean of the School or the Counseling Center. They might want to call a faculty advisor. A parent has a right to be heard. If the person on the line is not listening and taking your call seriously then go up the ladder. Call the President of the school if that is needed to get someone to listen. Your perspective as a parent is but one perspective but it needs to be considered. [More about this below when we talk about being alarmed by what you see.]

Q: What about when a child returns home on school break? What should a parent know or look for?

A: These are unique moments where a child may let down his defenses. In an unguarded moment, feeling the need to communicate, a child may turn to a parent and cue that they are having trouble. Alternately, if your child is especially withdrawn or reclusive, different from how she was, that is important to recognize. If your child goes from being a talker to someone who doesn't hardly say a word that is also something to note.

Significant weight loss can also suggest a mood or eating disorder. In other words, any significant change in your child may be a signal that you need to find out more, and perhaps do something about.

Q: What else can parents do besides ask their child?

A: A parent can make contact with the student's 'collaterals'. By this we mean others who may know their child. These can be parents of the youth's friends, even friends themselves. But be careful since you can really put off your child, as well as other parents or friends of your son or daughter. To do this tactfully, ask questions like "How is your child doing in school? Our children were such good friends before they left for college. Are they spending time together?" Calling friends is even more delicate: is you do, ask about them, as one would about a neighbor or a caretaking person would ask about someone they knew well before school began. The conversation aims to open an opportunity for that youth to say something about their friend if they are concerned. But reserve any call like this one for when you really need to use it.

Q: What about when a parent is alarmed by what she is seeing or hearing?

A: Alarm should mean alarm. Like when a child has been missing for a day or two. Or efforts to reach your child have been unsuccessful for a day or more. Or another student has contacted you and wonders where your son/daughter is.

These are the moments to contact the school. Call the dean of students (general dean or a dean specific to your child's course of study) or a residence hall director (if your child is living in a school residence). You want to speak with someone with responsibility at the school. They should listen, or if they do not then keep going until you find someone who will. You need to provide information, like "My son has been missing since … ," and if you know more, like "The last time I spoke with him he said 'life is not worth living'" or "His roommates are very worried since he had been so discouraged after an exam … and now they don't know where he is." And you want to ask: "Can someone look into what is happening and get back to me?"

Responsible schools will take your call, gather what information they can, and look into your concern. They are apt to contact your child, if your child is to be found, and say why they are calling, as they should since after all they have to be responsible to their student as well as to you. A school can meet that responsibility by being transparent about what they are doing. Trust is maintained, even if privacy is intruded upon.

Q: What do parents need to know about the privacy rules that colleges and universities live under?

A: There are two types of privacy rules: one applies to academics, called FERPA—the Federal Rights and Privacy Act, and the other applies to health services (this includes mental health and counseling), called HIPAA—the Health Insurance Portability and Accountability Act. Schools typically do not prominently display these rules. Sometimes the school's policies will be on its website.

The US Department of Education has a good primer on FERPA (available at http://www.ed.gov/policy/gen/guid/fpco/ferpa/safeschools/index.html—click on For Parents: Parents' Guide to the Family Educational Rights and Privacy Act: Rights Regarding Children's Education Records). Parents have a right to review their child's academic record until that child is 18 or goes away to school, so that means for colleges and universities the information belongs to the student, not you. Schools can, however, disclose educational information in the event of a health or safety emergency (but see how this is curtailed by HIPAA—below). Schools also can inform parents of youth under 21 if there has been a violation of a law or policy related to alcohol or drugs. Finally, and this is notable, a school official can share information based on their personal observations or knowledge about a student.

HIPAA (The Health Insurance Portability and Accountability Act) is a Federal law enacted in 1996 to protect the health information of individuals. While it has various components it is the privacy part that is generally best known, and governs the actions of health care organizations, which include student health services (and hospitals). HIPAA makes it clear that your child, as an adult, has full privacy protection from anyone trying to find out health care information—and this includes parents.

Q: Doesn't the school have to contact a parent in an emergency?

A: This is a very good question to ask when you go to orientation or at parents' weekend (preferably in the sessions for parents, not the sessions with parents and their children). In general, the answer will be yes, but the way a school defines an emergency is all over the map. And parents can themselves have quite different ways of seeing something as an emergency.

In the end, a good student health service will make the decision to contact a family on the basis of clinical judgment: namely, when they decide that contact is in the best interests of the student. There is no legal requirement to notify a parent of anyone over 18, especially if that student says no. A school is obligated in an emergency to do all that is necessary to respond to that emergency. This may or may not include contacting the family which is a clinical judgment and depends on what has happened.

Some schools with tend to err on the side of contacting the family. But doing that can create a "chill" among the student body since word gets out and students become wary of the school and its services. As both doctors and psychiatrists we would rather violate privacy than create conditions, including limiting contact with family, that could worsen a student's state of mind and keep them from needed support and help.

Q: How can students seek help?

A: Help comes in many ways. Students, we hope, are already seeking support and help from family and friends. But when more is needed, more is usually available.

One place a student can start is with the resident hall advisor (RAs). These are their peers, often senior students who are well informed and well trained about how to respond to another student's distress. RAs can be very helpful to your child, and sometimes to you, in putting some things in perspective since your child is not the first one to have the problem she has.

Students can also turn to a faculty member, or a faculty advisor. Whom they turn to is often, not unexpectedly, someone that student sees as more approachable or responsive. As a rule, every student has an assigned faculty advisor. While the ratios of advisor to students vary considerably, and with that the time available, there is someone who has been designated for your child to turn to.

Finally, a student can always contact the health services. Any contact with the health services is by nature confidential. Some health services will have the professional staff to respond directly, some will refer your child to professionals that the school knows. Your child needs to understand that the health service is an important part of their lives as independent adults who, like everyone, may need services for an illness, trauma, or mental health or substance use problem.

Q: What are mental health services like at colleges and universities?

A: They too are all over the map. Most schools have counseling services—but they are staffed very differently. Some have staff, few have a lot of staff, and some are organized to assess and refer.

You want to consider your child's needs beforehand. Some parents and students will decide to arrange for private mental health services in advance of starting school for students with identified problems who were engaged and responding to treatment at home. When visiting schools with their child during the selection process a parent should find out about their health and mental health services; for some families this will be a factor in considering what school to choose. Alternately, orientation or parents' weekend are times to understand the capacities of the mental health service (though as I mentioned earlier, this is always best done in the context of overall health).

Q: Are counseling services available 24/7?

A: Their availability varies. It is pretty uncommon for a school to be able to operate a counseling service with this kind of coverage. After hours, counseling services generally refer to local emergency rooms.

Q: Will using counseling services threaten my child's academic career?

A: We won't say that a depressed, traumatized or dead child won't get very good grades.

All students, and their families, should know that mental health treatment is fully protected from the academic activities of the school. The records are not shared between a school and its health center—unless a student's behavior is a danger to self or others.

Most good schools recognize that mental disorders are common and treatable. Generally, good schools understand that mental health and substance abuse treatment actually improve a child's functioning, including academic performance. So, they are supportive of these types of treatments—and appreciate that a student can and should continue with treatment. Stigma, although still a barrier, is not what it was, especially with conditions like depression and with the use of antidepressants.

Q: Are there return to school policies for students who go on leave for a mental health condition?

A: Every school is required to post its policy, so ask for it or go to the school website to find it. If you cannot find it, check with the Dean's office.

The decision itself, however, is one that should balance the importance of school in a young person's life with their readiness to return. This decision can be nuanced and requires very good judgment, so having the student, parents, school administrators, and expert clinicians involved will help in coming to a decision that best fits your child.

Q: What are the challenges that student mental health services face?

First, the economic recession. Cuts in budgets are everywhere, and can erode mental health services at a school. Enhancing services, which often do not meet needs, is becoming more elusive than ever.

Second, we are seeing more students begin school taking medications for psychiatric condition prior to enrollment in colleges. Access to professionals who can prescribe psychiatric medication is challenging in an urban area such as NYC or Boston or SF; it is far more challenging for schools in rural areas. Students may have to turn to primary care physicians and nurses with prescribing privileges. Thus, it is important to plan how medications will be monitored (before school starts) if your child is taking a medication that is helping. Sometimes the prescribing can be done by a clinician in your home area who knows your child; if not, develop a plan for what can be done before your child leaves for school and avoid that moment, away from home, when they discover they are out of medication.

Third, we need to do more and do better regarding suicide prevention in colleges and universities. There needs to be less stigma, more information and more accessible paths for students to follow when they are having difficulties or see their lives as not worth living. In a sad way the Virginia Tech tragedy has underlined the need for student mental health services and many colleges and universities are doing a better job. Tragedy sometimes produces responses and resources we would otherwise not see.

CLOSING THOUGHTS

Colleges and universities are where the future leaders of our society are. Student mental health services provide direct benefits to youth in need that enable them to better succeed in school and in their careers, as well as to remain safe. There is also the important—if indirect—effect where every student who has a positive experience with mental health will feel less stigma about themselves and others—for a lifetime.

College and university mental health services pay exceptional dividends. Mental health conditions are highly prevalent and remarkably effective. Use them if you or your child needs them and support them for they are surely worth their price.

REACHING FOR THE PRESCRIPTION PAD

LIS: I describe here an experience I had in a doctor's office after a biopsy for a skin lesion. This was/is a fine doctor wanting to do something (more) for his patient, namely me. But I felt what had been done was excellent and there was no need for any medication, which would be for comfort not cure. I respectfully declined—easy for a doctor to do but not easy for a lay person—and left a satisfied consumer.As has been said, the most expensive doctor's tool of all is his or her pen.

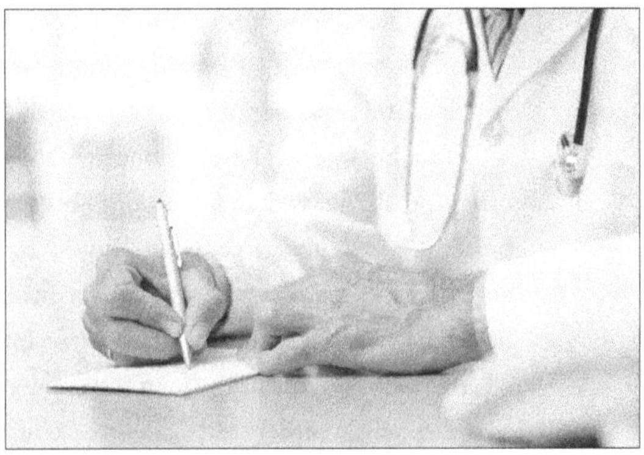

DOCTOR WRITING A PRESCRIPTION

I recently was at the office of a specialty doctor for a skin problem I have had for some time. He is a distinguished clinician and teacher in his field and I have consulted him for seven years. My appointment was a routine monitoring visit to check to see if my condition was the same, better or worse.

Dr. August (name is fictional) saw me promptly, a great courtesy not achieved in many a busy doctor's office, and took a careful history and inquired thoughtfully about how I was doing. He examined me thoroughly and concluded from history and examination that, in fact, I was doing better. He said so reassuringly to me. There was a resident in training with him so he took the time to explain matters to her as well as to me. I was a very satisfied patient. But then he reached into his white lab jacket pocket and pulled out a prescription pad to offer me a topical medication that I really did not need, might produce some minor side-effects, and of course would cost me money, if not directly at the pharmacy then through the insurance premiums I pay. I politely explained why I did not want the prescription and he put the pad back in his pocket—I think a little surprised. He suggested I return in six months for another monitoring exam, I thanked Dr. August for his help, and I left a very satisfied customer.

But I had to say no to the prescription of the medication. Imagine what someone who is not a physician would have done? Likely, dutifully taken the prescription to the pharmacy and began the treatment.

Why, I wondered, did this happen? This was a fine doctor with a patient who had his needs met. One common explanation of excessive medical care (and expenditures) in this country is the belief that more is better: more lab tests, more high tech imaging diagnostics, medications and more medications, and more invasive procedures. I don't doubt that in general but I think what happened with my doctor was different. I am a psychiatrist, you know.

Doctors are givers, as rule. The profession is meant for people who want, even need, to do something for other people. I fear we as a profession have lost sight of the fact that doing something can be all that my doctor did before he took out that pad. He did not keep me waiting, he thoroughly inquired and examined, he explained and reassured, and he made clear he was there for me by inviting me to return at a reasonable follow-up interval. I happen to think that was a lot. But I suspect that he felt the need to "give me" something—something more tangible than all that he had already given, namely a prescription. It was as if he was responding to Rousseau's caustic remark "bring me medicine but not the doctor."

For a busy general practitioner with eight to ten minutes to see a patient or with a busy psychiatrist often spending less than fifteen minutes seeing a patient there is one thing they can "do"—namely, write a prescription. With scarce time to investigate and precious little time to be a trusted physician who listens and discusses matters with a patient many a doctor is apt to want to "do something". And many a patient has come to equate leaving with a prescription as having been cared for.

As we rethink health care in the country, I hope we are thinking about the doctor as a doctor, not just as someone who orders tests, does procedures and writes prescriptions. Someone who listens and explains, assesses, and invites participation in the tough work of taking care of our health—and someone who is there when needed. Seems to me like a low cost way to get off the unaffordable health care conveyer belt we are on. As has been said, the most expensive doctor's tool of all is his or her pen.

NEUROENHANCERS: PAYING THE PIPER

LIS: "Neuroenhancers" are prescription medications to improve memory, concentration and mental functioning. Their use has become ubiquitous. An anonymous poll of students reading this post would surely reveal just how common their use is. Their touted ability as " … increasingly useful for improved quality of life and extended work productivity" makes them both highly seductive and perilous. The film and subsequent TV show, "Limitless", extols their virtues. Read this post at your own risk.

I read recently that the United States Air Force was "making available" the drug modafinil (Provigil®) to pilots on long missions. Modafinil is a type of stimulant approved by the FDA for narcolepsy and sleep apnea (resulting in severe daytime problems staying awake). I knew that stimulants like Ritalin® and Adderall® had extended far beyond their medically recognized use for Attention Deficit Hyperactivity Disorder (ADHD) and, like modafinil, were increasingly used by high school and university students to improve their performance on tests and papers. Those already in highly competitive financial and legal jobs were also discovering these drugs in order to keep up with the pace and productivity that success seemed to demand. It is now a reality that stimulant drugs have developed a role beyond their FDA approvals and become "neuroenhancers"—medications to improve memory, concentration, and mental functioning. They seem to provide an edge, a way of defying fatigue, achieving greater focus, and overcoming the boredom of everyday repetitive tasks. I started to wonder if I could use some modafinil.

In late 2007 the British Medical Association (BMA) took up the medical and moral challenges of neuroenhancers by publishing a "discussion paper" called Boosting your brainpower: ethical aspects of cognitive enhancements. Trying to "encourage debate" on efforts to "improve upon nature" they stressed that enhancers are creating vexing problems about how to balance individual freedom to improve performance with public health and ethical concerns about potential short and long term harm—for adults as well as the children whose parents will see fit to try to add octane to their child's brainpower. A commentary in late 2008 in the prestigious journal Nature called Use of Cognitive Enhancement Drugs implied the inevitability of these agents and that " ... Society must respond to the growing demand ... by rejecting the idea that 'enhancement' is a dirty word." Their policy recommendations aim to insert some intelligence and control into what appears to be the future of a society built on cognitive enhancers " ... increasingly useful for improved quality of life and extended work productivity." But I thought, when they say that something is too good to be true, it usually is too good to be true.

Fortunately, Dr. Nora Volkow, director of the National Institute of Drug Abuse (NIDA), and colleagues have been studying modafinil and in March 2009 published their findings in the Journal of the American Medical Association (JAMA). They were able to show that modafinil exerts its effect by increasing brain dopamine (as do the rest of the stimulant drugs, including cocaine and methamphetamine). What this means is that they have the potential for tolerance and abuse where more of the drug is needed to achieve the same effect and the brain craves for the drug if it is not present. The piper in these drugs may play quite a tune but you will have to pay the piper.

If you, your child or your loved one has a medical condition like ADHD or narcolepsy then the benefit of stimulants is likely to outweigh the risk (especially if combined with cognitive behavioral interventions). But if you do not, you are entering the world of performance enhancement—not the same thing as the treatment of a disorder—where many have tread and paid a great price. Neuroenhancers stand to become yet another cautionary tale in which promise is soon eclipsed by problems. So, I have decided to stick to coffee and tea, nourishing foods, learning a language or doing crosswords, reading and writing more, and getting some needed sleep—all of which ages of experience have shown enable us to think and perform better, safely, the old fashioned way.

A BLIND EYE TO ADDICTION

June 1, 2015
http://www.usnews.com/opinion/blogs/policy-dose/2015/06/01/america-is-neglecting-its-addiction-problem

LIS: Addiction is America's most neglected disease. 40 million people in the USA age 12 and over meet the clinical criteria for addiction involving nicotine, alcohol or other drugs. That's more Americans than those with heart disease, diabetes or cancer. Moreover, an estimated additional 80 million people in this country are risky substance users. Yet even as the epidemic of use grows, as does the body count, too little is being done to make a difference.

THE NOT-SO-NICE SPICE

August 5, 2015
http://www.usnews.com/opinion/blogs/policy-dose/2015/08/05/synthetic-marijuana-is-much-worse-than-weed-and-its-a-public-health-threat

LIS: The public's health is threatened by the illegal importation and distribution of synthetic "pot". Chemicals, hazardous to our health (and often manufactured in China or Russia), are sprayed on some green herb (like oregano or basil), and sold as Spice, K2 and with many other names. These drugs are cheaper than marijuana and draw the interest of youth, inner city impoverished residents, and people with mental and substance use disorders. They are sold in small groceries and delis, head shops and even truck stops in colorful bags meant to draw attention. They are poison and very hard to control.

DYING PREVENTABLE DEATHS

November 4, 2015
http://www.usnews.com/opinion/blogs/policy-dose/2015/11/04/white-americans-are-dying-because-we-ignore-mental-health\

LIS: An estimated half million, middle-aged white Americans have died between 1999 and 2013, reversing in this age group a long-term decline in mortality rates. These potentially preventable deaths are comparable to the lives lost during the AIDS epidemic from 1981 through the middle of this year. When causes of death in this impacted population were studied (by a Nobel economist) what emerged is that these people are dying of poisonings (i.e., drug overdoses), suicide and the consequences of alcoholism (including cirrhosis of the liver). In other words, alcohol and drug use and suicide appear to be the primary causes for the increased rates of death (and illness) in this country's white middle-aged population.

THE POLITICAL PROMISE OF A DRUG

January 19, 2016
http://www.usnews.com/opinion/blogs/policy-dose/articles/2016-01-19/obama-is-right-fighting-drug-addiction-is-a-bipartisan-issue

LIS: Carly Fiorina, former Florida Gov. Jeb Bush and New Jersey Gov. Chris Christie have spoken about a close family member or friend devastated or destroyed by addiction. While Donald Trump was silent, we know his older brother died at age 43 of complications from alcoholism. Ohio Gov. John Kasich, having seen the scourge of addiction in middle-America and his home state of Ohio, appealed to our humanity when it comes to caring for people in need. Both sides of the Congressional aisle have personal experiences with the devastation that addiction can bring. The Comprehensive Addiction Recovery Act (CARA) is a good start, though it lacks adequate funding. But personal issues make for needed bedfellows.

TAKE ACTION AGAINST ADDICTION

February 1, 2016
http://www.usnews.com/opinion/blogs/policy-dose/articles/2016-02-01/10-ways-to-combat-americas-drug-abuse-problem

LIS: The opioid and other addictions epidemic has seized this country, and has a firm and deadly grip. What can be done to contain this epidemic? Unnecessary deaths can be averted, and we can do far better to protect against the personal, community and economic devastation that addiction wreaks on a society. In this opinion piece I recommend 10 actions that individuals, families and communities (including our policymakers and insurers) can do.

BETTER THAN A WAR ON DRUGS

March 21, 2016
http://www.usnews.com/opinion/blogs/policy-dose/articles/2016-03-21/cdc-opioid-guidelines-are-a-step-forward-to-end-painkiller-abuse

LIS: The Centers for Disease Control and Prevention (CDC) has issued a set of prescribing guidelines for opioid medications. These only suggest (do not require) conformance. They are meant for primary care clinicians (doctors, nurses and physician assistants), and apply not to patents in active cancer treatment, palliative care or for the comfort of people receiving end-of-life services. The guidelines are clear, concise and useful—no small feat. But changing doctors' practices is notoriously difficult to do. We need Guidelines and now we have to figure out how to effectively use them.

AMPLIFY OBAMA'S DRUG ABUSE ACTIONS

March 30, 2016
http://www.usnews.com/opinion/blogs/policy-dose/articles/2016-03-30/obamas-plan-to-curb-drug-abuse-is-only-the-beginning

LIS: In a major policy address at a national drug summit in 2016, President Barack Obama advanced a set of actions, largely executive in nature, aimed at curbing the death and destruction that opioids have rained on this country. These include expanding access to treatment; aiming to better ensure that federal parity legislation is more than merely a law on the books as well as expanding the law to cover an additional 23 million youths and adults; using naloxone to help prevent overdose deaths; promoting community heroin policing; and supporting more than 60 medical schools that have committed to educating their students on the prudent prescribing of opioids, especially for chronic pain. Executive actions can make a difference, especially when Congress is paralyzed and inaction is too costly.

THE FOLLY OF SUPPLY-SIDE DRUG INTERVENTION

April 19, 2016
http://www.usnews.com/opinion/blogs/policy-dose/articles/2016-04-19/substance-use-treatment-works-better-than-any-war-on-drugs

LIS: In the first Season of HBO's "The Wire," the fictitious but alarmingly real Baltimore deputy police commissioner remarks, "Buy-bust … that's what we do." He was talking about undercover police practices where officers buy drugs from dealers and then bust them. Photo-ops often ensue, with a folding table covered with packages of drugs, money and usually an assortment of weapons. Sounds good, but what remains unchanged is the ubiquity of available, illegal drugs; unsafe neighborhoods; the murderous violence of the drug culture and its leaders; and the power and financial success of the dealers who become heroes for the young to emulate creating the next generation of dealers and users. "Supply Side" efforts to control drugs (through for example crop control, interdiction and policing) have persisted for hundreds of years, despite their virtual utter failure. This post illustrates why these control efforts fail, and what alternatives exist.

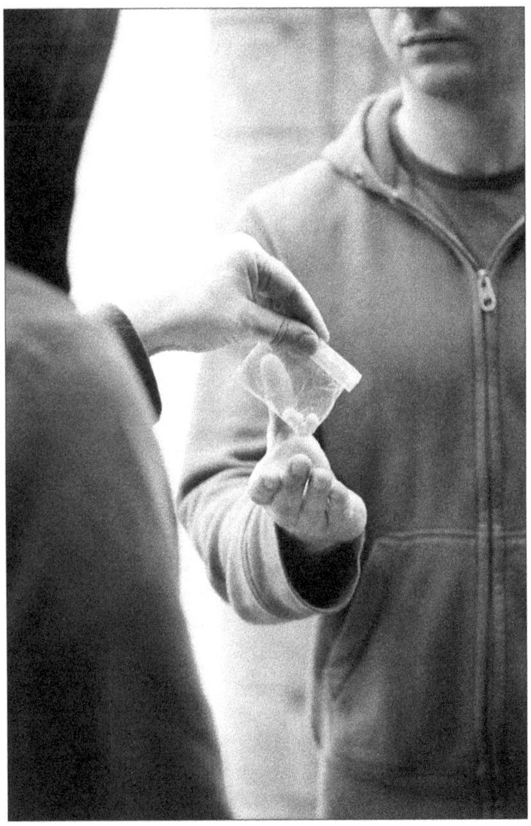

A DRUG DEAL

PAINFUL SHADOW OF PRINCE'S DEATH

May 10, 2016
http://www.usnews.com/opinion/articles/2016-05-10/what-were-overlooking-about-opioids-pills-and-princes-death

LIS: Prince's march to his death followed an all too familiar trajectory: orthopedic problems in his hip from too much wear and tear, to surgery, then to prescribed opioids, and then likely to their regular, unregulated use. This is a deeply familiar and perilous course. We need more than parroting the negative consequences of drugs or supply side control efforts in order to effectively change addictive behaviors. The answers ahead may be found in neurocircuitry and electrophysiology, eastern yogic practices, religion, art, culture, family, community, nutrition and what we have yet to learn. Prince's death may help catalyze what we need to do to get out of the past and into the future of a more balanced—and successful—approach to the addictions.

PRINCE

ON THE MOVE BY OLIVER SACKS

LIS: The late, great neurologist and medical writer Oliver Sacks had an especial fondness of taking drugs when he was a young doctor. Over his life, he advanced the treatment of many medical conditions, using medications among other interventions. He was a power weight lifter, and a prolific writer. His life tale, told in this autobiography, is riveting.

ON THE MOVE: A Life
By Oliver Sacks, Knopf, NY, 2015

ON THE MOVE

But for his extraordinary gifts as a clinician and medical writer Dr. Sacks' life could have been a disaster.

Oliver Sacks fled England, where he had gone to Oxford and medical school, and began his medical career in San Francisco, then onto Los Angeles, finally settling in New York City to this very day (though he never surrendered his British citizenship). But his time anywhere can hardly be characterized as settled, as the title of his new autobiography conveys. England was too risky for a gay man, as Alan Turing had discovered around the same time as Dr. Sacks completed medical school and was active in the underground gay world.

When first in the US, Oliver Sacks plunged into rather extensive, peripatetic, high speed leather-clad adventures on his beloved Norton motorcycle. He had one turbulent training or research experience after another. There was also one job loss after another, with periods of returning to the UK (or Norway) with no money and no job, to write and try to conjure up direction. For many years he seemed as dedicated to power weight lifting as to neurology, and set a California record for a full squat with 600 pounds (likely producing the source of back spasms that recurred throughout his life). For over four years, he was heavily addicted to amphetamines, and had transient drug-induced psychoses; he also used LSD and other hallucinogens liberally. He had many an accident, some serious, and lost or impetuously burned a number of extensive notebooks and manuscripts.

We read all this in Dr. Sacks' self-effacing, poetic prose. We are treated to some of his early notebook writings inserted into the book. We meet some of the notables who befriend and emotionally support him for he depicts himself as often a naïf, besieged by self-doubt. These include WH Auden (a fellow Oxford alum who lived in the USA for decades), the poet Thom Gunn, the Soviet neuropsychologist AR Luria, Stephen Jay Gould, Robin Williams, the Laureate Francis Crick, and his devoted but complicated family with (very conventional) physician parents and three brothers (one who suffered from schizophrenia).

Today may be an era of disruptive thinkers and innovation. But not when Dr. Sacks was casting about well into his 30s; he was often regarded as troublesome and even eroding of medical professionalism for his narrative portrayals of patients and their conditions. But he became too great an artist to overlook or disparage—too riveting in his literary elegance, empathy for patients, and his resolute insistence on humane care for those with medical and mental illnesses, as well as those with developmental disorders.

Dr. Sacks has again succeeded in gently revealing our collective foibles, fears, and endless capabilities, this time using himself as the central subject. His candor is courageous and his intelligence astonishing. His boundless capacity for discovery, ever fresh, has kept at bay the demoralization that could have come from his retinal melanoma, agonizing neuropathic pain, and progressive visual and physical impairments. His capacity for love, renewed in his 70s, may be the universal antidote to despair we all can find, if we are lucky and try. But it is his millions of words woven into stories that illuminate, transfix and transport our imaginations that is the legacy this great and original man continues to provide the fortunate reader.

A COMMON STRUGGLE—CONGRESSMAN PATRICK KENNEDY'S AUTOBIOGRAPHY

LIS: Former Congressman Patrick Kennedy has been extraordinarily candid about his struggles with addiction and mental illness, and how those problems affected many others in his family. This autobiography, written with Stephen Fried, is revealing, absorbing and inspiring.

A Common Struggle: A Personal Journey Through the Past and Future of Mental Illness and Addiction
By Patrick J. Kennedy & Stephen Fried
Blue Rider Press, New York, 2015

In 1995, at the age of 27, Patrick J. Kennedy became the youngest member of the Congress of the United States, having been elected to the House of Representatives from his home state of Rhode Island. When he left Congress in 2010 a more than 60 year era of a Kennedy serving in Washington ended.

Patrick Kennedy is the son of the famed former US Senator Ted Kennedy and the nephew of President John F. Kennedy and former Attorney General Bobby Kennedy. He is a member of America's royalty. His story, as candidly and intelligently told in this co-written autobiography, is a needed and welcome addition to the political and dynastic history of our country.

Three narratives run through this book: One is about politics; another about family; and the third is about mental illness and addiction. For the Kennedy's, and not just Patrick, these are quite inseparable. And while the politics are ever present in the stories we read in *A Common Struggle*, it is what we are made privy to about family and mental and addictive illnesses that makes this such a fine and illuminating read.

The heart of the family story is of course that between the father and the son; the particular stage where the drama appeared was in Congress. Patrick had great fealty to his father but discovered he would have to fight him to achieve the passage of one of the most important pieces of health legislation for people with mental and addictive disorders: The Mental Health Parity and Addiction Equity Act of 2008. This Act, still yet to achieve its full implementation and power, requires that health insurers deliver benefits (as measured by numbers of visits/days covered and dollars paid *and* by the provision of rehabilitation services such as partial hospital programs) for these conditions no different than those for the physical illnesses the insurers also covered. Ted Kennedy thought a more limited bill was needed for passage but Patrick proved him wrong, winning the support of the House Speaker and members of both parties. The Bill was signed by President George W. Bush in the Oval Office, with Ted already suffering from a brain tumor and ambulating with a cane.

Their fierce but quiet battle also was over addiction in the family. Patrick makes the case that his father was an alcoholic, albeit a remarkably high functioning one. He believes his father was profoundly traumatized by the public murders of his two brothers and the Mary Jo Kopechne/Chappaquiddick incident that foreclosed what might otherwise have been his ascent to the Presidency.

Joan Kennedy, Patrick's mother, is a self-admitted alcoholic with a long history of treatment, with some periods of recovery but sadly with an overall deterioration. Many other family members suffered from mental and addictive conditions, and their names are prominent in the worlds of celebrity and politics. But the Kennedy ethos was silence and suppression. Patrick discovered that secrecy was the enemy. He began speaking out about his illnesses in 2000 at a campaign appearance by Tipper Gore, the then Vice President's and Presidential candidate's wife. His breaking the no-talking taboo continues, and his candor and bravery are remarkable.

Perhaps the over-riding political message I took from *A Common Struggle* is that politics is personal. As Patrick outed himself and fought for proper mental health care in the US he found great allies in fellow politicians who themselves had an addiction, mental illness or an affected close family member—including those who had a loved one who died from suicide.

Patrick is unsparing in his revelations about himself, dating back to his teenage years. He reports having depressive, anxiety and manic symptoms and that he has Bipolar (Manic-Depressive) Disorder. His use of alcohol and then mixing that with cocaine and for many years narcotic pain pills like OxyContin and Percodan was severe. Like his dad he was so hardy he could press on. But the day of reckoning came when he met and married Amy, his current wife and mother of their three children; that was his turning point. He was going to make recovery work for himself, his family, and for those who could benefit from his efforts.

Today, Patrick Kennedy has about 5 years of sobriety. His openness about himself and others in his family has stirred some contention in the wake of this book's publication. But this is no tabloid or sensational memoir. What we read, delivered with his co-author Stephen Fried, are the reflections of a highly informed, dedicated and loving son and family member who appreciates with laser clarity that denial is part of an illness and that stigma feeds on it.

Patrick Kennedy's mental health, political and personal mission continues in many ways, especially through his creation of two non-profit organizations—The Kennedy Forum, uniting the community of mental health advocates and practitioners, and One Mind, dedicated to global brain research. Mental and addictive disorders are a civil rights fight for Patrick, and like the best of the Kennedy tradition he is showing himself a true fighter.

Reprinted with Permission from Lancet Psychiatry

GOD'S HOTEL

LIS: "God's Hotel" abounds with stories of patients (and their caregivers) with all variety of chronic neurological, heart, lung and liver conditions, strokes, cancers, AIDS, and psychoses sent from acute care facilities to Laguna Honda for what might be a chance to find life again or to die with dignity. Dr. Victoria Sweet went to work there planning on staying for few months and remained for 20 years. She teaches us about "slow medicine", which taps natural healing and time—things that have been generally lost to "modern" medical care.

GOD'S HOTEL BY VICTORIA SWEET

Riverhead Books, NY, 2012

I bought God's Hotel in 2012, when it was published, at the urging of a number of friends whose wisdom minds taking. But it went into a pile of good intentions to read and sat there untended. Then some months ago I went to find it and it was gone! Without much detective work I discovered my wife had taken it to read and joined my other advisors in saying, "You have to read this book!"

Now I can say I have. And its release as a paperback gives me the opportunity to write about this remarkable piece of creative non-fiction. I imagine its author, Dr. Victoria Sweet, would appreciate that it took time for me to journey to and through her work since that may be one of the many compelling messages she so eloquently, yet simply by storytelling, conveys: We're all on a journey, and when we see the way, value it and use it, then we have found The Way.

There is an ancient pilgrimage, 1,600 kilometers to walk, from south central France to the frontier of Spain and then due west to Compostella. In France, the path is called le chemin and the route the Saint Jacques de Compostelle Pilgrimage. In Spain, it is el camino and known as the Santiago de Compostella Pilgrimage. But the term that pilgrims for a thousand years have used is The Way. It is a journey of body and soul, a means of seeing, feeling and being that a person unleashes from within: This is a spiritual force, non-sectarian and universal, and a means of finding the purpose and human connection that are as essential to a life well lived as they are hard to achieve (Journey for Body and Soul).

Dr. Sweet has walked the pilgrimage trail in Europe. And she walked it, as well, as a physician practicing in the very last of the alms houses in this country, The Laguna Honda Hospital in San Francisco. She committed to working there for two months and stayed 20 years. When she began Laguna Honda had 1,178 patients whose medical conditions were so severe and persistent that there was no other place for them to go.

Terry, in her late 30s, had a bedsore on her back bigger than a dinner plate and had failed numerous grafts and needed "slow medicine" to heal.

Paul had amputations of both legs, finally at the hip, the result of clots that shut off circulation and produced gangrene, and needed slow medicine to rebuild a life in a wheelchair from which his skills with computers and bootlegging DVDs made him one of the more popular people in the hospital.

Radka, an older woman and immigrant from Bulgaria, had been sent from the county hospital to die from lung cancer, but she rallied with human warmth and slow medicine before she chose to go to hospice and then let go of life.

Steve, a former truck driver and present-day pain in the ass, was thought to have had a stroke (and was not taking well to the idea of rehabilitation) until careful observation and critical thinking revealed he had a rare form of familial muscular dystrophy. He too was the beneficiary of slow medicine.

God's Hotel abounds with stories of patients, and their caregivers, with all variety of chronic neurological, heart, lung and liver conditions, strokes, cancers, AIDS, and psychoses sent from acute care facilities to Laguna Honda for what might be a chance to find life again or to die with dignity.

Slow medicine does not disavow fast medicine: A broken bone still needs to be set, a heart attack kept from killing someone, and appendicitis requires surgery. But when acute care has done its job then recovery needs the right milieu, a different form of medicine, where the barriers to healing are removed, including unnecessary medications, abuse of drugs, alcohol and cigarettes, inadequate nutrition, and fear and hopelessness.

Dr. Sweet, also an historian of pre-modern medicine, wrote her Ph.D. while working at Laguna Honda. She studied the writings of a 12th century German nun, Abbess, philosopher, writer, composer and medical practitioner named Hildegard of Bingen—a course of study which, like The Way, makes all the sense in the world once you read Dr. Sweet. Hildegard regarded the body as more like a plant than a machine and thus needed a way to reawaken its capacity for growth (greening or viriditas) rather than to be fixed like a machine (the metaphor of our industrial age). Hildegard's work led Dr. Sweet to consider how to remove the barriers to recovery and fortify a person with the basics of healthy sleep, nutritious food, and protection from toxic substances and people while permitting "tincture of time" to also do its job.

The great irony expressed by the book (and sharply portrayed in Dr. Sweet's TEDx talk The Efficiency of Inefficiency) is that slow medicine is actually efficient! Sometimes doing less is actually more, and it can save a lot of money. She takes to task consulting companies hired to update and improve medical facilities, politicians, myopic or ambitious administrators, and agonizingly entrenched or zealous government agencies and regulators that don't know how to save themselves from themselves, no less the people they are charged with serving.

I may have missed God's Hotel the first time around, but not this time. Nor should you if you want to feel hopeful that (and see how) modern medicine may come to realize that slow medicine can—and should—co-exist with fast medicine. Or as Dr. Francis Peabody of Harvard Medical School said in 1927, well after Hildegard of Bingen but true to her tradition: "The secret of the care of the patient is in caring for the patient."

A HERO'S JOURNEY: *WINTER'S BONE*

LIS: While cooking methedrine is going on in the Missouri Ozarks, a 17 year old teenager is left to care for what remains of her family. She is surrounded by relatives and neighbors who are friends and foes, addicted to the product they make, often without care or concern for anyone, without prospect of exit, and living in a culture of violence. This film is a testimonial to human survival without a hint of pretense.

Winter's Bone, A Review
Starring Jennifer Lawrence, Directed by Debra Granik, from the novel by Daniel Woodrell

What do you do when home and family are in peril? When your mother lives in a psychotic fugue too far removed to help, when your siblings are too young to care for themselves, the relatives too deranged to let them take over, and dad is missing and sought by the law?

Ask Ree Dolly. While only 17 she has come of age in the lost land of the Missouri Ozark mountains. While called "child" by those who seek to dominate her she long ago discarded any innocence. Yet she has integrity and drive, qualities that are about to be assaulted, literally and figuratively, by those closest to her.

We enter Ree's life as the sheriff drives onto property that seems a burial ground for cars, tires and lost souls. Winter is setting in and frost permeates the air. Warmth comes in small and fleeting doses. "The law," as he is called by everyone, brings bad news: Ree's father, Jessup Dolly, has skipped bail and cannot be found. Unless he appears in court next week his bond, made by putting up the family home and woodlot, will be seized. She, her brother, sister and mother will be homeless as the cold hardens around them. The law cannot find her dad but she says "I will."

Jessup was awaiting trial for cooking crank (running a home lab that makes crystal methedrine) before he disappeared. In fact, most of the Dolly family is in this business as a generation of ill fate, glimpsed from photos in an album, has delivered them to poverty and its desperations. Even their farm 'crop' has changed from marijuana to meth. They are also consumers of their product—at least the men are—so their brains are on fire with the drug and their behavior is as unpredictable as the mountain weather.

The accounting unfolds as Ree begins her search for her father. Like every hero's quest there are abundant dangers, surprising and shifting enemies and allies, and resolve to be tested every step of the way. Men menace their women but it is the women who are strong. Family loyalty is in constant tension with doing what is just. Ree's journey fills us with suspense as prospects for finding Jessup and saving her family dim.

The pain Ree suffers is hard to take. She seems so strong, but no one is that strong. Can it be worth it? Yet she acts without hesitation to retain her land and the meager future it will yield. Some of the scenes are deeply primal. Jennifer Lawrence's capacity to render agony, grit and tenderness is a sight to behold, if you can stand it.

Winter's Bone may be one of the best films we will see this year. It is an independent film with a two million dollar budget that spells promise for American movies. A movie of this power, that depicts a journey of necessity and determination, embodied by an ageless young woman, inspires and lends hope about those we might otherwise count out.

This film is a testimonial to human survival without a hint of pretense. All is shown, nothing has to be said: the story line and character portrayals do all the work. We encounter savage meanness and we witness transcendence. We are confronted by family in their terrible and wonderful ways. We see that when there is everything to lose that choices narrow and love shows us the way. This is the crucible which makes the (wo)man.

'LIMITLESS': WOULD THE FDA APPROVE?—A FILM REVIEW

LIS:

One pill makes you larger
And one pill makes you small
And the one that mother gives you
Don't do anything at all
Go ask Alice
When she's ten feet tall
—From "The White Rabbit" by Jefferson Airplane

ALICE IN WONDERLAND

A drug has the ability to take limited brain functioning (after all we use a fraction of our brain's capacity) and totally unharness its power. The protagonist, played by Bradley Cooper, becomes limitless—soon making a fortune and is featured in the NYC tabloids as its latest phenom. But the devil must have its due, and the film depicts how merciless that devil can be. Though, being Hollywood and Bradley Cooper, all's well that ends well.

'LIMITLESS': WOULD THE FDA APPROVE?—A FILM REVIEW

Starring Bradley Cooper, Robert DiNiro and Abbie Cornish

> One pill makes you larger
>
> And one pill makes you small
>
> And the one that mother gives you
>
> Don't do anything at all
>
> Go ask Alice
>
> When she's ten feet tall
>
> —From "The White Rabbit" by Jefferson Airplane

And I thought that tune was dated. But not after I saw "Limitless," the film starring Bradley Cooper (Eddie Morra) and the legendary Robert DiNiro (Carl Van Loon), and directed by Neil Burger.

A writer, Eddie, who cannot put two words in a row on a page finds himself unable to deliver on the book he somehow has had an advance on, his beautiful and talented girlfriend (Abbie Cornish) hands him back his apartment keys and says goodbye, and dishes and debris pile up around him in the shambles of his apartment in New York's Chinatown. He has been drinking too much and now has cause to drink more. But chance happens upon him as his ex-wife's brother spots him on the streets of New York, asking if indeed that is his address. Vernon (Johnny Whitworth), a former drug dealer we learn, looking quite dapper and well to do, takes the sad sack Eddie out for a drink, not hard to do, and offers him a pill that will change everything. One pill makes you larger. What the hell, what does Eddie have to lose?

And so begins his adventure, as Vernon supplies him with NZT (why does my mind go to AZT, an antiretroviral medication for HIV/AIDS?), a drug that takes his limited brain functioning—we use a fraction of our brain's capacity—and delivers it to its totally unharnessed power. He becomes limitless—soon making a fortune and is featured in the NYC tabloids as its latest phenom.

It is an ascent meant to inspire envy as he rockets to success on Wall Street and in the trendy bars of NY, where one beautiful woman after another cannot resist him. He woos a billionaire investor, Carl Van Loon, into taking him on as his principal advisor as the tycoon plots the largest (sic) corporate merger known to mortals, ironically involving Libya and oil! Hah, hah!

However, though NZT makes you larger, it then makes you small. The drug begins to destroy the brain and the body through which it streams. The outcome is fatal unless the user continues to employ the drug, and even then it has a track record of debilitating its host. As if that were not enough, Eddie becomes the target of a variety of bad guys, each with his own special and savage evil intent.

Inside and outside his corporal existence, Eddie is in big trouble. The acting is terrific, the film pace brisk, and the story line hurtles forward. It is not looking good for all wrapped up in the NZT and corporate worlds. Soon the body count exceeds many an Arnold Schwarzenegger film, though the causes of death are more varied.

I was on board for all that. It was the resolution that troubled me. Remind you, I am a psychiatrist and public health doctor. Eddie, now looking All-American, is no longer a sketchy writer, a drug addict in withdrawal, or a corporate icon in hand made suits; in fact, he is about to become a Senator (and not a state senator) from New York. Carl Van Loon tries to co-opt him by taking control over Eddie's supply of NZT, so he thinks. But Eddie, smiling brightly, his blue eyes ever more radiant, has him beat. Eddie says he is off the drug, even suggesting he has found ways to make it less toxic. Although off the drug Eddie is, no less the incomparable genius he has become. We get some line about his brain having been altered in ways that make Einstein look like Harpo Marx. Eddie's brain has incorporated the drug's benefits, has no residual adverse effects, and is now the man that stands to rise to President of the United States of America. Obama beware.

I have written about cognitive enhancers ("Neuroenhancers: Paying the Piper"). In fact, the film mentions the "enhanced Eddy." "Limitless" seems to proffer that we can dodge the damage of drugs, that you can take a neuroenhancer, a pill as potent as can be envisioned, and come out the other end of your own drug deal of sorts as a Senator, if not a President, with your love life restored, your crimes forgotten and your wealth, uh, oh yes, limitless. Go ask Alice, When she's 10 feet tall. Maybe the FDA should be asked to review this film?

LIMITLESS—THE TV SHOW

LIS: A good movie was turned into a bad TV show, at least in this reviewer's mind. But by general audience standards it sold, and has been renewed for a couple of years. The film's protagonist has even achieved more—become a US Senator—and thus we have a new "limitless" fellow, a government agent in fact. This might be good fun, preposterous of course, but it fans the kind of fantasies that promote drug use and abuse among youth and adults alike.

'LIMITLESS'—THE TV SHOW, A REVIEW

September 23, 2015
http://www.huffingtonpost.com/lloyd-i-sederer-md/limitless-the-tv-show_b_8180770.html

In 2011, Bradley Cooper starred in the film version of Limitless, co-starring Robert DiNiro and directed by Neil Burger. I reviewed the film for the HuffPost feeling a bit uneasy about its message of grandeur delivered by a capsule.

In the movie, Eddie (Mr. Cooper) is a writer who cannot inscribe two decent words in a row on a page and his talented and beautiful lady friend hands him back his apartment keys and says goodbye. He descends into a life of dishes and debris piling up around him. His drinking blossoms into an unending bender. But chance happens and a former drug dealer (not Mr. DeNiro, for his job is to bring corporate malfeasance to the table), now a dapper man about town, offers him a pill that will change everything. One pill makes you larger. What the hell, what does Eddie have to lose?

In the TV show, which premiered on CBS on September 22, 2015, we meet Brian Finch (Jake McDorman) and rejoin today Eddie, now a superstar and U.S. Senator (played by superstar Bradley Cooper). We also go from corporate America in the movie to government in this TV network show, but don't worry it's the FBI not the IRS. Jennifer Carpenter plays FBI "special" agent Rebecca (can someone tell me what makes an agent special?) who used to think that dangers lurked outside the office; now she has to worry about the soon to be new agent on the block, Brian. But when he is good, boy is he good.

Brian can run and jump like Tom Cruise, think like IBM's Watson, fight like Mike Tyson, play chess like Bobby Fisher, play music like Eric Clapton, and make Dr. House look like a freshman medical diagnostician. Yet mere days earlier he was a loser, a big loser. The difference is NZT—rendering Brian ... ten feet tall. However, and here's the rub, NZT makes you larger, and then it makes you small—commensurate (like any drug) with a person's blood levels.

Rewind to 2011 and NZT, the super cognitive enhancer that the Feds know about and but have gone dark for reasons we will have watch more episodes to discover (though if we had NZT we could surely divine the answer). NZT is what Brian gets from his former band mate, Eli, who is soon a homicide erroneously attributed to Brian. Now we have not only Limitless but The Fugitive, all rolled into one. Brian's problems are amplified as a consequence of the drug's duration, which is a mere 12 hours. He is on a mission to secure more drug to quiet his tremulous withdrawal, not to mention to save his terminally ill father, solve a batch of murders, and it wouldn't be a bad idea if he took a shower.

Out of the blue (eyes) comes the Senator (a bearded Bradley Cooper) who is about to become Brian's savior because he has a better brand of NZT—and the star power that might enable this series to last beyond the five episodes that have been shot.

The action continues. Brian breaks into a bank, uncovers evidence about the murders, and wins the trust of Rebecca, the FBI agent, who unimaginably convinces her superior to make him an "asset". It might take some NZT to comprehend how preposterous this all is.

But that is just fiction, and I have a great appetite for fiction. But as a public health doctor I don't have much of an appetite for cognitive enhancers (see Neuroenhancers: Paying the Piper). Limitless is very seductive, proffering that anyone can take a powerful neuroenhancer, with no side effects—and no effort—and become a Senator, if not a President, with your love life flourishing, your crimes forgiven, and your wealth, uh, oh yes, limitless. Go ask Alice, When she's 10 feet tall.

Will the FDA and the DEA review this show? I hope so. It needs a controlled substance rating.

DISCUSSION AND CRITICAL THINKING QUESTIONS

Why are drugs so popular? Why is substance use and abuse such a popular and contentious topic?

Every society on earth, since time immemorial, has used psychoactive drugs. That is no accident and it is not going to change. The clinical and public health challenge we face is to not pretend we can wage a successful "war" but, instead, find ways to prevent, mitigate and even use substances in more healthful and psychologically enhancing ways, without the consequences of addiction and brain and body damage that can ensue.

What clinical strategies might be employed to improve the public's health and mental health?

What public health strategies might be employed to improve the public's health and mental health?

What strategies can be employed to change the public discourse and often misguided policies that often do more harm than good?

IMAGE CREDITS

Fig 1.1: Copyright © Shutterstock Images LLC.
Fig 1.2: Copyright © Depositphotos/ventanamedia.
Fig 1.3: "Talking Pathways to Patients: Addiction." Image by Chris Karampahtsis, MD, MPH courtesy of the National Neuroscience Curriculum Initiative. Copyright © 2014 by National Neuroscience Curriculum Initiative. Reprinted with permission.
Fig 1.4: Copyright © Depositphotos/BoxerX.
Fig 1.5: Copyright © Depositphotos/alexraths.
Fig 1.6: Copyright © Depositphotos/GeorgeRudy.
Fig 1.7: Copyright © Depositphotos/Wavebreakmedia.
Fig 1.8: Copyright © Depositphotos/Highwaystarz.
Fig 1.9: Copyright © Zarateman (CC BY-SA 4.0) at https://commons.wikimedia.org/wiki/File:Vitoria_-_Graffiti_%26_Murals_1238.jpg.
Fig 1.10: Copyright © Erik Charlton (CC by 2.0) at https://commons.wikimedia.org/wiki/File%3AOliver_Sacks_at_TED_2009.jpg.
Fig 1.11: Copyright © Depositphotos/Dazdraperma.

OPENING COMMENTS

Mood disorders, known widely as depression and bipolar (manic-depressive) disorder, impact every country, every demographic, and every socio-economic group. They strike throughout the life span, from early childhood through senescence. Depression, in particular, is a highly common co-traveler (co-occurring condition) seen in about every chronic physical disease, including diabetes, asthma, heart and lung disorders, cancer, Parkinson's, auto-immune disorders, and so on.

Mood disorders have a strong genetic component, with first-degree relatives (like children of people who are depressed or have bipolar illness) at greatest risk. Substance use increases the risk of a mood-related condition. Untreated, these disorders damage lives—through functional impairment and disability, great strain on relationships, and inability to maintain work or school.

WOMAN WITH DEPRESSION

The greatest public health problems with effectively managing these conditions are not their treatments, which can help the predominance of people affected, but rather how infrequently these illnesses are detected, properly diagnosed, and evidence-based treatments offered in a comprehensive, continuous manner. Stigma adds to the problem of under-detection because people affected, and their families, feel ashamed and blamed for an illness that they certainly did not chose to have.

Medications and psychotherapy have been the mainstays of treatment for both major depression and bipolar illness. The more severe the condition, the greater the necessity is for medication—for a year after onset and often considerably longer. But that is no different from diabetes or hypertension, where ongoing medication, with critical lifestyle management, is essential to controlling a disease and having a good life.

The articles below examine these conditions from biological, psychological, and social perspectives and offer an optimistic view that the public's health can be improved when it comes to these highly prevalent and painful conditions.

DEPRESSION: IT'S NOT JUST IN YOUR HEAD: IT'S ALSO IN YOUR GENES

LIS: We all want to know about telomeres, especially our own. These are the "caps" at the end of our DNA strands, and they forecast health (such as heart disease and stroke, dementia, diabetes and osteoporosis) and longevity, or not. In this post, I also describe research done on daughters of mothers with depression (and controls) where shorter telomeres were associated with greater stress responses as well as onset of depression. And if you are not blessed with longer telomeres, what can you do? Take a read.

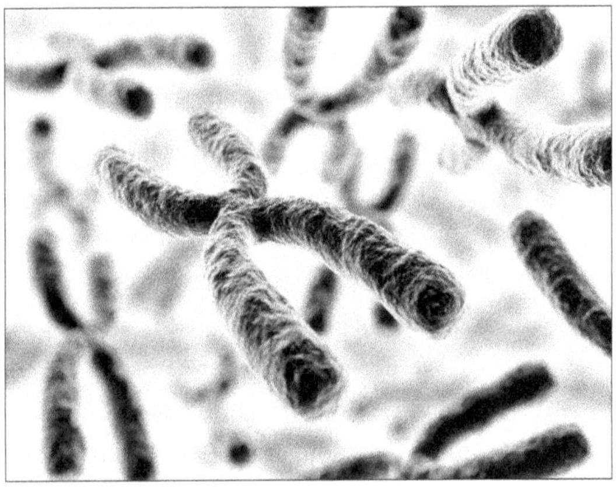

TELOMERES

Ninety-seven healthy girls, ages 10 to 14, had saliva DNA samples taken. About half of them had moms with histories of depression, and about half had moms who did not. None of the girls had histories of depression. (1)

The girls whose moms had suffered depression had significant reductions in the length of their telomeres. We all want to understand telomeres, the caps at the ends of our DNA strands, because the longer they are the longer we tend to live—and live freer of age related illnesses like heart disease, stroke, dementia, diabetes and osteoporosis. The girls whose moms didn't have histories of depression, the control group of the study, did not show the same changes in their DNA as a result of reductions in the length of their telomeres.

The researchers took the study another step: they compared both groups of girls, the former or "high-risk" group and the control or "low-risk" group, by measuring their response to stressful mental tasks. The children of moms with depression had significantly higher levels of cortisol, our stress hormone, released during these tasks than those in the control group; both had normal levels of cortisol before the stressful tasks.

These findings are what scientists call associations, namely highly significant events found together that are unlikely to co-occur randomly. In themselves, they don't prove one caused the other, but they suggest that something important, not accidental, is going on. This study demonstrated shorter telomeres in daughters of moms who had depression and greater hormonal reactivity to stress in these girls.

When the girls were followed until age 18, 60 percent of those in the high-risk group developed depression, a condition that was not evident when they were first studied. The telomere was a biomarker, an individual hallmark that a person is at higher risk for an illness—in this case for depression. We already knew that shortened telomeres were a risk factor for chronic, physical diseases but now the evidence is emerging for its likely role in depression.

Should you go out and get your saliva tested? There are labs happy to provide the test. But your decision should depend on whether you have reason to suspect being at risk, like a family history of maternal depression—which may be all you actually need to know. But information is only valuable if we can do something about it.

And we can. We have a growing set of tools to help control our stress responses: these include yoga, yogic breathing, meditation, cognitive training techniques, exercise, diet, and working to have supportive, stable relationships, and home and work environments. People at greater risk for stress-related diseases (mind you, we all are at risk it's just a matter of degree) would be wise to learn and master these techniques early in life, and use them to live a healthier and longer life.

We also need to better detect and treat mothers who suffer from depression. We have strong evidence that untreated depression in moms impairs their attachment to their children and is associated with these children developing behavioral and emotional problems in childhood. If the moms are properly treated not only do they do better, so do their kids (2).

As we try to undo a long history of stigma about mental disorders and demonstrate they are illnesses that call for identification, early intervention, effective treatment, and prevention whenever possible, this telomere study is more evidence that depression is " … not just in our heads."

Understanding our genetic predispositions, developing reliable biomarkers, managing our environment and stresses, protecting ourselves from our harmful hormones, and having access to effective treatments are our best prescriptions for healthier and longer lives.

REFERENCES

1. Telomere length and cortisol reactivity in children of depressed mothers, Gotlib, IH, LeMoult, J, et al, Molecular Psychiatry advance online publication, 30 September 2014; doi:10.1038/mp.2014.119
2. Weissman, M, et al, Remissions in Maternal Depression and Child Psychopathology A STARD CHILD Report , JAMA, March 22/29, 2006

HUMAN MASKS AND MENTAL ILLNESS

LIS: We all wear masks. As did two iconic performers whose masks hid their mood disorders, use of substances and suicidality: Philip Seymour Hoffman and Robin Williams. Williams hung himself and Hoffman died with a needle in his arm. Each of their deaths produced a wave of bewilderment among their legions of admirers. How could they do this to themselves, these extraordinarily gifted people who lived a life replete with success and wealth? The answer lies behind their masks. We do know that almost everyone who survives a suicide attempt is (in time) grateful to be alive. Depression can be treated if a person does not die by their own hands before they get better. That's possible when someone feels able to take off the mask that conceals their pain and their illness, and turns to others to seek life-saving help.

PHILIP SEYMOUR HOFFMAN

We all wear masks. Ordinary life would not otherwise be possible. But these everyday masks are different from the masks that conceal what need not be hidden.

Performers are exemplars in wearing masks. The show must go on. We celebrate their capacity to suspend reality, theirs and ours, and take us on flights of imagination. Performers can don masks of mirth, yearning, fear, desire, bliss, pain, worry, sadness, and much more. When they excel, their masks are convincing: we don't see what's going on behind the mask.

Two iconic performers left their families, friends, and audiences in recent months: Philip Seymour Hoffman and Robin Williams. I knew neither of them personally, and like many fans I had the illusion of knowing them. But I did not. I imagine there were few who knew them past their professional masks.

Each had his mental demons. Credible media and self-reports tell us that they both suffered from serious mood and substance use disorders. Each died as a result of these demons—Williams hung himself and Hoffman died with a needle in his arm. Each of their deaths produced a wave of bewilderment among their legions of admirers. How could they do this to themselves, these extraordinarily gifted people who lived a life replete with success and wealth? The answer lies behind their masks.

In the past few decades we have demystified many diseases and learned to speak aloud about them: breast cancer, Parkinson's, HIV/AIDS, Alzheimer's, even PTSD (somewhat), to name a few. But clear thinking, understanding, and open dialogue about mental and addictive disorders still elude us. We continue to judge rather than recognize these conditions as illnesses that do not warrant the discrimination and blameworthiness they too frequently receive.

As a result, when these disorders have a fatal outcome we are puzzled. When these diseases take someone we love or value we wonder how that could happen. When we are fooled by masks we look for reasons other than the illnesses themselves.

As a psychiatrist who has worked with patients for many years, I have learned three things about depression—especially when it is coupled with the excessive use of alcohol and drugs:

—The psychic pain it can produce can exceed the greatest of physical pain; mental pain is all the more difficult to bear because a person can't answer the usual question of 'where does it hurt?'

—Hopelessness is depression's dark co-conspirator; a severely depressed person believes there is no hope for recovery, no end to the pain, no exit from the hell they inhabit.

—People who are depressed realize they are a burden to family and friends: their bleak mood pervades a room and their inability to function results in demands upon others (including assuming their responsibilities and covering their lost income or medical bills); ironically, suicide can have an altruistic appeal when a depressed person thinks being gone will relieve others of their burden.

Many people with mood disorders (including depression and bipolar disorder) turn to alcohol and drugs to ease their psychic pain. Substances work, but only transiently leaving the person in an even deeper hole, and one that calls for more chemical numbing.

Alcohol, narcotics (like heroin and pain pills), and stimulants (like cocaine, meth, and amphetamines) also add to the deadliness of depression because these drugs induce dis-inhibition and impulsivity. The usual mental reservations we have to not act on a troubling idea or feeling are dissolved by drugs; alcohol has been called the 'universal solvent' (solvent is from the Latin, meaning to loosen or untie). When the impulse to die as a means of ending psychic pain, hopelessness, and guilty burden is given freer reign, as it is when intoxicated, the risk of suicide dramatically escalates.

While not the case for Robin Williams and Philip Seymour Hoffman, we know that half of the more than 39,000 deaths by suicide in the US (2011 data, the most recent available) were from gunshot wounds. Ninety percent of suicide attempts by firearm are 'successful' (result in death) while only 10 percent of attempts from overdose (usually with pills) are fatal. Access to deadlier means of suicidal behavior, like guns, contributes significantly to its tragic outcomes.

What helps to explain suicide (and many deaths by drug overdose) is that these were people overcome by the demon of depression. A great proportion of them also had taken substances that blunted their most basic instinct, namely to stay alive.

These are facts that seldom emerge and were too hidden in the wake of the deaths of these two international icons. We cannot know what they would want the public to know—or others skirting the same precipice as did they. But we do know that almost everyone who survives a suicide attempt is (in time) grateful to be alive. Depression can be treated if a person does not die by their own hands before they get better. That's possible when someone feels able to take off the mask that conceals their pain and their illness, and turn to others to seek life-saving help.

Have a story about depression that you'd like to share? Email strongertogether@huffingtonpost.com—or give us a call at (860) 348–3376, and you can record your story in your own words. Please be sure to include your name and phone number.

Need help? In the U.S., call 1-800-273-8255 for the National Suicide Prevention Lifeline.

DEPRESSION: THE EVERYWHERE AND EVERYONE ILLNESS

LIS: Clinical depression (Major Depression) is no passing phase or simply a bad day. It has haunted the human condition as far back as we can know. No race, ethnicity, age, socioeconomic group or country is spared its grip. It causes great psychic pain, physical distress, and functional impairment. It aggravates any coexisting chronic health condition, including asthma, heart and lung diseases, diabetes, Parkinson's and other neurological disorders and pain syndromes. Depression also is highly associated with the excessive use and abuse of alcohol, prescription pain and tranquilizing medications, and illegal substances. This post launched Stronger Together, The Huffington Post's 360-degree view on what it's like to live with depression in America today.

ROBIN WILLIAMS

Twenty-five hundred years ago, well before Christ, Hippocrates, the Greek father of medicine, identified melancholia as a common condition of dark mood and physical malaise. He even attributed melancholia, which today we think of as clinical depression, to a biological disturbance, namely an excess of a bodily fluid he called "black bile."

Melancholia—severe depression that is no passing phase or simply a bad day—continues today to haunt the human condition. No race, ethnicity, age or socioeconomic group is spared its grip. We find depression in every country on Earth. It causes great psychic pain, physical distress, and functional impairment. It aggravates any coexisting chronic health condition, including asthma, heart and lung diseases, diabetes, Parkinson's and other neurological disorders and pain syndromes.

Depressed patients also have twice the risk of developing cardiac and artery disease (CAD) and stroke. They are four times more likely to die within six months of a myocardial infarction (MI or heart attack). They are three times more likely to be non-compliant with treatment—a reflection of how the illness diminishes our ability to, or interest in, taking care of ourselves, as well as its harmful effects on the body's stress response, immunity and hormones.

Those people with diabetes and depression average health expenditures that are four times greater than those who are not depressed. Individuals with major depression make an average of twice as many visits to their primary care physicians as do non-depressed patients—not for their depression, but for myriad other symptoms, which are explainable when the depression is uncovered.

Depression is highly associated with the excessive use and abuse of alcohol, prescription pain and tranquilizing medications, and illegal substances. The dysphoria of depression prompts its sufferers to seek relief through these substances. But any relief is short lived and the user finds himself in a deeper hole.

Depression, as well, is found in more than 80 percent of people who take their lives by suicide. The vast predominance of people over 60 (still the highest risk group, especially among men) visited their primary care doctor's office in the past month. In other words, a chance to reach them was lost.

Yet of the estimated one in 15 who suffer with this condition annually (one in six lifetime) fewer than half are diagnosed properly or at all, and only half of those get any treatment. One in eight gets good care. This is not because of bad doctors or bad patients. It is the unfortunate consequence of stigma, persistent views of a disease as a character fault, and a very broken health and mental health system. (See my two viewpoints in JAMA: "Fixing The Troubled Mental Health System," and JAMA Psychiatry: "What Does It Take For Primary Care Practices To Truly Integrate Behavioral Health Care?") Depression is a treatable disorder. Like any serious illness, it takes comprehensive, ongoing, scientifically based care, an effective working patient-clinician relationship, and the support and patience of loving others.

It is hard to turn away from depression after losing (as their family, friends, and we the public just did) two iconic figures—Robin Williams and Philip Seymour Hoffman. We have in the wake of their respective tragedies, a moment to face squarely the demon of depression, and to try to ensure the fate of others affected is not a deadly one.

There was a time when you or a loved one would have gone to a family doctor and you would not have had your blood pressure measured. A time when we did not measure blood sugar (much less the ongoing measure of glucose control, the hemoglobin A1c), or cholesterol. A time when "care paths" were places to walk in shaded glens, not treatment protocols. That not need to be the case today.

The Huffington Post will be adding its voice to improving the recognition, care, and social acceptance of people suffering from depression. An effort like this, of course, pertains to the many other mental disorders that exist—but let's start with this most common one.

Stronger Together will take a 360-degree view on what it's like to live with depression in America today. We want to lessen stigma by fostering a conversation that includes all voices. We want to hear from people who struggle with depression—what do they wish others knew about their condition? What are they proudest of in terms of their management of the disease and their lives? There also will be articles from our staff, essays and blogs on personal experiences from thought leaders, as well as op-eds from mental health professionals.

Some day we will look back and wonder how we did not measure and treat depression, and other behavioral health disorders more effectively. We are on the transformation road now. It will be uphill and bumpy. So is all change.

Have a story about depression that you'd like to share?

Email—strongertogether@huffingtonpost.com, or give us a call at (860) 348–3376, and you can record your story in your own words. Please be sure to include your name and phone number.

Need help? In the U.S., call 1-800-273-8255 for the National Suicide Prevention Lifeline.

BIPOLAR DISORDER: WHAT A FAMILY (OR FRIEND) MIGHT SEE AND WHAT A FAMILY CAN DO

LIS: Approximately 1 percent of people in this country suffer from Bipolar Disorder (sometimes referred to as "manic depression"). It is a mental illness characterized by major mood swings of mania (bipolar I) or hypomania (a less intense form of mania called bipolar II) and depression. In this post, I describe 1) what the condition might look like to families and friends—who represent the best early warning system to identify the problem and the most essential of actors to a person with this condition getting critical help and 2) what families and friends can do.

BIPOLAR DISORDER

Nearly 1 percent of people suffer from bipolar disorder (sometimes referred to as "manic depression"). Bipolar disorder is a mental illness major mood swings of mania (bipolar I) or hypomania (a less intense form of mania called bipolar II) and depression.

We see in the press that Catherine Zeta-Jones has admitted herself to a hospital for treatment of what has been identified as bipolar II: This form of bipolar disorder can produce considerable distress as well as difficulty meeting life's demands—but without (yet) resulting in a full blown manic attack.

People with bipolar disorder, I or II, with good treatment, self-care and supportive family and friends can—and do—live full and productive lives. Without effective treatment, bipolar disorder can have a devastating effect on the person and their family, relationships and work.

What Might Bipolar Disorder Look Like to Family or Friends?

Because bipolar disorder involves both depressive and manic states, either mood problem can herald the recurrence of the condition. But I will focus here about what you might see during an emerging manic or hypomanic episode. In fact, mania typically progresses from excitement to hypomania and, if not controlled, can escalate to mania. So what you will see first is probably hypomania.

Over the course of days to weeks, your family member or friend starts sleeping less and less. He or she seems to have rather unlimited energy and is full of ideas. At first, the person may be funny and pleasant to be around, but soon that mood will become more irritable and unstable. Your loved one may start drinking more or using drugs secretly—a very common problem in people with bipolar conditions. If the person was on medication for bipolar disorder, he or she has probably stopped taking it (causing the problem to come back) or will want to discontinue because it can dim the feeling of excitement, a very desirable, though problematic, feeling for someone with this illness.

Money may be missing from where you keep it or from your bank account. Bad judgment is common during a hypomania, or in a full manic state: Your loved one may spend money recklessly and engage in risky behaviors, including casual (and unprotected) sex, gambling, driving at high speeds, and frequenting neighborhoods and settings where no good is known to happen. Your loved one may accuse you of being boring, oppressive, or ruining his or her life or hopes. As time goes by and if the illness is not treated, the excitement mounts and a person will be unable to get anything done; behaviors can become progressively more threatening to the safety and wellbeing of the family. Commonsense talk seems to go when you try to reason with the person who is now ill.

WHAT CAN YOU DO?

Faced with mounting evidence of serious problems and a family's efforts at reasoning defied, with worry and love driving them, a family may want to push harder, insist that their loved one faces facts—does something! Tempers can escalate and each side digs in more deeply.

The first thing you can do is what not to do, which is to not get into fights with your loved one. This may be the hardest prescription of all. What can work is a combination of listening and leverage. There is much to say about this, which I do in my book for families. I believe that all behavior, even illness behavior, serves a purpose. We just may not know yet what it is. By listening and asking questions, you may find out—not by crossing swords.

Leverage is about a family being a two-way street: You get and you give. As a family or friend, what supports are you providing? Like a cell phone, money, car, even a place to stay. These are leverage points that can be used to negotiate for what needs to be done. What does a loved one need to do—ultimately in their interest—to continue to receive money, use the car, or stay together?

Avoiding a fight is not the same thing as being disengaged. In fact, it's staying just as involved—in a different way. It is hard to not get into a fight, you may need help.

The second thing, therefore, is don't go it alone. Mental health problems, including addictions, are among the most common medical problems that exist. That means that there are others—in your extended family and among their friends and co-workers—who have been down the same road.

Who can you confide in? Is there a spouse, brother, sister, aunt, uncle, friend, or someone who has had a depression, addiction, traumatic disorder or other mental problem and is open about it (and, thankfully, more people are)? That's someone to turn to. You can turn to a primary care doctor or clergy, someone who has known your loved one for some time. Families can turn to school counselors or employee assistance programs at work. Advocacy organizations, like a local chapter of the National Alliance on Mental Illness (NAMI) or the Mental Health America (MHA), are terrific resources that I almost always suggest; these organizations are staffed by experienced and trained people. NAMI has families who have been there. These organizations provide information and referral, by phone or in person. And they are free!

Don't go it alone. This lesson has been learned with every persistent illness, including diabetes, colitis, cancer, Alzheimer's and countless other conditions. Mental disorders, including bipolar disorder, are no different.

Third, learn about the mental health system of care, its treatments, its rules and how to work with and bend the rules. I am not talking about going to psychology graduate school. I am talking about becoming an informed and vocal advocate for your loved one. Health care in general—not just mental health—now demands informed and assertive families and consumers.

Fourth—and this is also hard, but no different from illnesses of all sorts—you will need to think of managing the illness as more of a marathon than a sprint. Managing all but short-term illnesses (like infections or broken bones) means taking a long view. Sticking with it.

A family's morale and determination will be tested. "Never, ever, give up." While often difficult to predict, a person's involvement in care or their illness improves. Mental health professionals have seen this again and again. You need to know this. Don't lose hope, don't give up. Take the long view, in your mind and with your efforts.

RECOVERY

Recovery is a word that does not only apply to addictions. Recovery is about having a life of meaning, purpose, dignity, relationships and contribution. It is what we all want, and it is possible with mental illnesses like bipolar disorder, and the many other faces of mental illness.

As we watch how Ms. Zeta-Jones manages her illness, there may be much to learn from someone so talented—so successful, and yet ill—about how to not let bipolar disorder, or any mental or addictive disease, derail or destroy a life or a family.

BIOMARKERS FOR DEPRESSION: PROMISE OR PRIME TIME?

LIS: World Health Organization (WHO) has defined a biomarker as " … any substance, structure, or process that can be measured in the body or its products and influence or predict the incidence of outcome or disease" Depression biomarkers potentially could provide objective, physical evidence to demonstrate the presence of the illness; they might inform doctors how to better select which medication for which patient. But there is often a long road, full of right and wrong turns, between promise and practical application. Are biomarkers for depression ready for prime time? This post says, not yet—and explains why.

I scanned the table of contents of the British online journal BMC Medicine soon after it appeared in my email. A title caught my eye: "Depression Pathogenesis and Treatment: What Can We Learn From Blood mRNA Expression?" I thought about the many families that have asked me about biomarkers, especially for depression.

At a recent conference, a young woman came up to me, accompanied by her parents. She described how though she was in treatment for a major depression she had not, as yet, seen enough improvement to be able to regain good functioning at work. Her parents said they had read about blood tests that could better detect and inform the treatment of depression. They asked: Did they exist? Should they get them for their daughter?

So when I saw the journal article, I wondered if there was something new that could better explain how depression comes on in a person (called pathogenesis—or how a disease process is born). Might there be new information about how to improve depression treatment?

Biomarkers are tests that uncover valuable information about a disease. Doctors, patients, and families all seek biomarkers that might help in the treatment of very common conditions that produce great suffering and burden, like depression.

Depression affects about 7 percent of adults in the U.S. annually, and about one-third of those people have severe symptoms that markedly decrease functioning. That's about 17 million people over 18 who suffer this condition, about 6 million severely, every year. We all know someone who has depression, and one in 10 Americans are on antidepressants. Controversy continues to brew, as well, about whether this disorder is over-diagnosed and whether antidepressants are effective. Might there be biomarkers to better resolve who needs and can benefit from which treatment(s) for this condition?

The article described people they studied with major (clinical) depression who demonstrated " ... an altered pattern of expression in several genes ... compared with healthy controls." What was especially intriguing about this study was that it focused on how our genes express themselves, not simply the actual genes.

Humans have 22 chromosomes plus a sex chromosome (X or Y). On these chromosomes are about 3 million DNA "base pairs"—the small molecules wound into the iconic double helix structure that pass genetic information from one generation to the next. But the information on the DNA must be sent out in message form to operate the way the cells in our body operate. That is the work of RNA (ribonucleic acid), especially messenger RNA (mRNA), miraculous compounds that decode and guide the expression of the genetic lineage that our DNA supplies. While DNA has the blueprint for human life, RNA is required to orchestrate the protein synthesis that will tell individual cells throughout the brain and body how to function, including moving muscles, digesting food, seeing, smelling and hearing, and the astounding ability we have to feel and think.

The report in BMC Medicine focused on mRNA in blood cells, which might serve as an easily obtainable proxy for the mRNA in the brain where it influences neurotransmitters, stress hormones, inflammatory proteins and cell growth factors, all of importance in the development of major depression. What's more, mRNA (in the brain and body tissues) has incorporated how our environment has affected our genes (called epigenetics or nurture) and the dynamic gene interactions that have altered the final expression of what nature (DNA) has provided. Might these scientists have found a way of identifying, through mRNA found in blood, a biological marker for the disease of depression?

The young woman I met and her family, like so many others, could benefit from biomarkers if:

1. There were definitive biological markers of psychiatric disease, in this case depression. Mental disorders are real, yet there is no measure like high blood sugar, bad lipid levels or elevated blood pressure to demonstrate the presence of a physical illness.

2. If there existed more of what is termed "personalized" treatment. Some medications work better for some people than others. This is true in cancer as well as with mental illness. But how can we know—aside from trial and error—which one is better so it can be used sooner and more effectively?

Depression biomarkers potentially could physically demonstrate the presence of the illness and might inform doctors how to better select which medication for which patient. But there is often a long road, full of right and wrong turns, between promise and practical application. People with mental illness, and their families, are often on the watch for useful innovation. But their precious resources, financial as well as hope, must be carefully protected. Biomarkers are being marketed today, including those for depression. Should you spend your money on these tests? Are they ready for prime time?

The authors of this study conclude that while there was a " ... pattern of altered expression in several genes of interest ... the temporal [timing] relationship with other factors, such as exposure to stress, is still unclear." They add that: " ... we also do not know whether some of these changes in gene expression represent the marker of a genetic predisposition ... [or might represent an] association between depression and inflammation."

In other words, there is promise but not more, not yet. My answer to the family I met would not change: I had said that while there is reason to believe we will see reliable biomarkers in the future, I would not advise they go for this type of testing right now.

Genetics and neuroscience rival the complexity of the physics of the universe. With genetic inheritance alone, there is hardly a single or simple pathway. Often, many genes are involved in complex diseases like diabetes and depression. The genes themselves actually vary in their form and expression (called genetic alleles). Those many genes, and their alleles, also are subject to highly-variable expression as a result of the physical and emotional environment they encounter in individual human beings—with genes being turned on and off continuously by countless factors to which the person is exposed. And even within the specific cells that the genes send their messages to (via mRNA), ever-changing intracellular activity exerts further influence on what proteins are then synthesized that drive cellular functioning. As if that cascade were not complex enough, genes mutate. They change. Some changes are quite common and some rare, but our genes are constantly undergoing changes that may be adaptive or maladaptive to our everyday lives.

Yet science is remarkable, and by dint of effort, good luck and (often accidental) discovery our species enjoys vastly greater health and life prospects than our ancestors. But brain biomarkers are not what distressed patients and families should invest in right now as they seek better diagnosis and treatment of depression. Careful clinical assessment, systematically-developed and followed treatment plans created between patient and doctor, ongoing monitoring, and course corrections when needed remain the state of the art and science. That is how the predominance of people with depression today can improve and experience greater pleasure, purpose and productivity.

RAPID CYCLING BIPOLAR DISORDER: IN THE OFFICE AND ON 'THE STREET'

LIS: With this condition, a person experiences four or more major (clinical) mood shifts in the course of a year. For some that can happen many times in a given day. People with this illness are especially vulnerable to triggers, events and physical states, which can set off their illness. This disorder is notoriously difficult to treat and has a poorer prognosis than non-rapid cycling Bipolar Disorder. We need better prevention and treatments for this disease.

Rapid cycling bipolar disorder is a turbulent and psychologically painful condition characterized by four or more major mood shifts in the course of a year (sometimes even in a week). Moods go up or down in this condition and are demarcated by a rapid switch to a state of the opposite polarity. Rapid cycling states can come at any time, and are known to appear and disappear.

Rapid cycling bipolar disorder is perilously vulnerable to outside influences, notably both those that are troubling and deleterious or, alternatively, uplifting and beneficial. Stressful events are famous for precipitating shifts into low or high states of mind. The condition begs for a stable environment and a predictable and reliable future.

This disorder is notoriously difficult to treat. Among the remedies used are mood stabilizers, anti-convulsants and anti-psychotics(!). When one intervention fails, as often happens, another is piled on; then another. In some tragic cases, all this effort is to no avail. In other cases, where the cycling abates, the myriad of interventions leaves little clue as to which one may have made a difference.

Lives are put in shambles, families rendered asunder, workplaces disrupted and resources dangerously stretched when rapid cycle bipolar disorder sets in and affects individuals and their communities.

Rapid cycling is typically associated with a poorer longer-term prognosis. One cycle, up or down, seems to trigger another, and another. The more cycles there are, the more likely another cycle will explode upon the scene leaving those affected thunderstruck and anxious as to whether they will ever escape the condition's grip. Over time, hope can fade. Over time, resources dwindle. With little to live on and scarce opportunity for a better future individuals may have little choice but to rely upon government entitlement programs.

You might think I am talking about my business, psychiatry, where we recognize a condition with these features and call it "rapid cycling bipolar disorder." But, instead, as I tuned into relentless media reports coming from Wall Street to Tokyo all this past week, I started wondering about the equity markets—and our societies. What we are witnessing seems to meet all the diagnostic criteria for rapid cycling bipolar disorder. Without effective interventions, reductions in stress and a good dose of hope (see "Raising the Hope Ceiling") the prognosis is not good. We need a game changer for this condition wherever it may appear.

DEPRESSION TREATMENT: TREATING DEPRESSION THE OLD-FASHIONED WAY

LIS: A pioneer in alternative medicine over 150 years ago treated his depressed patients with baths, vigorous exercise, adequate sleep and proper diet. Perhaps the one thing we all can do, more than anything, to improve our well-being, protect against Alzheimer's, and extend longevity is exercise. The use of exercise in treating depression, as an invaluable component to its acute and maintenance care, is what this post discusses.

GROUP OF WALKING ON BEACH

Were he around today, I could imagine referring one of my patients or a family asking about help for a loved one with depression to Vincenz Priessnitz. But he died in 1851. Priessnitz was a pioneer in alternative medicine, where diet, exercise, and non-medicinal interventions (like hydrotherapy, namely baths with robust currents and minerals added), were provided to people with depressive illness, among other disorders.

Practicing in Austria (in a region that is now part of the Czech Republic), Priessnitz gained fame throughout Europe, the UK, the New World, and as far as New Zealand for curing his patients by combining baths with vigorous exercise, adequate sleep and proper diet. Exercise consisted of long walks in fresh air or sometimes (the season permitting I suppose) walking barefoot in fields of grass.

What do they say? What goes around, comes around? Especially, what we could call 'the walking cure.'

Several recent studies, a mere 150 or more years after his death, validate Priessnitz's contention about exercise. More general support for the medicinal, or health, value of exercise was reported in a review article on 29 studies that showed that attention, memory and speed of mental functions were substantially improved in individuals who engaged in aerobic exercise (1). More specific, anatomic brain volume increases were found in people with schizophrenia who exercised aerobically (2). General mental health has been shown to be associated positively with how vigorous and frequent adults exercise (3).

But my favorite is the work of Drs. Dunn, Trivedi and their colleagues in Texas and Canada who demonstrated the salubrious effects of exercise on depression (4). Before I describe their work, I want to stress, as I have elsewhere, that if you or a loved one has severe depression, or depression with suicidal ideas or loss of reality (called psychotic depression), get thee to a doctor. Alternate treatments like exercise or evidence-based psychotherapies, like cognitive-behavioral and interpersonal therapy, are highly effective for mild to moderate depression but for more severe depressive illness—which can be life-threatening—medication is generally needed. When illness is severe, alternate treatments become complementary treatments, which is to say they can add, or complement, the action of medical interventions.

But back to the 'walking cure.' The work of Dunn and Trivedi showed that exercising three or more times a week to the level recommended by the American College of Sports Medicine and other public health consensus reports improved symptoms of depression. They called this the "public health dose" of aerobic activity, which means vigorous exercise (walking, running, stationery bicycle are all good) for at least 30 minutes at a time, several or more times a week. No differences were found between those that exercised three times versus five times a week. But those who did not get the "public health dose" (either because they were in a group that did less exercise or were controls, people who did not engage in the treatment but were monitored as a comparison group) did not have the clear improvements in depression that those that exercised did, judged by significant reduction in symptoms or full remission of their condition.

You don't have to start at the "public health dose." Like with most treatments, wise counsel is to start low and go slow. Begin with short walks, or time on an exercise machine. Do it twice a week, and then get to three or more times. Find the right time for you: some people prefer to exercise in the morning, some in the late afternoon or evening (when our muscles are more warmed up and flexible). Work, school or home schedules, of course, may make it plain enough what times are possible.

How does exercise work? We don't know for sure. Release of neurotransmitters instrumental to mood regulation (like serotonin and norepinephrine) or pain control (like endorphins) may play an important role, or perhaps reductions in stress hormones. The discipline and self-mastery of committing to a task and doing it faithfully helps with self-esteem and self-confidence. We may not know the mysteries of the neurophysiology and neurochemistry of exercise, but we know it works!

What does not work, however, is not exercising. It can be hard to exercise even if you are not depressed. Exercise takes time, and for people not used to it can produce aches, pains and fatigue. But those 'side-effects', if you will, go away soon—replaced often by a feeling of well being, clearer thinking and improvement in mood; some people even lose weight. For people who are depressed, doing almost anything can seem too great a task, or they feel that their condition is hopeless or that they do not deserve to feel better. That is where family and friends come in. Exercise that is done with others, or encouraged and supported by others, is more likely to happen. Priessnitz had a captive population, so if you were at his spa or under his care you got up and walked—not negotiable if you want to get better, he might have said.

The question for a person with depression, then, is what are you willing to do to feel better, to be able to feel energy and hope again in your life? What do you not only owe yourself, but what do you owe your loved ones, friends and others who rely on you at home, work, school and in your community?

The answer may be old-fashioned, but not out of style.

REFERENCES

1. Smith, Blumenthal, et al: Psychosomatic Medicine: 72:239–252, 2010
2. Pajonk, Wobrock, et al: Archives of General Psychiatry: 67:133–143, 2010
3. Medical Sciences Sports Exercise: December 1, 2010
4. Dunn, Triveti, et al: American Journal of Preventive Medicine 5:28:1–8, 2005

CAN ELECTRICALLY STIMULATING THE BRAIN IMPROVE MENTAL HEALTH?

LIS: Mental disorders have a long and mixed history of biological treatment by pharmaceutical agents. The search is on to treat these conditions, substance use disorders as well, in ways that intervene differently in the brain—and that are effective, safe and perhaps with fewer side-effects. One technique is known as CES, cranial electrical stimulation, where a weak, alternating current to the scalp is used to treat depression, anxiety, insomnia and stress; and it has been used to aid in long term abstinence in people with alcohol and drug dependence. A second technique is known as TMS (or rTMS), transcranial magnetic stimulation. rTMS (r for repetitive) delivers alternating magnetic fields to the scalp that induce electrical currents in the brain cortex. Both these techniques are non-invasive and appear to be safe. Studying their effectiveness is underway. More details are in the post below.

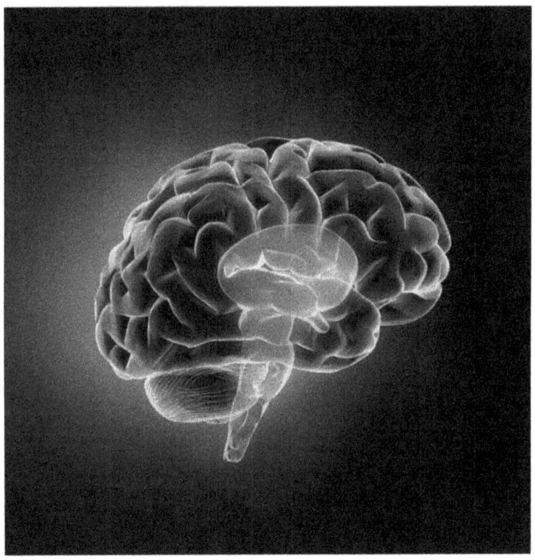

HUMAN BRAIN

So many people think that ECT (electroconvulsive therapy, sometimes erroneously called "shock therapy") is the only way to apply electrical stimulation to the brain as a treatment. Not so. In fact, there are a variety of proven and promising electrical (or magnetic) techniques that affect the brain—from those with virtually no side effects, nor an invasive procedure, to those that are surgical in nature.

Why consider applying a current to the brain? Primarily to offer an alternative to psychopharmacological (medication) treatments. We need different yet safe and effective ways of improving mood and anxiety disorders or reducing insomnia and stress.

Medications affect levels of neurotransmitters, or chemicals such as serotonin, norepinephrine or dopamine, naturally present in the brain (within or between nerve cells) known to affect how we feel, think and act. Electrical stimulation and magnetic fields induce currents that change the way that brain cells, called neurons, fire. In other words, medications work on molecules and brain stimulation works on cells. Brain stimulation, notably, has no known interaction or effect on medications a person may be taking, unlike most other treatments we have. Neuroscientists and psychiatrists have been searching for alternatives to pills for centuries because too many individuals do not fully respond or have side effects and medical complications from the medications so far developed.

Interest in electrically stimulating the brain dates back to the 1930s when Italian scientists developed a means of inducing a brain seizure by applying an intense electric current to the scalp—which we now call ECT. While ECT remains an important treatment today for those individuals whose condition, especially severe depression, does not respond to medication and therapy—it does require anaesthesia, produces at least short-term memory problems, frightens many people, is costly and is often transitory in its effects. Hence, the search for alternative means of improving brain functioning in people with psychiatric disorders.

Remarkably, over 60 years ago (1949) scientists in the (then) Soviet Union began applying a very low voltage alternating current to stimulate the brain, CES or cranial electrical stimulation, which they called "electrosleep" to treat insomnia (cranial refers to the skull or cranium, where the electrical leads are placed and the scalp stimulated). This treatment does not deliver any where near the electrical current needed to induce seizures. The repertoire of brain stimulation techniques grew in the mid-1980s when magnetic fields were applied around the cranium to stimulate the brain, a technique known as TMS, or transcranial magnetic stimulation. More recently, brain stimulation has been done surgically by deep brain stimulation (DBS) and vagal nerve stimulation (VNS), which were first used for neurological conditions such as epilepsy and Parkinson's disease, then adapted for psychiatric conditions. Of all the brain stimulation procedures available recent interest has been greatest about CES and TMS.

CES, cranial electrical stimulation, applies a weak, alternating current to the scalp usually by leads placed on a person's temples or earlobes. CES has had FDA approval for over 30 years as a device (grandfathered-in, or approved without specific study) to treat depression, anxiety, insomnia and stress; it has also been used to aid in long term abstinence in people with alcohol and drug dependence. The current is of micro-voltage (ECT has 1000-fold more current), can hardly be felt, has little or no side-effects, or evident harm. While there are many testimonials to its benefits we lack rigorous study of its therapeutic effectiveness. CES devices can be purchased over the internet and a variety of companies will sell you one, with a medical prescription, which you can apply to yourself at home. CES is quite safe but its benefits remain to be scientifically established: we have promise, but not proof.

TMS, transcranial magnetic stimulation also known as rTMS, delivers alternating magnetic fields to the scalp that induce electrical currents in the brain cortex, or outer layers of the brain. The electrical currents are about 100–200 times more powerful than CES but do not require anesthesia; TMS is not meant to induce seizure (though this is a low risk of the procedure). The electric current induced by the magnetic field produces immediate and very brief nerve cell activity, or firing of brain cells. TMS recently achieved FDA approval for treatment resistant major depression but must be prescribed and administered by a professional; insurance coverage for this FDA approved treatment is spotty. TMS is proven to work and thus represents an important choice in the treatment of major depression for individuals who are not responsive to properly selected and administered medication and therapy.

Mental illnesses are highly prevalent, cause great suffering in those affected and their loved ones, and can produce disability and heavy financial burden to families and society. As a result, we are on a continuous quest to discover new, safe, effective and acceptable treatments for people with illnesses such as depression, anxiety disorders, substance use disorders, and psychotic illnesses (such as schizophrenia and bipolar disorder). In addition, safe and affordable interventions for distressing symptoms like insomnia, stress, and low or anxious mood that do not reach the proportions of a mental disorder are needed. While medications tend to get the most press when it comes to treatments for mental conditions they are but one approach.

We know that psychotherapy works, especially structured forms of therapy like cognitive-behavioral therapy, interpersonal therapy and desensitization techniques; we know that alternative forms of treatment like acupuncture, meditation, yoga, homeopathy, and forms of eastern body work (shiatsu and sugi massage) can be helpful in disease states and everyday suffering; and we have means of brain stimulation that work or show promise.

Knowing what works for whom at what point in the course of illness is the science and art of psychiatric medicine. A diverse set of therapeutics is essential since no one treatment works for everyone, nor meets the important preferences that individuals bring to the therapeutic encounter. The more diverse the alternatives the better the chance that each person will find something that relieves their suffering and enables the functioning we all want to have a life lived with others and of contribution.

LET'S NOT GET TOO DEPRESSED ABOUT DEPRESSION

LIS: Major Depression is terribly common, affecting youth and adults, impairs functioning, can be disabling, and it is seen as the predominant, active mental condition in people who take their lives. Most people with depression do not go to see psychiatrists, psychologists and social workers; they go to their primary care physician complaining of some vague set of problems or show up frequently because their heart disease or diabetes just doesn't get better. This post describes work underway in many states (and spreading substantially) to introduce depression screening, treatment to target, quantifiable and sensitive to change measures, and clinical management in primary care settings—where the patients are and where they are not apt to leave even if referred to specialty mental health services.

Depression is the poster child of mental health. It is everywhere: we all have a relative or friend or co-worker that suffers from depression. It is understandable: like a blue day—but 50 times worse and it won't go away. Celebrities, authors, and athletes tell us tales of their depression. It is historical: melancholia dates back to Hippocrates. It is universal: no race, ethnicity, or country is spared; it strikes along the age spectrum from youth to old age. And it is treatable.

Depression is painful, disabling and a major driver of suicide. It reduces the productivity of our businesses through absenteeism and presenteeism (showing up but not being able to do much). It appears all the time, an unwelcome intruder, in people with diabetes, heart disease, cancer, Parkinson's and asthma, and impairs their ability to recover from their medical problems. Depression escalates health care spending for other diseases unless it is detected and treated. For all its prevalence and impact on our society—and one in five Americans will have a depression in their lifetimes—depression just doesn't get the respect it deserves.

My evidence for that claim is not its popularity in the media but its second class status in medical care. Most people with depression do not go to see psychiatrists, psychologists and social workers; they go to their primary care physician complaining of some vague set of problems or show up frequently because their heart disease or diabetes just doesn't get better. Those who go and say they feel depressed are frequently inadequately treated or told it's because of age or illness (75 percent of seniors who kill themselves were in their primary care doctor's office in the month before they took their lives). Reliable studies indicate that 75 percent of those afflicted with this treatable and too often debilitating or fatal illness do not receive effective care. One highly noted national study reported that 13 percent of people treated in the general medical sector get "minimally adequate" mental health care.

This is not because there are bad doctors (though there are some of those). This is because depression has not gained a foothold in the standard operations of your doctor's office. When we go to our doctor we get a set of numbers: we are weighed, our blood pressure taken, pulse too—all numbers we have come to understand. We know it is really bad to have a BP of 170/110, and if we tell someone who cares about us they say "what are you doing about that?" Then we get more numbers: labs are drawn for sugar, good and bad cholesterol, iron in our blood cells, PSA in men, and on and on. We know it is really bad to have a sugar of 400 and pretty good to have a total cholesterol below 200. Doctors and patients (and families) understand numbers and manage to numbers.

But for the longest time mental health conditions, like depression, did not have a number. Chart records might say mood was "pretty low" or "about the same" or "discouraged" or "crying a lot". Quality medical care is hard to achieve with just descriptive terms; it relies on quantitative measures, principally numbers. What's more, there is not much chance to compete for a doctor's precious time if she is busy fixing the numbers for sugar and BP. Mental health has been losing in the competition for fair time and proper management without a numerical measure of a disease. How about starting with its poster child disease—depression—to remedy that?

The good news is that there is a simple, nine item questionnaire called the PHQ-9 that someone can fill out in the waiting room, before seeing the doctor or nurse, that provides a highly reliable number that tells the doctor the likelihood (almost 90 percent sensitive) that you have a depression. The PHQ-9 gives a score from 0–27 and over 10 is the line in the sand that says depression is likely present; over 20 means it is severe. The patient, once diagnosed by the doctor, has a number—say 18—which goes in the medical record and the patient, family, and doctor have the job of getting that number below 10. Just like the person with the BP of 170/110 needs to get that number to (or below) 120/80.

Doctors are good learners. If they need to do something they will learn to do it. If you measure their performance they learn how to do better. We see this with rates of immunization, mammography, surgical complications, and the treatment of a host of common and serious diseases like diabetes, asthma, and heart disease. But they have not yet had to tackle depression, even though it is ubiquitous in their practice, because it has not been systematically measured and monitored. Clear treatment care paths exist that doctors can follow that make for success in treating depression, just as they do with other prevalent conditions that carry great suffering and disability. Improvement rates seen from well-studied depression treatments are in the 70–80 percent range—as good as or better than treatment responses to diabetes and heart disease.

One hundred percent of primary care practices that see adolescents through adults of all ages should be screening for depression and using standardized treatment guidelines. New York City began a journey toward that goal in 2005 (see New York Times April 13, 2005, p1). Initial progress was good when the City's municipal hospitals, which care for one in six New Yorkers, decided to make the PHQ-9 a standard screen to be completed in the electronic medical record. Other care systems have begun to adopt the practice but change has been slow. Some selected health systems around the country are using it, but to my knowledge no state, county or municipality has made depression screening and management a standard of care.

When we ran the public relations campaign for depression screening in NYC our tag line was: HAVE YOU ASKED YOUR DOCTOR ABOUT A SIMPLE TEST FOR DEPRESSION?

Have you? For yourself or your loved one? Why not? Are you not giving depression the respect it deserves?

THE GOOD NEWS ABOUT THE 'BAD' NEWS ABOUT ANTIDEPRESSANTS

LIS: For years, literature and debate has raged about whether antidepressants "work" in the treatment of depression. For people with mild to moderate depression, they have many interventions to choose from: medications, psychotherapy (like cognitive-behavioral therapy, interpersonal therapy, psychodynamic therapy); even for some with mild conditions what used to be called "watchful waiting". For severe depression, where a person is paralyzed by this illness and at risk for suicide, antidepressants can be life-saving. This post notes two publications expanding on these ideas.

There's been a lot of buzz in recent weeks saying that antidepressants don't work, or that they don't work better than placebos—or sugar pills. This controversy is not new. Previous studies have suggested that people with mild to moderate depression respond to psychotherapy as well as they do to antidepressant medications. Other studies even suggest that placebo treatments, the power of suggestion coupled with ongoing attention and concern, may work as well as any "active" treatment, whether it is medication or psychotherapy.

We can expect important scientific rebuttals to the celebrated "anti" antidepressant study in the Journal of the American Medical Association (JAMA, January issue) by Fournier and colleagues. I hope those whose lives are affected by depression will read the forthcoming challenges to Fournier's findings, and that journalists will cover what they say, since the conclusions arrived at by him are debatable. More importantly, antidepressants do work, especially for people with severe depression—who are also at greatest risk for suicide. Aside from this debate I was surprised to read that many regarded the JAMA article as bad news about antidepressants. Bad? Why bad?

The good news I read is that depression is amenable to many interventions, so people have choices: medications, psychotherapy (like cognitive-behavioral therapy, interpersonal therapy, psychodynamic therapy), even for some with mild conditions what used to be called "watchful waiting", which is very different from indifference. Placebos are not just sugar pills—they are means by which people who are suffering are attended to by trained, caring and attentive individuals—that sounds a lot like watchful waiting to me.

Depression is terribly common (and far more untreated than it is properly treated—see my Huffington post article). The fact is that far too few people get diagnosed or receive any treatment. Take a look at another journal article by Gonzalez and colleagues in the January issue of the Archives of General Psychiatry; this report tells the story of those who do not get the care they need, especially people of color.

People with depression, if their condition is recognized and they are helped to engage any one of a variety of effective treatments—and for some kindly concern, support and hope—will get better. That sounds like good news to me.

DISCUSSION AND CRITICAL THINKING QUESTIONS

What do we know about mood disorders, especially depression, their genetic influences and about potential "biomarkers" to help identify these conditions early and to choose treatments selectively?

How do people with mood disorders hide their conditions? Why? What are the dangers of hiding and isolation?

What do families of people affected face, and what can they do to help their loved ones?

Treatments are varied, and many work. What is the current thinking about medications, psychotherapy, electrical stimulation of the brain, and life-style management (including exercise, diet, meditation, yoga, etc.)?

IMAGE CREDITS

Fig 2.1: Copyright © Depositphotos/creatista.
Fig 2.2: Copyright © Depositphotos/sashkin7.
Fig 2.3: Copyright © Depositphotos/kozzi2.
Fig 2.4: Copyright © Eva Renaldi (CC BY-SA 2.0) at https://commons.wikimedia.org/wiki/File%3ARobin_Williams_2011a_(2).jpg.
Fig 2.5: Copyright © Depositphotos/stocksnapper.
Fig 2.6: Copyright © Depositphotos/michaeljung.
Fig 2.7: Copyright © Depositphotos/CLIPAREA.

OPENING COMMENTS

In the United States, more than 42,000 people take their lives each year, and every one of them is potentially preventable.

Suicide is the exit strategy for a person beset with unbearable psychic pain, all too isolated, and convinced that there is no exit from the state they are in. In approximately 90% of deaths, there is an active mental disorder, usually major depression, often accompanied by the use or abuse of substances like alcohol, which disinhibit protective aspects of our nature that want us to survive. In this country, half of the deaths from suicide are due to gunshot wounds, which are almost always fatal or irrevocably destructive.

Yet, as vital as the diagnosis and treatment of an active mental or substance use disorder is, that is not enough. We have learned that a second track must be instituted immediately to keep a person alive until

PREVENTING SUICIDE

they want to live again. Most everyone who survives a suicide attempt later says they are glad to be alive. Specific techniques, many described in the articles that follow, are available to make contact with and enable people to stay alive until their disease state and hopelessness abate.

There are also public health actions that can be taken to protect against the deadly co-occurrence of suicide and homicide, illustrated in two *HuffPosts*, one on the Germanwings plane crash that killed 150 people and the other a national campaign for suicide prevention in Australia called "R U OK?"

I offer as well both a book and documentary review to take readers to other media that tell the story of the tragedy of suicide and what we can do to avert it.

HOW DOCTORS THINK: SUICIDE PREVENTION

LIS: More than 42,000 people die by suicide annually in the United States. Of the 10 greatest preventable causes of death this one is the only one where the rate continues to climb, year after year. It is not enough to treat an underlying mental or substance disorder, and they are almost always there, though that must be done. This article specifies current thinking on suicide prevention in the US. We now know that "suicidality" must be seen as a co-occurring condition, to be detected and measures taken immediately to help someone stay alive, including "safety plans, "warm handoffs", and reducing access to deadly means of self-destruction (especially guns).

Second in a Series about "How Doctors Think"*

By Lloyd I. Sederer, MD and Jay Carruthers, MD**

About 10 years ago, one of us (LIS), as mental health commissioner of NYC, was providing budget testimony before a committee of the City Council. One of the City Councilors asked what my agency was doing to reduce suicide attempts and deaths in the City.

In addition to funding Lifenet (now a national crisis line), I spoke about my agency beginning an audacious initiative to implement depression screening and management in all primary care practices in the city.

We knew clinical depression was present in a vast percentage of people who make serious suicide attempts. By detecting and effectively treating depression in primary care settings, where most people appeared—especially seniors—in the days and weeks before an attempt, we envisioned reducing suicide attempts among residents of NYC by treating the mental disorder that was instrumental to prompting people to this form of self-destruction. We had launched a depression treatment campaign; we even had a poster and media campaign at doctors' offices, on buses and the subway and at ATMs!

However, that was what we knew then. Since then we have learned more about how best to reduce suicidal behavior. While a social media and public education campaign about depression was (still is) needed and detecting and effectively treating depression in primary care (and other) settings was (still is) necessary those did not translate into immediate reductions in suicidal behavior.

We have since learned that to reduce suicidal behaviors we will need to separate intervening in the acute, transitory suicidal state from other efforts to treat any accompanying mental or addictive disorder, including depression. In other words, detection and treatment of an underlying mental health condition is still necessary but it is not sufficient if we are going to reduce suicides in NYS (or elsewhere).

Doctors, mental health clinicians, and community health workers now must learn to think (actually practice, not just think) differently to save the lives of suicidal people. First, they need to ask (as they always have), in ways that do not rush or shame, whether someone is or has reached the point where living has become a form of intolerable suffering. After asking, today's clinicians will principally need to learn to do three things for those at risk:

1. Establish a "Safety Plan", a preplanned way to get support and reduce the impulse to act (an educational video on Safety Plans is available here).
2. Maintain phone or in person contact (called a "Warm Handoff") in the days following a suicide attempt, an emergency room visit, or a psychiatric or addiction hospital stay.
3. Reduce access to deadly means of self-destruction, especially guns.

Each of these is described in more detail below. The need to treat any active mental and substance use disorder does not go away—but that will take time. A person has to be helped to stay alive until the treatment works and any deadly impulses abate.

A Safety Plan is a prioritized list of supports and coping strategies to be used when suicidal urges arise. A trained clinician works collaboratively with the patient to construct an individualized safety plan. Core to this effort is the view that the suicidal individual is the expert on his or her life; the clinician is the expert on interventions that can help. Together they craft a plan that is then practiced and refined over the course of treatment, in which specific self-management skills and action steps to obtain support are employed during times of distress.

It has been identified that the period immediately following discharge from an inpatient psychiatric unit or Emergency Room as high risk for suicidal individuals (especially within the first 30 days). Clinicians now need to carefully attend to these transitions in care and ensure that services bridge the gap between the hospital/ER and the patient's engagement in outpatient services. One such approach is called "structured follow-up" where the hospital team develops a Safety Plan with the patient just prior to discharge. Equipped with a copy of the hospital safety plan, a trained staff person calls the patient within 24 hours of discharge. In a series of brief calls—often lasting fewer than 15 minutes—the clinician does a quick mood and safety check, reviews the safety plan (refining it if needed), and problem solves around any barriers that might limit additional treatment and social supports. Calls can continue until all agree that what is needed for safety is in place.

Finally, we know the vast majority of individuals contemplating suicide experience some measure of ambivalence about taking their life. For many, the time from first thinking about ending their life to the time of attempting suicide is often minutes to a few hours. These brief, but transient, moments of acute suicidality can come on powerfully and suddenly—and exceed a person's capacity to use a Safety Plan or seek help. In those instances, what is critical is whether a person has immediate access to lethal means of dying, especially firearms. Guns account for over 50 percent of all suicides in the U.S each year and are lethal in over 85 percent of cases. Thus, doctors now need to think and ask about access to deadly means of suicide, especially weapons. Taking steps to "suicide-proof" a home with safe storage of firearms, using gun locks, and reducing access to dangerous medications can prevent a brief period of overwhelming distress from turning into the tragedy of a family suicide.

Doctors and other health and mental health clinicians are learning to think differently about suicidality, and thereby reduce its grave consequences. They need to learn, as we have and you will as well if you have a loved one with a mental illness or addiction, to uncouple treating the disease state from intervening to keep someone alive. The three practical approaches described here work. When they become broadly adopted and consistently used in clinical care many lives will be saved.

....

* The first in this series was: How Doctors Think: Addiction, Neuroscience and Your Treatment Plan, The Huffington Post, June 29, 2015.

** Dr. Carruthers directs the Suicide Prevention Office at the NYS Office of Mental Health and is an Assistant Professor of Psychiatry at Albany Medical College in Albany, NY.

SUICIDE, VIOLENCE AND MENTAL ILLNESS

LIS: This article was written in the wake of the Germanwings mass murder, where a 27 year old pilot with a mental illness crashed his plane killing 150 people, including himself. I propose two paths for protecting the public—while at the same time protecting people with serious mental illnesses. The first involves revisiting the limits of privacy. The second urges the use of clear measures to monitor all individuals with direct responsibility for others whose job places the public safety in their hands. Delaying action in these two areas will limit the introduction of preventative measures that can and will save lives.

PLANE CRASHING

The story of 27-year-old Andreas Lubitz, co-pilot of Germanwings Flight #9525 who, reportedly, resolutely defied medical letters not to work because of illness and took 150 people, including himself, to a brutal end will surely ignite yet another round of confusion, consternation, and pitched comment about what to do:

—About the dangers posed by mental illness—including the 42,000 suicides (and rising) annually in this country and the 22 American veterans who die at their own hands every day;

—About the horrific, episodic violent events that rock our minds and disrupt the peace of our families and communities, which include Adam Lanza (Newtown, Connecticut); James Holmes (Aurora,

Colorado); Jared Loughner (Tucson, Arizona); Elliot Rodger (Santa Barbara, California); Seung-Hui Cho (Virginia Tech, Virginia); and Andreas Lubitz. What may seem like random acts of violence are not so random;

—About the inestimable and disproportionate human and economic toll taken by that very small percent of individuals whose serious mental illness impairs their capacity to recognize they are sick and to take steps to ensure their wellbeing and that of their communities.

I fear that Lubitz's story will unleash a fresh round of fear and vitriol regarding people with mental illness. I fear that simplistic reactions known not to work (like "lock them up and throw away the key") may again be seen as attractive answers to problems whose solutions can be understood but difficult to achieve. I fear that work towards protecting the public's safety will be lost in the fog of the war of words that are already descending upon us in the wake of this latest tragedy.

Andreas Lubitz does not fit the familiar profile of a person with serious mental illness who goes on to kill others and (typically) himself. Lubitz reportedly was not a loner, did not have a long history of isolation and alienation from family and friends, did not have an undetected mental illness (and he was presumably in treatment), and maintained at least a patina of competence and responsibility. As far as is known to date, he was not a terrorist. He apparently left no notes to explain his actions or take responsibility for the lives he took.

We thus face a different set of problems to tackle if we are to find direction from the wreckage of Flight #9525 and the fate of its passengers and their families.

I want to propose two paths for protecting the public as well as protecting people with serious mental illnesses. They call for real time performance information on those entrusted with our safety.

First, we need to revisit the limits of privacy, balancing both individual and community rights. Second, we need to consider measures that could reduce the risk of another deadly scenario, especially the potential for employing technological advances to identify problems before it is too late.

Privacy often takes the quality of a hallowed right, especially in this country. But privacy is not universal or unlimited. Privacy, particularly in mental health, can have both its needed place and its proper limits, especially when circumstances may be life-threatening. Those whose service involves our safety have that as their primary and overriding responsibility. Regular, random drug testing is a common example for many service employees whose work involves the health and safety of others.

Yet organizations whose employees are directly responsible for the public safety—like doctors, police, firefighters, bus drivers, nurses, and pilots—usually are not contacted when an employee is deemed medically not safe to work, as we painfully see with Germanwings (and Lufthansa). Has privacy trumped public safety? Would not the public safety be served if select groups of service workers with jobs that can impact safety and are in treatment for a medical condition (including psychiatric, neurological, and certain chronic illnesses that can impair cognitive functioning) consent to having their doctor report to their employer should they be determined unfit to work? Andreas Lubitz would not have flown that day were that the case. Impaired physicians and nurses would not endanger their patients were that the case. The right to return to work when fit would have to be guaranteed. Safety must always be the first priority, and the privilege of serving others should rest on that principle.

However, professions, mine included, do not have a stellar record of protecting those they serve. Do we have reason to believe that professional organizations or corporate entities can be trusted to protect their clientele? Self-interest, concerns about liability, and economic forces too commonly eclipse the integrity of purpose that is their mission.

R. Buckminster Fuller did not believe pressure could change people or organizations when he said, "You never change things by fighting the existing reality. To change something, build a new model that makes the existing model obsolete." We need something besides the imposition of external regulations and reporting requirements to achieve real and lasting change. Advances in technology and data systems may now allow for a new models of monitoring that heretofore were not possible.

We can, thus, today pursue a second, and parallel, path that adds clear measures to monitor all individuals with direct responsibility for others, such as the service personnel mentioned above and others whose work places the public safety in their hands. Here technology may offer feasible solutions that in the past were too intrusive and burdensome.

In NYC, for example, a combined multi-year effort by NYS and NYC monitored a very high-risk group of individuals with serious mental illness using administrative data to identify when they failed to attend their medical appointments or pick up prescribed medications, or had a sudden re-emergence of acute illness as evidence by ED or hospital admissions. This work focused on the clinical providers, not the patients, responsible—where data alerted everyone involved about who was not doing well. Responsibility then lay with the provider organizations to act when patients were not succeeding. This initiative now is evolving into more accountable care organizations to ensure that those in trouble are reached and engaged.

This high risk initiative (or others like it) is, however, far too limited and focused on individuals with known histories of serious problems. That appears not to be the case for Lubitz or many others who have flown below the radar of responsible monitoring. What could work are real time measures of the performance of service personnel, agreed to by those given the privilege of bearing the responsibilities they do. Wearable devices far beyond Fitbit are emerging that can track and report changes in social behavior and functioning that correlate with impaired performance (often the result of illness) thereby alerting service organizations (as well as caregivers and health professionals) that a person's capacity to do his or her job may be compromised.

We don't want someone with a fever of 105 degrees operating heavy machinery or flying a NASA mission. We don't want someone whose cognitive capacities are transiently impacted by a mental (or other medical) illness or drug use driving our bus or operating on our abdomen. When someone is impaired, he or she needs to stand down, or not be allowed to work, until their functioning is again normal, as evidenced by real time performance measures. Perhaps a universal approach used for all workers the public relies upon for safety even could avoid the traps of diagnosis and stigma we see when a mental disorder limits functioning.

We need professions and service organizations to invite innovation from technology companies researching human performance measurement to build, test, and promote solutions that serve the public safety. We can find answers that balance individual liberties with collective needs, that prioritize safety, and that create the expectation that with certain privileges comes accountability for performance.

Regaining the public trust and professional pride are possible. But we will need a different glide path than that we have been on. We can use Flight #9525 as an impetus and a reminder that delays only invite yet another collective grave and failure of will when prevention could be possible.

DO NOT GO GENTLE INTO THAT GOOD NIGHT

LIS: This HuffPost (HP) was produced as a partnership between my agency, The New York State Office of Mental Health (the largest state mental health agency in the country) and The HP, on the occasion of World Suicide Prevention Day. Suicide is a preventable event. This article launches a public education and action campaign to enable the preventative efforts that can happen and by which lives can be saved.

Stronger Together for Suicide Prevention—a partnership between the New York State Office of Mental Health and The Huffington Post.

I know too many people who have taken their lives—and not just because I am a psychiatrist.

These people include family members, friends, colleagues, and neighbors, as well as those in the public eye whose deaths, some very recent, have riveted our attention. While I have had the good fortune of having no patient under my direct care die by suicide, because I have led many clinical services, I have seen too many times the indelible tragedy that suicide can usher in.

Do you know someone who died by his or her hands, or tried (including perhaps you)? If you do, whether near or far from your heart, we hope you will join New York State and The Huffington Post in our campaign to help prevent deaths that need not happen. Almost everyone who survives a suicide attempt is glad to be alive. Our challenge is to figure out how to keep those people alive until they want to live again.

More than 39,000 people die each year from suicide. That is more than twice the rate in this country of homicidal deaths. One million people, annually, make a suicide attempt in the U.S. We need to think of these losses as preventable, as we already approach deaths from accidents and illnesses where prevention, early detection, and employing effective interventions are lifesaving.

Suicidal deaths are inextricably tied to mental illnesses. We estimate that in nine of every 10 completed suicides the person was suffering from an acute mental illness, clinical depression in particular. In a great many instances, the deadly action was enabled by the use of alcohol or drugs, or both, which disinhibit our protective instincts and fuel impulsiveness. What this means is that detecting and treating mental and addictive disorders will be critical to preventing suicide deaths.

Today, Sept. 10, is World Suicide Prevention Day. The World Health Organization (WHO) reports on the basis of 10 years of research from around the world that someone dies by suicide every 40 seconds. Their findings tell us that approximately 800,000 people kill themselves every year, and that suicide is the second leading cause of death in young people, aged 15 to 29, though it is people over 70 who are the most likely to take their own lives. Men are three times more likely to die from suicide attempts than women, but as access to deadly means of self-destruction increase (like firearms, narcotic pills and heroin) this gap in fatal outcomes may close.

The Huffington Post's Stronger Together campaign (see my introduction to that initiative) found a public that is powerfully interested in understanding mental and addictive disorders, having people tell their own stories, and identifying where help is available.

Building on this campaign and on the occasion of World Suicide Prevention Day, New York State and The Huffington Post are launching Stronger Together for Suicide Prevention. We believe this is the first public mental health campaign that brings together the government of a major state and an international, Pulitzer Prize-winning media outlet.

On HuffPost today, we will have contributions from the NYS Office of Mental Health, Lifeline (the national suicide prevention hotline: 1-800-273-TALK), the Iraq and Afghanistan Veterans of America (IAVA, with its priority of preventing the 22 veteran suicide deaths that happen every day—We've Got Your Back), The Jed Foundation (a leader in protecting the emotional health of America's 20 million college students), and The Mental Health Association of New York State (MHANYS, with its focus on the role of families and communities).

In the days and weeks to follow, we will be providing more online posts as well as a Twitter chat and a HuffPost Live segment focused on suicide prevention. We invite readers and concerned individuals and organizations to join in the conversation. More details on these events will be provided soon.

Suicide is a preventable event. But it will take all of us, as individuals, advocacy organizations, government agencies, workplaces, and medical (not just mental health) services to step forward and do what can be done to help people before they act in an irrevocable way. Stronger Together for Suicide Prevention will show how we all can help.

The Welsh poet Dylan Thomas wrote: "Do not go gentle into that good night … Rage, rage against the dying of the light." His words are a beacon for the fight against death—and should be for when death threatens to come by a person's own hands.

THE GUARDIANS—AN ELEGY—*A HUFFPOST BOOK REVIEW*

LIS: A gifted young man kills himself. I knew his dad from medical school. He jumped in front of an oncoming train north of Manhattan. The Guardians is a tightly-written, powerful "elegy" by Sarah Manguso to her friend, this man who took his life. He had deftly escaped the psychiatric hospital where he had been admitted. While there is so much we cannot know about what drove this man to suicide we do know that suicide is preventable. The author, Sarah Manguso, is a lesson herself in how life can go on, despite illness and tragedy. Her path shows that love, creativity and contribution can be achieved in the wake of a tragic event.

Harris Wulfson died July 23, 2008. He had walked for some 10 hours from midtown in New York City to the Riverdale Metro-North train station (north of Manhattan), where he jumped before an oncoming train to his crushing death.

His loss is beyond measure to family and friends who loved him and relished his abundant talent, energy and quirkiness. Because his death was from suicide while in the throes of an acute psychotic illness, likely bipolar disorder, his death is yet another preventable tragedy.

In this country, 35,000 people annually succumb to death by their own doing; there are no doubt more where the cause of death is less clear. Each is a life that need not have ended and inestimable grief for those who held that person dear.

Sarah Manguso delivers a tightly-written, powerful "elegy" to her friend Harris. She wonders:

"Why is it easier to think 'Harris killed himself' than to think 'Some unknown invasive pathology entered Harris without my knowledge and, while I wasn't looking, murdered him?'"

She asks a question that plagues my field: psychiatry. She asks what is the disease that extracts the ultimate price from its host. By inference, she also asks how we can learn to protect against its invasion and, if not effective in doing that, at least avert a fatal outcome.

The Guardians, an allusion I imagine to the angels of antiquity who look after we mortals, weaves Harris' and Maguso's often tormented, creative paths—with his death seemingly to have permitted her escape from a similar fate. Manguso holds no animus to her friend for leaving her: She believes in " … the possibility of unendurable suffering." At once darkening and heartening to their stories is also her depiction of the catastrophe that befell New York City on Sept. 11, 2001—9/11 brought horror, resilience and recovery to so many like them who lived through the attack.

Harris, who I never met, though I have known his father since medical school, was a spirited genius, a young man whose gift for creating music and computer software were head-turning. Scattered as he was, that did not matter; what counted was the way his remarkable brain operated and the ways by which he was a friend. Those were the treasures that Manguso enjoyed, and she dolefully laments their loss. We feel her pain since none of us is spared grief.

Serious mental illnesses can be agony: They are as painful as physical illnesses but further bedeviling because there is no broken bone, no dead heart or lung tissue, no cancer or non-functioning organ to point to. For some people with psychotic illness, their capacity to appreciate that they are ill has been pirated away by the "invasive pathology" that is mental illness. When intractable psychic pain seems like it will never end, without evident cause or hoped for remedy, the soul is taken over by a horrific state that Sartre called "no exit." Those are the conditions that drive a person to suicide.

Harris deftly escaped the psychiatric hospital where he had been admitted. He may have been on medication that made his distress even greater, so speculates Manguso. There is so much we cannot know since he is not here to tell us what feelings and thoughts preceded his irrevocable act. But we do know that suicide is preventable. Manguso herself is a lesson in how life can go on, despite illness and tragedy; her path shows that love, creativity and contribution can be achieved.

Suicide is a public health problem. Like other mortal and disabling conditions there are fundamental ways to beat it. Solutions begin with early detection of mental illness: 50 percent of psychiatric disorders begin by age 14 and 75 percent by age 24. Even before that are the behavioral problems that occupy more often in pediatric practices than for any other reason that kids and families are in the waiting room. Yet gaps as long as nine years are typical from the time symptoms appear to when a diagnosis is made. Another basic, yet often unmet, public health principle is to assure the delivery of effective treatments; sadly, in this country, less than one in five affected individuals receive treatments—medications and psychotherapies—proven specific to their conditions.

We know that early intervention and evidence-based treatments can prevent the progression of a disabling psychiatric condition. Offering accessible services is also vital; clinics and offices need to be welcoming and responsive to patient and family preferences and without unbearable wait times to appointments, insurance hassles and denials. The role of hope, persistence despite setbacks, and exposure to and support from others who themselves have lived through the "noonday demon" (as Andrew Solomon described) can never be underestimated. Mental disorders are highly prevalent and can be treated. The pain and cost of not doing so, which is too often the case today, is egregious and exorbitant.

We have Sarah Manguso to thank for her revelatory candor and the beauty of her prose. We have her to thank for this tribute to her friend, whose loss cannot be reversed but whose story can impel a health and mental health care system to do better from here on in.

Need help? In the U.S., call 1-800-273-8255 for the National Suicide Prevention Lifeline.

I HEAR YOU: RESPONDING TO CRIES FOR EMOTIONAL HELP

LIS: I was asked to write this HuffPost after Sinead O'Connor declared on Twitter: "does any1 know a psychiatrist in dublin or wicklow who could urgently see me today please? im really un-well ... and in danger." In my work, I understand how people reach out and that we need to listen. Their greatest fear often is that they will find no one there. Suicide, as has been said, is not just the product of hopelessness; it is the result of believing that you are all alone, with no one to turn to and no means of exiting from the psychic pain that is crushing your soul.

HELP!

Cries for emotional help come in all forms. We witness these cries in ways direct and indirect: from outright requests to help me stay alive to the less direct but no less obvious self-starvation of anorexia or leaving empty pill bottles or illegal drugs in plain sight.

We recently witnessed a modern-age cry for help when Sinead O'Connor declared on Twitter: "does any1 know a psychiatrist in dublin or wicklow who could urgently see me today please? im really un-well ... and in danger." Why a celebrity needs Twitter to find a psychiatrist is beyond me. Sure, we can all quip about how hard it is to get an appointment with a doctor, but I suspect that is not what this was about.

Nor can I know since I am not personally familiar with this celebrity, her medical community or resources, or for that matter her state of mind when she turned to such a ubiquitous form of social media for help. But as a psychiatrist I understand how people reach out in ways that we need to listen to: The ultimate fear is that they will find no one there, which is the saddest situation of all. Suicide, as has been said, is not just the product of hopelessness; it is the result of believing that you are all alone, with no one to turn to and no means of exiting from the psychic pain that is crushing your soul.

Mental or emotional pain hurts no less than physical pain. In some ways, mental anguish can be more unbearable because it is often laced with several horrible additives. The first is a common tendency for a person to blame themselves for the condition they are in: They feel guilt, shame, a failure for not having willed themselves better. In addition, there is stigma: The way that people with mental disorders are shunned, castigated and marginalized as if that person is a low-life who needs "to get a life." External injury is thus added to personal agony and self-blame. Topping it all off, there is no broken bone, tumor or infection to point to that explains what's causing the pain. This can create upheaval in a person's sense of self as they search for a way of comprehending what does not have the same explanatory power as do the myriad of conditions that appear visibly on the body, or by blood or imaging tests, or by looking at cells under a microscope.

The Australians launched a social media campaign a few years ago called "R-U-OK?". The Aussies suggested something far more personal and meaningful than waiting for someone to arrive at an emergency room after an overdose or sending a distress signal by email, Twitter, Facebook or some other channel in our rapidly-expanding universe of social media. If you see someone in emotional distress or displaying the consequences of psychological problems (such as social isolation, compromised work performance, poor self-care), they urged to reach out to that person: Ask, R-U-OK? and then sit back and listen non-judgmentally and support the part of that person that wants to live, to love and to be connected to their family, friends and work community. It is there, I assure you, but often buried under hurt and disappointment and hopelessness.

Don't be afraid of saying the wrong thing. Saying nothing, letting somebody stew in their psychic pain, is far more likely to result in something unfortunate happening than is offering a kind word and support for taking what steps are needed to begin to change a situation or treat a problem. When no one asks, when no one notices, cries for help generally escalate—and not only by tweeting.

Human behavior is purposeful. We do things for a reason. Sometimes that reason (or reasons) is obvious and sometimes not. Behavior is "crazy" only until we understand it, then it is not crazy anymore. Self-destructive behavior happens for a number of reasons, including a need to communicate with others how bad the pain and loneliness is.

You may not be able to answer a celebrity's Twitter cry. But you can listen for cries for help from those you love, from friends and from co-workers. You can answer their cries for help. If not, who knows where or how the cry will next appear?

Need help? In the U.S., call 1-800-273-8255 for the National Suicide Prevention Lifeline.

WHAT DOES SUICIDE PREVENTION HAVE TO DO WITH HEALTH CARE?

LIS: This article reports on a suicide prevention symposium hosted by my agency, The New York State Office of Mental Health, where I am the Chief Medical Officer. We put on this event to fashion a state-wide plan for reducing deaths from suicide in our state. While New York has significantly lower rates than the preponderance of other states, every death is one we see as preventable. Since this meeting, NYS has built a plan, in conjunction with national partners, to achieve "Zero Suicide"—an aspiration we mean to do all we can to achieve. This post describes a number of clinical and public health strategies that can reduce suicide deaths.

At a recent suicide prevention symposium hosted by the NYS Office of Mental Health (Disclosure: I am the agency's Medical Director), Dr. Lee Goldman, Dean of Columbia Medical School, began the day by remarking that there has been an 80 percent (!) reduction in deaths from heart disease in the past 50 years. Dr. Goldman was highlighting how what seemed like inevitable mortality rates two generations ago could be systematically and dramatically altered by reducing risk and intervening early and effectively; lives can be saved and pain and suffering for potential family survivors can be blessedly mitigated.

That was a heartening opening in light of why this meeting was called: 10 years ago a national strategy to reduce suicides in this country was launched built on a platform created by Former Surgeon General David Satcher. Yet despite many well considered efforts there has been no reduction in deaths, which now are greater than ever, about 36,000/year according to the latest statistics. NYS Mental Health Commissioner Mike Hogan called this New York meeting to consider what this state of near to 20 million people might do to reduce deaths by suicide, and the grim consequences they cast. Our work would build on and resonate with a national effort underway.*

We began by hearing several success stories. First, we heard how Henry Ford Health System in Michigan, a large health insurance plan with some 500,000 members that delivers medical services to its subscribers and others (~10,000 visits/business day), set a goal for what they called "Perfect Depression Care." The vast predominance of people who complete suicide have an active mental illness, particularly depression. Not willing to tinker around the edges, they pursued a radical approach that set zero deaths as their goal. They implemented screening, proven principles and practices for the care of all chronic illnesses (including diabetes, heart disease and depression), immediate access to appointments, and continuous and robust quality improvement—and after several years of progressive reductions in deaths they achieved and maintained 2 ½ years of zero deaths by suicide.

We next heard how Kaiser Permanente of Northern California, an HMO with over 3 million members and 20 medical centers, instituted a remarkable plan for primary care suicide prevention (i.e. in general medical services not mental health clinics). They introduced screening for depression, anxiety, substance abuse, and intimate partner violence, coupled that with treatment practices known to work, and scrutinized every suicide for what improvements could be made.

Finally, we heard how Magellan Health Services, a large national mental health managed care company, implemented suicide prevention in Arizona by focusing on those people whose risk for suicide was 6–12 times the general population, namely those people with a serious mental illness. They trained clinicians, standardized the provision of best practices, stressed community based care, and engaged families and those who survived an attempt; they have reduced deaths by 48 percent and inpatient admissions among their subscribers by 51 percent, indicating risk reduction as well as cost savings.

What was so notable from the presentations was that "suicide … was just the tip of the iceberg," as the last speaker remarked. The vast problem below the surface, one that can be avoided, is not doing the right thing. We actually know what is right: setting very high standards (don't be afraid of perfection); systematically identifying people at risk; relentlessly providing proven methods of intervention; crossing boundaries between general medical and mental health care and staying with people when they move from one care setting to another (like from hospital to home); regularly assessing performance with measures that are as clear and understandable to patients and families as they are to clinicians; and zealously pursuing opportunities for improvement when problems appear, as they always do.

Deadly consequences happen, in effect, from suicide just like from heart disease, when we do not do the right thing as unfailingly as we can. Good medical care does not know the difference between illnesses. The same principles govern health care for every disease, physical and mental. Reducing rates of suicide is about improving health care. We will need to abide by these very same access and quality standards in order to manage the diseases that afflict our generation, especially those that derive from habit disorders and age, including diabetes, hypertension, asthma, obstructive lung diseases, Parkinson's and Alzheimer's disease, and the multiplicity of ails that derive from smoking, overeating, sedentary life styles and stress.

A colleague from the NYS Health Department, Dr. Foster Gesten, in the summing up at the end of the day suggested that strategies for saving lives could be "deep and wide." Deep are those that health care systems with accountability for identified individuals or populations could implement in NYS—as we learned are going on in Michigan and Northern California (as well as the very notable work throughout Washington State). Wide are the practices known to work universally that are ready for prime time and wide application, like screening to identify high risk people, treatment care paths, open access to appointments, careful attention to transitions from one service site to another, informed and 'activated' patients and families, and health information technology that provides decision support and communicates essential information to those who need to know. Reducing death by suicide would be one of many fortunate outcomes from improving our health care system.

Achieving change in health care is very hard to do. It entails an unwavering ambition for excellence and zealous attention to details. I am reminded about something Michelangelo was reported to have said: "Trifles make for perfection, but perfection is no trifle."

* Last year, Federal Secretaries Sebelius (Health and Human Services) and Gates (Defense) launched the National Action Alliance for Suicide Prevention bringing together government and military officials, experts, people with mental illnesses, family members, foundations, and others to fashion a plan that would be more focused and successful than the efforts of the past decade. Commissioner Hogan and a number of those who attended the NYS symposium are members of the Action Alliance.

SUICIDE PREVENTION: WE CAN DO BETTER

LIS: A second national strategy for suicide prevention was launched in 2010, ten years after the first—which unfortunately did not achieve reductions in deaths. In fact, suicide deaths have increased every year since then. At this new, 2010 launch, Secretary Kathleen Sebelius, Health and Human Services, and Secretary Robert M. Gates, Department of Defense, accompanied by former U.S. Senator Gordon H. Smith (now CEO of the National Association of Broadcasters), the Secretary of the Army, John McHugh, other officials and experts announced a public and private partnership called the National Action Alliance for Suicide Prevention. Maybe this time we can do better. We certainly have the right people at the table.

Statistics can be chilling: 34,000 (at the time this article was written) people die by their own hands in the U.S. each year (that's a suicide every 15 minutes, nearly twice that of homicides) and more veterans of Iraq and Afghanistan take their lives than die in combat. But it is the emotional agony that precedes the deadly act for the person and the legacy of lifelong pain that follows it for the survivors that haunts the world of those who take their lives.

Few families are spared—if not death then suicide attempts and the maelstrom they stir. As a doctor, a psychiatrist, who has treated many patients, I had one man who ran away from a hospital on the day I met him, decades ago, and drowned himself in a freezing river. As a clinical administrator of mental health services and medical director of a psychiatric hospital, I know of many people who have taken the ultimate step and ended their lives. But it was a close relative by a former marriage who hung herself many years ago whose memory to this day still sears my mind and stirs doubt about myself and what might have been done.

Ten years ago, a National Strategy for Suicide Prevention (NSSP) was built on the foundation created by Dr. David Satcher, the extraordinary U.S. Surgeon General who had issued a "Call to Action to Prevent Suicide." A common understanding of suicide was established by the NSSP, advocacy efforts begun, public awareness campaigns launched, local and state prevention plans written and commenced; all the best minds and influential people were involved. Shortly thereafter, the then President George W. Bush ordered the President's New Freedom Commission on Mental Health and its report candidly identified what needed to be done to improve a very broken mental health system in this country.

A very auspicious start. But when we take its measure today, a decade later, we cannot show any evidence that the suicide rate across this country has been reduced. We have not "bent the curve" on self inflicted death. Preventable deaths continue. We can and have to do better.

While no specific, single preventative intervention or technique has worked we have seen notable instances where an impact was made in reducing death by suicide. Two remarkable examples stand out. One is the "Perfect Depression Care Initiative" that began in 2001 in the Behavioral Health Services Division of the Henry Ford Health System, a large Health Maintenance Organization with 200,000 members operating in southern Michigan and adjacent states. Since 2008, they have achieved the perfection they sought: 10 calendar quarters have now passed where not one person has died from suicide. The second example was by the U.S. Air Force in the mid-90s to prevent suicide among Air Force personnel; this initiative was driven by top leadership in the wake of growing deaths and produced an 80 percent reduction, initially, and a 50 percent reduction over time.

In September 2010, recognizing that 10 years had passed with disappointing national results, Secretary Kathleen Sebelius, Health and Human Services, and Secretary Robert M. Gates, Department of Defense, accompanied by former U.S. Senator Gordon H. Smith (now CEO of the National Association of Broadcasters), the Secretary of the Army, John McHugh, other officials, and experts announced a public and private partnership called the National Action Alliance for Suicide Prevention. A second meeting of the Action Alliance met on February 9 to build on the efforts of various workgroups and change the static state of suicide prevention. Many ideas are now in play, so focus, feasibility and leadership will be needed.

What works, then, I ask? Some aspects that pertain to Henry Ford Health and the U.S. Air Force are revealing. What about starting with the setting rather than with any specific intervention to reduce suicide? In other words, first identify an established group to work with. This can be a health plan, a university, a government agency or institution, or a business organization. It can be an organization that has information on all its members, the capacity to reach them all, has clear and committed leadership and is well disposed to innovation. One that can specifically measure what will be done to change practices as well as report on the results while using a quality improvement framework to sustain and enhance any gains that are achieved.

Once the setting, or population is chosen, then is the time to identify specific clinical or social interventions (like depression screening, care paths for the suicidal person or for specific mental disorders, reducing access to weapons, engaging spouses and families, treating alcohol and drug abuse, education campaigns, etc) that would fit each unique setting (or population).

This approach inverts a customary approach to suicide which begins with an intervention and looks to where it can be implemented. Since no single intervention has been proven effective it may be time to turn the field on its head: begin by establishing what contexts offer opportunity for getting something done rather than starting with what can be done.

If we can reduce suicidal deaths by 25 percent in the next 10 years near to 90,000 lives will be saved—that we know of—not to mention reductions in serious suicide attempts and the catastrophe that suicidal behavior rains upon a person, family and community. If we can send a man to the moon, we can figure out how to save lives on earth.

R U OK?

LIS: Aussies are among my favorite people. I have been there a number of times and have had the privilege of working with some of their state governments, as well as with gifted colleagues especially in Sydney and Adelaide. This post was written shortly after what was called the "R U OK Day" in Australia. The term refers to a national campaign on suicide prevention, starting with the premise that those who might help someone in distress often don't have the words to begin. R U OK? is a simple, doable script for reaching out to someone you know in distress. Doing so may end their isolation and begin their path to safety and recovery.

HELPING ONE ANOTHER

Sunday November 29th was R U OK Day in Australia.

R U OK? (are you ok?) is an Australian national suicide prevention effort developed by an organization that seeks to reduce the rate of suicide by breaking the isolation and helplessness that characterizes people at risk to take their lives. This organization had its genesis from the death of Barry Larkin, a businessman and consultant who took his life in 1995; his three sons decided to introduce a conversation they never had the opportunity to have with their dad. Australians at work, home and among friends are now prompted to break the silence and ask 'are you ok'?

To help everyday people ask this not so easy question, R U OK? offers suggestions, which I paraphrase:

- Be open and receptive, take the lead and ask 'are you ok?'; convey that you have time to talk.
- Say something that suggests concern and opens the conversation, like 'I've noticed you have looked really stressed' or 'I understand this is a very tough time for you'.
- Listening is more important than telling. You need not know answers. Your interest and your seeking to end a person's isolation and aloneness is what counts
- Be hopeful, but not superficial. Periods of serious stress and depression can and do pass—especially if someone feels that others care and that there is help they can get.
- Don't expect someone to cheer up, or get over it. Instead, suggest to a person who says 'no, I'm not ok' that there are ways to get better—which start with their taking one step at a time. Sometime that step is talking with others, taking better care of themselves, or speaking with a doctor or mental health professional.

In the United States, 31,000 people commit suicide each year (data at time this post was written). This does not count those who disguise their suicide in the form of an accidental death or where natural causes are attributed to what was an act of self-destruction. This is three times the homicide rate in this country. And the suicide rate is increasing, for the first time in a decade, especially among Caucasian women aged 40–64.

I recently heard about a man I had known, a very successful lawyer, who had suffered from depression. He was no complainer: the bigger the demand the more he was there to meet it. But a difficult financial time coupled with developing diabetes were the stressors that prompted his depression. The strain showed, at work and at home, but those that cared about him felt awkward; how could they say something to him, since it was he who always took care of everything and everyone? This story does not have a happy ending. He took his life, alone, in his car, far from home. Who knows if the outcome could have been different? But we do know that the mix of depression, health or financial problems, a personality that has difficulty asking for help, and no one daring to ask 'are you ok' can be a deadly combination.

For you to have the confidence to initiate an 'are you ok' conversation, you may need to know what to do if you uncover an immediate crisis. In Australia, and here in the USA, there are National Help Lines if you ask someone 'are you ok?' and then sense that person may be in imminent danger of doing something self-destructive—and perhaps irrevocable. If you are not familiar with local services or who to turn to there is a National Suicide Prevention Hotline (1-800-273-TALK) in the USA. It is free, confidential, 24/7, and connected to crisis centers throughout the country.

We are entering the holiday season—a time where many are not so merry and feelings of isolation often peak. One kindness we can offer friends, family, fellow students, or colleagues at work is asking 'are you ok'? This is a good time to ask and to take the time to listen. It may be the greatest gift of all.

HERE ONE DAY: A DOCUMENTARY FILM REVIEW

LIS: This is a film by a loving daughter, Kathy Leichter, about her mother. Nina Leichter was the mother of two children; the wife of a New York state senator; a gifted artist; a political activist and advocate; and a person whose fires burned intensely (sometime too much so) until she extinguished the flame. She was ill with bipolar disorder—manic-depressive illness. Suicide is hardest on the ones left behind, as this film poignantly conveys. The film culminates with Nina's suicide note: She asks her family to live well, even though she no longer could. But her death remains the ineradicable tragedy that has befallen this family. Only by finding better and more sustaining ways to effectively treat mental illnesses will we help to spare other families what the Leichters have had to endure.

Here One Day
A Documentary Film by Kathy Leichter
Reviewed by Lloyd I. Sederer, MD

How can a person overcome the basic instinct we all possess to survive and take one's own life? The families, friends, coworkers, and many other intimates of the more than 39,000 people who suicide annually in the USA may wonder. Those close to the 22 veterans every day, men and women, who die by suicide may wonder. Doctors and other health and mental health professionals try to comprehend and explain. But words are often a limited means of communication, however earnest and heartfelt they may be.

Here One Day, in the tradition of fine journalism, shows you, rather than tells you. This award-winning documentary has many answers to the unnerving questions that suicide evokes.

This is a tough film to watch—because it is done so well. It is a daughter's homage, her eulogy and loving tribute, to her mother who at the age of 63 jumped, no longer able to bear going on, from her dining room window into the abyss of a NYC apartment building's inner concrete courtyard.

Nina Leichter was the mother of two children; the wife of a New York state senator with more than two decades of public office; a gifted artist; a political activist and advocate; and a person whose fires burned intensely (sometime too much so) until she extinguished the flame. She was ill with bipolar disorder—manic-depressive illness. This mental illness, which came on in her 40s, had (in her case) a relentless progression that left her, by the mid-90s, "ravaged" and "deteriorated." The images and the deeply personal storytelling of this film reveal to you how she came to the point of no return.

Kathy Leichter, the producer, director and daughter of Nina Leichter, exhumes, after 16 years, the artifacts of her mother's life, career and condition. She was 28 when her mother died. In this film, Kathy uncovers and dusts off her mother's recorded audiotapes, handwritten notes, drawings, a stunning mosaic table, photos, videos, record albums and—yes—a handful of still partially filled pill containers. We witness the arc of a woman, child of immigrants, who made a good life in New York until mental illness perturbed it deeply. It was Kathy, the daughter, who returned to her childhood home—the NYC apartment from which her mother had jumped—to live with her father, grieve and eventually discover these buried mementoes of a life lived and lost.

Suicide is hardest on the ones left behind. In the Leichter family, we see its corrosion on each member, still flush with feelings almost two decades after their loss. This is one reason, I think, why some regard suicide as "selfish." Its multigenerational impact is captured in this documentary, a legacy not just in this family but in countless others. There is a segment in the film, towards the end, where the ensemble of daughter, son, and father/husband unveil their broken hearts. The pain and its emotional scars seemed acute and deep, not that of a distant event. This portrayal, like looking into a therapy session, could be helpful to some and may be difficult to others.

The film culminates with Nina's suicide note. It is generous to others, as she had been. She asks them to live well, even though she no longer could. But her death remains the ineradicable stain on that wish. Only by finding better and more sustaining ways to effectively treat mental illnesses will we help to spare other families the tragedy that befell the Leichters.

For more information about Here One Day, go to: www.Hereoneday.com

DISCUSSION AND CRITICAL THINKING QUESTIONS

Why do people take their lives? How do they overcome our fundamental instinct to survive?

How is suicide related to the presence of an active mental or substance use disorder, and how is it not? How do we keep people alive until their mental disorder comes under control, and their hopelessness abates?

What is the impact of suicide on a family, and friends?

How is it that death by suicide continues to increase, year after year in this country, despite public campaigns of awareness?

What are the clinical and public health strategies that can make a difference?

What can any one person do, and how?

IMAGE CREDITS

Fig 3.1: Copyright © Depositphotos/Wavebreakmedia.

Fig 3.2: Copyright © Depositphotos/juanjo39.

Fig 3.3: Copyright © Depositphotos/iqoncept.

Fig 3.4: Copyright © Depositphotos/leremy.

OPENING COMMENTS

CHILDHOOD TRAUMA

Trauma knows no boundaries. Its nefarious reach extends to natural and human-made catastrophes, terrorism, war, forced displacement and immigration, childhood neglect and abuse, and domestic violence—among other horrific events.

Trauma mobilizes a chronic stress response, putting natural stress mechanisms into persistent overdrive. The results are ongoing inflammation in blood vessels (in the heart and brain) thereby reducing blood flow and increasing the risk of heart attack and stroke; organ damage in the pancreas (producing insulin insensitivity and later adult onset diabetes) and joints; and compromised immune functioning, with increased risk of cancer and auto-immune diseases. Trauma and chronic bodily inflammation has been shown to be highly associated with the expression of a host of mental disorders (including depression, PTSD, substance use disorders, and likely schizophrenia as well). "Chronic stress is the enemy," as I wrote in my recent book, *Improving Mental Health: Four Secrets in Plain Sight.*

This section explores a variety of traumatic disorders, their pathogenesis, and the clinical and public health strategies for mitigation they demand.

COMMUNITY POLICING AND CHILD DEVELOPMENT: AVERTING TRAUMATIC DISORDERS

LIS: When the police met up with mental health professionals it was a beautiful thing. I went to New Haven, CT, to sit in on the weekly "rounds" between the New Haven PD, The Yale Child Study Center, and the Connecticut Department of Child and Family Services. This had been going on for 22 years, and still is. The week's caseload of incidents that involved a family where a child was exposed to trauma were systematically reviewed, under the careful watch of the Police Chief and Dr. Steven Marans of Yale. They discussed what more could be done, by whom and that was carefully planned for action. Their aim is to reduce the consequences of trauma a child may develop, and thereby enable that child to continue on with everyday life and development, without the damage and limitations of a traumatic condition.

You could tell the police sergeants in blue from the lieutenants and chiefs in their white shirted uniforms. But 11 were there, including Dean Esserman the New Haven Chief of Police, representing their respective precincts for the weekly meeting with about as many clinicians from the Yale Child Study Center as well as staff from the Connecticut Department of Child and Family Services. This remarkable collaboration has run for over 22 years orchestrated by Dr. Steven Marans, a psychoanalyst and professor at Yale and an innovator in the prevention of and intervention in the often devastating effects of childhood trauma.

The meeting began with one sergeant describing a domestic violence incident in which a six year old child witnessed a stabbing in the home. Police, mental health, and child protection professionals sat around a large conference table with wooden arm chairs (that barely allowed the utility belted, armed police to nest within them) as if it were a graduate seminar. The university location at Yale meant that the participants discussed not only the safety measures taken but also what evidence-based, clinical interventions had been provided for the family and child, and what else might be done.

Other incidents on the day I visited followed, all characterized by a child witnessing or directly being a victim in his or her home. These are the kind of nightmares that the youth does not awaken from to reassuring words that it was just a dream. As many as ten new incidents are reviewed each week, and a group of follow-up cases are then worked through. In 60 minutes, in crisp, definitive and compassionate ways, these professionals try to avert the very probable consequences of a witnessed or actual trauma to the child (including beating or rape) by providing proven, effective interventions that call upon all their collective efforts.

The CD-CP (Child Development-Community Policing) program, originated by the Yale Child Study Center's National Center for Children Exposed to Violence, understands that problems don't disappear once the immediate violence is contained. Inside the mind of the child—witness or victim—the trauma begins to do its insidious and destructive work. The program began in New Haven out of concerns about two wars in the early 90s: the Persian Gulf War calling up fears that another Vietnam-like event would be our ghastly nightly TV experience, and the cocaine gang wars that were ravaging New Haven (and many other cities). Trauma was the enemy the CD-CP program sought to fight.

After a trauma, over time, a child's functioning at school or home deteriorates as attention wanes and distress becomes paramount; symptoms of post-traumatic stress disorder (PTSD) and related disorders appear, often months later, and can include withdrawn or aggressive behaviors, difficulties with sleep and eating, stomach pains and headaches, tearfulness or severe anxiety. Before traumatic disorders set in is when we can make the greatest difference: prevention trumps illness, with its trajectory of impaired educational and social development, and its association with later criminal justice involvement as well as health and mental health problems.

The scope of violence exposure in children in this country seems beyond our emotional comprehension. How do we appreciate the impact of ~ 800,000 children annually confirmed by child protection agencies as victims of neglect or abuse? How can we get our heads around the 2 million (!) youth, ages 12–17, who have been victims of sexual abuse; or the 4 million (!) who have been physically assaulted; and the 9 million (!) who have seen with their own eyes serious violence. The public health and mental health consequences in these legions of victimized youth (and in all our communities) are well known (ACEs: Adverse Childhood Experiences—http://www.huffingtonpost.com/lloyd-i-sederer-md/adverse-childhood-experiences_b_4256732.html; http://acestoohigh.com/2014/03/17/vermont-first-state-to-propose-bill-to ...), with chronic physical illnesses, teenage pregnancy, and mental and addictive disorders setting in before a child reaches the age of majority.

The CD-CP program has mental health professionals join police calls. The social workers, psychiatrists, and psychologists I met go out in the evenings with a New Haven police officer in a cruiser, partners from the moment of trauma, each complementing the other because the problems they encounter are without clear criminal justice or mental health boundaries. After they respond to an incident they go back, together, after safety has been restored to reconnect with caregivers and children and to offer more.

The home visit happens within 72 hours of the event and focuses on maintaining safety, mobilizing resources, and showing that police do more than take people away. The CD-CP program includes cross training, consultations, and case conferences. And it delivers what is called "trauma-focused treatment."

The trauma-focused treatment, called The Child and Family Traumatic Stress Intervention (CFTSI), involves 4–6 sessions with caregiver(s) and impacted child(ren), ages 7–18—also done in the immediate wake of the incident. It aims to detoxify the trauma and avert its producing a disorder, and a deepening pit of psychic and physical pain, illegal activities, and long term disability. It is free and confidential—and voluntary. A controlled study in 2009 found that CFTSI served youth were 65 percent less likely to develop PTSD at three months and 73 percent less likely to have full PTSD or its partial expression.

Trauma, as Dr. Marans says, is at the "hub of the cycle of violence, circling from childhood exposure to violence to adult perpetration of violence ... " The CD-CP program is now going on in over 15 U.S. cities, including New Haven, Providence, Charlotte, NC, and Wilmington, DE. Some families continue in treatment at the CSC, or with other community services, and some are lost to follow-up—likely to appear again when police return to a site of domestic violence. Imagine a neighborhood, even yours, where cops and clinicians—and government—demonstrate (not just say) that an ounce of prevention is worth a pound of cure.

REFERENCES

Marans, S, Smolover, D, Hahn, H: Responding to Child Trauma: Theory, Programs and Policy, in Handbook of Juvenile Forensic Psychology and Psychiatry (Grigorenko, EL, editor), Springer, 2012

Finkelhor, D, Ormrod, RK, Turner, HA: Lifetime assessment of poly-victimization in a national sample of children and youth. Child Abuse & Neglect, 33(7), 403–411

The Safe Horizon-Yale Child Study Center Partnership: Offering Hope for Abused Children (https://www.safehorizon.org/images/uploads/misc/1333460124_ChildAbuse_CFTSI_WhitePaper_Final.pdf)

Child Development-Community Policing, 2008 DVD, by The National Center for Children Exposed to Violence

ACEs: ADVERSE CHILDHOOD EXPERIENCES—AND PROBLEMS FOR A LIFETIME

LIS: ACEs are "adverse childhood experiences" that can usher in a lifetime of misfortune—and frequently then pass troubles on to succeeding generations. These are events beyond a young person's control. The principal types of ACEs that children are exposed to are abuse, neglect and seriously troubled households. While ACEs occur before the age of 18, their effects typically endure, producing (via the mechanisms of chronic stress and inflammation in blood vessels and organs) problems like depression, substance abuse, obesity, heart and lung diseases, teenage pregnancy, suicide attempts, and much more. What is not known hardly at all is that Lady Gaga and her mother (Cynthia Germanotta) established The Born This Way Foundation, with its message to be brave and to be kind, to not be daunted by challenges of this magnitude. This post marked early efforts to collaborate with their efforts, which I regret to say did not materialize—at least not yet.

The Born This Way Foundation is opening doors for many youth to have the full life they are born to live. Many youth experience events in their early life, through no choice of their own, which can be deeply stressful to a developing mind and brain—both highly sensitive to beneficial and detrimental influences.

ACEs are "adverse childhood experiences" that can usher in a lifetime of misfortune—and frequently then pass troubles on to succeeding generations. These are events beyond a young person's control.

The principal types of ACEs are abuse, neglect and seriously troubled households. More specifically, ACEs are emotional, physical and sexual abuse; emotional and physical neglect; and homes that have domestic violence, or mental and/or substance (alcohol or drug) disorders, or parental separation or divorce, or a family member who is incarcerated. While ACEs occur before the age of 18, their effects can endure.

Doreen, for example, was born of a teenage mother who was herself physically abused and suffered severe traumatic stress disorder. By the time Doreen was 14 she was markedly obese with pre-diabetes and using synthetic marijuana on a daily basis. She lived with her grandmother, who was physically disabled and unable to care for herself, no less Doreen.

Alberto, for example, was 15 and had behavioral problems in school dating back almost a decade. His father was in prison and had been a drug addict. His mother had divorced his father and her search for a stable male partner and father figure for her two sons yielded a series of unstable, volatile and sometimes exploitative relationships. Alberto had multiple school suspensions and was at risk for expulsion because of fights and truancy. He started using tobacco, alcohol and drugs when he was eleven.

The stories of these two teenagers are as tragic as they are common. They are the faces of the impact of ACEs—in this or any other country. ACES put our youth, and the generations they spawn, at risk for developing many of the following conditions and problems:

- Alcohol and drug abuse
- Depression
- Heart, lung or liver disease
- Sexually transmitted diseases (STDs)
- Intimate partner violence
- Smoking, including at an early age
- Suicide attempts
- Unintended pregnancies

As the number of ACEs a youth experiences increase, so too does his or her risk for these health and mental health problems—often before they depart their teen years! In fact, the greater the number of ACEs a youth experiences—and the presence of one ACE usually means there are others—the greater the likelihood of multiple problems.

The initial study that identified ACEs was done almost 20 years ago, involving over 17,000 people, by the Centers for Disease Control and Prevention (CDC) and Kaiser Permanente Health Plan.

We can appreciate how a progression of consequences begins with one or more ACEs. These unwelcome and unavoidable (to the youth) experiences adversely impact that youth's social, emotional and cognitive (intellectual) development and foster increased rates of unhealthy behaviors including smoking, alcohol and drug use, indiscriminate and unprotected sex, a sedentary life style and a diet rich in sugar and fats.

ACEs seem to do their damage in two principal ways: First, by inducing a chronic stress response in the brain (and thus body), which lowers immunity to disease and is instrumental to the development of a variety of mental and physical illnesses—as well as our capacity to recover from them. Second, by the long-term disease-producing effects of behavioral and habit disorders. The combined effects of chronic stress and risky behaviors and habits induce a host of disease states and social problems, often by adolescence and, if not, by young adulthood. In short order, disease and disorder mount, limit functioning and quality of life, and go on to produce disability and early death.

With this degree of scientific information on the profound impact of adverse experiences on youth (and their later lives) it remains a puzzle that so few people know about this work. But lack of appreciation of ACEs is only one element in limiting the development of interventions to reduce their awful impact. Preventing abuse, neglect and seriously troubled households are among the most daunting of social challenges to try to tackle. Yet their prevalence, and the suffering and cost these problems produce, are the measure of the necessity for our families and societies to find ways to intervene—and spare youth from a life marred by pain and dysfunction.

The Born This Way Foundation, and its message to be brave and to be kind, is not daunted by challenges of this magnitude. Lady Gaga and Cynthia Germanotta, co-founders of the Foundation and daughter and mother, recognize social-emotional development as a crucial building block in the lives of youth, and have made this and what impacts it, negatively and positively, a focus of their work. In the future, I will report further on what they are doing to change the world for and through young people.

WARTIME PTSD: WHAT WORKS AND HOW TO CARE FOR A LOVED ONE

Sandro Galea & Lloyd Sederer
June 11, 2013
http://www.huffingtonpost.com/lloyd-i-sederer-md/veterans-ptsd_b_3408128.html

LIS: Hundreds of thousands of war returnees from Iraq and Afghanistan have or will develop post-traumatic stress disorder. As have a great many other veterans of other wars. What might PTSD look like to a family member? What are its effective and promising treatments? What can those affected and their families do? What public health actions need to be done to identify those in need and help them engage and remain in care? This post discusses all these questions.

WAR

June is PTSD Awareness Month, so declares the Veterans Administration. Hundreds of thousands of war returnees from Iraq and Afghanistan have or will develop post-traumatic stress disorder. It is a condition that induces suffering in veterans—and their families, who can be repeatedly separated from their loved one, live with more limited resources as a member is gone and emotionally contend with anxiety about the possible injury or death of their soldier.

The risk of developing PTSD is increased when military personnel experience combat, are wounded, witness death, are taken captive or tortured, handle remains, or are sexually harassed or assaulted. The most stressful of combat experiences include exposure to unpredictable attacks, including IEDs, sniper fire, and rocket-propelled grenades. Longer and multiple deployments as well as greater time away from base camp add to a soldier's likelihood of developing PTSD.

The Institute of Medicine/National Academy of Sciences issued "Treatment for PTSD in Military and Veteran Populations (Initial Assessment)" after reviewing Department of Defense and VA data on prevention, screening, diagnosis, treatment and rehabilitation of PTSD. Its aim was to inform and direct future efforts to more effectively respond to a condition that profoundly impacts soldiers, families, and our communities.

WHAT MIGHT PTSD LOOK LIKE IN YOUR FAMILY?

Your loved one was exposed to a life-threatening or horrific event, which may have happened in recent months or perhaps happened in the past—even years ago. Your soldier becomes inward, isolated, and preoccupied, with difficulty concentrating on and completing tasks. He or she has changed profoundly, leaving you confused and even afraid. Some will startle very easily at something as minor as the sound of a door closing or a telephone ringing. Some will be highly vigilant, as if a sniper were on a rooftop nearby. If you can get the person to talk about what is happening, he or she may describe feeling scared, numb, or both. Images of the trauma erupt into the person's conscious mind, sometimes without a clear trigger. Sleep is terribly restless and full of anxious dreams. Alcohol and drug abuse is very common, and if a person smokes cigarettes he or she may smoke a lot more.

Suicidal thoughts are common. (In fact, the number of completed suicides among veterans of Iraq and Afghanistan now far exceeds the deaths suffered in combat.) A well-validated screening tool is the PTSD Checklist, a version of which exists for military personnel and can be accessed on the Web to help in identifying this condition.

TREATMENT OF PTSD

We have much to learn about what are the most effective treatments for PTSD for which individuals and at what point in the course of their illness. A principle that applies to PTSD, as it does to every serious medical illness is that early detection and early intervention can help slow the progression of the disease. Another principle is that comprehensive treatment is essential: Interventions are often best when they combine medications, therapy, ongoing self care (exercise, nutrition, yoga and meditation), supportive friends and families, and control the use of alcohol and non-prescribed drugs. Still another principle is that treatment be continuous—because interrupted treatment allows illness to gain the upper hand producing relapse (falling ill during an episode of illness) or recurrence (falling ill after recovery).

Studies indicate that the therapy treatments that work for PTSD are exposure therapy, cognitive behavioral therapy (CBT), anxiety management programs, and EMDR (eye movement and desensitization reprocessing—a new finding given its unclear results in the past). It is critical to detect depressive illness and substance use disorder, highly common co-occurring conditions to PTSD, because unless these are recognized and treated a soldier cannot recover from the primary traumatic disorder.

Medication treatment has proven less clear, especially for the commonly used selective serotonin uptake inhibitors and serotonin reuptake inhibitors (SSRIs and SNRIs). Studies of U.S. veterans have yet to show conclusive efficacy, though there is considerable debate about this finding because of more sanguine findings with veterans in other countries. Findings about other antidepressant medications like tricyclics and monoamine oxidase inhibitors have been even less conclusive.

Complementary and Alternative Medicine (CAM) treatments show promise and include herbal compounds, yoga (especially breathing techniques), acupuncture, and meditative techniques. But here too the evidence is at best preliminary and contested.

WHAT CAN YOU DO?

It is not enough for doctors to ask "Why are you here?" Patients and families often wonder, "How will I be able to tell if the treatment is working?" So doctors need to ask their patients and their families what they want to achieve. If you are not asked, come prepared to say what that is. Establishing clear goals for treatment is a simple and practical way of determining if the treatment is working. In addition, the use of standardized questionnaires, simple checklists that quantify symptoms and functioning, like PTSD and depression scales, are also good ways of monitoring if a person is responding to treatment. While mental health disorders have yet to have blood tests, these paper and pencil scales are as reliable in determining treatment response as are blood sugar, hemoglobin A1c levels and lipid profiles.

Psychiatric conditions, including PTSD, depression and substance use, often have the additional vexing problem where those affected fight against receiving the care that can make a difference. Sometimes it is the illness itself that blinds a person from knowing they are ill. Stigma, shame, hopelessness that anything can help, bad experiences with care, not wanting to be a burden, and fear of unemployability as a result of mental illness (especially in uniformed personnel jobs like police, fire, and EMTs) all conspire to deter a person with PTSD from getting care. Sometimes this is the greatest problem a family will face.

Families will need to be clear about what they see in the person affected, validate their experiences with each other and ally together, listen to understand why the veteran is behaving as he or she is, and carefully use their leverage to help their loved one act, ultimately, in his or her interest. Families can learn how to best help their loved one, but they generally cannot do so without the support and coaching of others.

WHAT WE CAN DO NOW FOR VETERANS AND THEIR FAMILIES

The IOM report urges that PTSD screening be carried out at least once a year in primary care settings. Standardized screening is an important way to rise above a "don't ask, don't tell" policy of medical evasion by doctors and patients.

Families need to be an ongoing part of the treatment of war returnees with mental health conditions. While consent is always needed, it helps to create family involvement as an expectation of good treatment, not tack it on after the fact. The family may prove not only the best early warning system of danger but also can be the greatest asset a person with an illness may have.

We must measure the quality and outcomes of treatment programs to ensure that they are consistently providing the evidence-based practices (such as they are) and are producing results. We can evaluate program performance to determine patient retention in treatment so they have a chance at recovery.

We must also seek innovative and alternative treatments that may prove not only effective but more palatable to soldiers, their families, and even are less costly than conventional interventions.

WHAT LIES AHEAD

The IOM has also called for observing clinical services and practices on military bases as well as ongoing assessment of new and emerging treatments and practices. It speaks to an ongoing need—and commitment—to help veterans and their families recover from the "invisible" yet profoundly evident consequences of war on the minds and souls of combatants.

The fight ahead is not only to "wage war for peace," to paraphrase The Carter Center, it is also for the peace of mind of those individuals (and their families) who served and are serving in Iraq and Afghanistan.

Need help? In the U.S., call 1-800-273-8255 for the National Suicide Prevention Lifeline.

TRAUMA AND ADVERSITY IN CHILDHOOD: HISTORY NEED NOT BE DESTINY

LIS: This article followed the release by the American Academy of Pediatrics of two groundbreaking reports—"The Lifelong Effects of Early Childhood Adversity and Toxic Stress" and "Early Childhood Adversity, Toxic Stress, and the Role of the Pediatrician: Translating Developmental Science Into Lifelong Health". Their position is that brain and emotional development are profoundly disrupted by childhood adversity and trauma. This post describes the mechanisms by which trauma does its damage, the role of pediatricians, and existing programs that can help children and families impacted by trauma. This is medical leadership at its best, though going from concept to practice, changing doctors' behaviors, is one of the harder things to do—I know that since I have spent a career trying.

Once again, the American Academy of Pediatrics is demonstrating its clinical leadership. Two recent, groundbreaking reports—"The Lifelong Effects of Early Childhood Adversity and Toxic Stress" and "Early Childhood Adversity, Toxic Stress, and the Role of the Pediatrician: Translating Developmental Science Into Lifelong Health"—by the Academy boldly declare what has been known but too hidden from sight: Namely, that brain and emotional development is profoundly disrupted by childhood adversity and trauma.

The pediatric academy quotes Frederick Douglass who said "It is easier to build strong children than to repair broken men."

Toxic stress, or early environmental trauma, has been proven to disrupt normal brain development and trigger genetically predisposed diseases. The tragic results include impairments in the ability to regulate emotions and learn, to adapt socially with others and produce, in adolescence and adulthood, lifelong physical and mental disorders, including heart disease, asthma, arthritis, obesity, diabetes, cancer, depression, substance abuse and PTSD. Trouble staying and succeeding in school are also common, as are brushes with the law.

Adverse Childhood Events, or ACEs, were initially studied by Kaiser Health of Southern California and then by the World Health Organization (WHO) World Mental Health Survey Initiative. ACEs include:

1. Direct psychological abuse
2. Direct sexual abuse
3. Direct physical abuse
4. Substance abuse in household
5. Mental illness in household
6. Mother treated violently
7. Criminal behavior in household

The greater the number of ACEs, the greater the risk of developing a chronic disease, or multiple chronic diseases. From post traumatic disorder research we know the greater the severity and frequency of the trauma the more like it will burn itself into the brains neural circuitry.

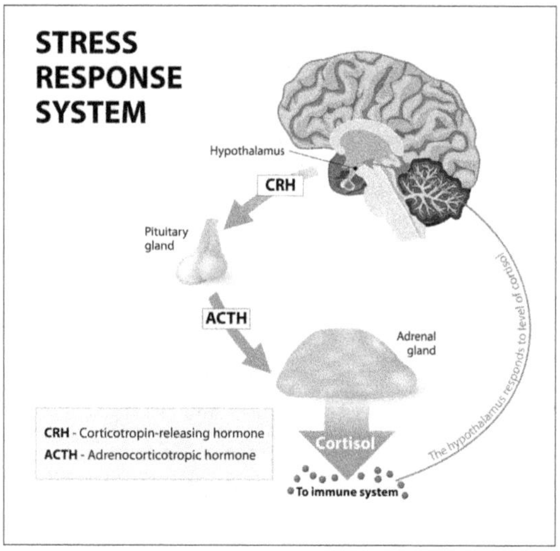

THE STRESS RESPONSE SYSTEM

The mechanisms by which early childhood adversity lays its toxic roots are numerous and complex. The manifestations are as specific as youth engaging in impulsive and dangerous behaviors (well beyond normal adolescent risk taking), including reckless (and drunk) driving and unprotected sexual behaviors, which can result in sexually transmitted diseases and teenage pregnancies. The mechanisms are as fundamental as the unregulated and ongoing release of stress hormones, including cortisol and adrenaline, which weaken body defenses (compromising the immune system's ability to protect from infection and cancer or to turn our immune systems against us in the form of autoimmune diseases), raise blood pressure, promote plaque formation in arteries, and are linked, neurologically, to depressive and post-traumatic stress illnesses.

The specialty of pediatrics was first to develop "medical homes" (popularized today with federal enabling legislation) designed initially for the young with serious and chronic illnesses whose proper care needs to be monitored and clinically managed by one responsible (accountable) doctor and clinic.

Pediatricians have long used screening tools to track childhood development and more recently many have introduced depression screening (and treatment paths) as basic tenets of good care. Their declaration, through these recent reports, of the impact of childhood trauma is a rallying call for what heretofore was another example of "don't ask, don't tell."

There are many proven approaches to these problems. Among them are:

—Home visits by nurses to mothers identified as being at high risk for emotional problems (e.g., Dr. David Olds' Nurse Home Visiting Program)
—Primary care screening and early intervention for depression in moms
—Pediatric screening and early intervention for depression and addictive disorders in youth
—Parental skills training programs (e.g., Positive Parenting, The Incredible Years, Bright Futures, About Our Kids)
—Youth support programs (e.g., Big Sister, Big Brother, after school programs)
—Pediatric medical homes that holistically support child development and deliver health, mental health and wellness services
—Trauma-focused mental health programs (for youth already affected)

The health of our youth, today and into their futures, can be protected. We can prevent the diseases and disabilities that result from childhood adversity and trauma. State and national budgets can be protected from decades of preventable health, correctional and social welfare expenditures. By following the wise counsel of the American Academy of Pediatrics, and other professional and policy groups, early experience need not be destiny for countless children, their families and their communities.

HAITI: TRAUMA AND RESILIENCE A YEAR AFTER THE EARTHQUAKE

Drs. Lloyd Sederer & Cassis Henry*
January 12, 2011
http://www.huffingtonpost.com/lloyd-i-sederer-md/haiti-earthquake-trauma-resilience_b_808054.html

LIS: The picture is a grim one, one year after the massive, deadly earthquake in Haiti. Trauma has set in, along with horrific, disease producing living circumstances and an epidemic of sexual assault on women and children in the camps. Yet, even under such extraordinary corrosive conditions, resilience is possible. Some individuals faced with traumatic circumstances find a way to make a life, or try. This report is informed by Dr. Henry's work in Haiti, and by Partners in Health.

The earthquake that hit Haiti a year ago today was the sharpest single shock in a 400 year history characterized by very hard times. This country's history begins with the extermination of the native people, slavery of a brutality unequaled in the Western hemisphere, the persistence of an unequal society with almost uniformly limited political concern about the poor majority, and dictatorship and foreign intervention.

The majority of Haitians have a lifespan shortened by malnutrition, infectious disease (including HIV and tuberculosis), poor maternal health care, environmental destruction, and the toll of back-breaking labor. The earthquake brought additional plagues. One of these has been a cholera epidemic engendered by poor access to clean water (already a problem before the earthquake), poor management of sewage, limited access to coordinated health care and poor routes of public health communication—all problems of the sort we call in medicine "pre-existing conditions," but exponentially worsened by social disruption and the re-organization of the population in Port au Prince into fundamentally unsound living conditions—barely alleviated by only a fraction of the external aid that was promised.

Living conditions have played a central role in the epidemic of sexual assault that is suffered by women and children living in the Internally Displaced Persons camps, promoted by living conditions including insecure structures made of bedsheets and tarps, the absence of light at night, and the absence of the social protections offered by familiar neighbors and social networks. Yet another is the year-old existence of a large disabled population, including individuals who suffer from amputations after crushing injuries, loss of function, minimal access to rehabilitation and prosthetic devices, joining those who were disabled prior to the earthquake. Those who struggle with the burden of loss of limbs and function are joined by the millions who suffered the loss of family and friends. Those individuals who already suffered from mental disorders—almost certainly untreated—prior to the earthquake have had to deal with worsening of their conditions and an almost total absence of a mental health care system.

Under such extraordinary corrosive conditions, resilience is possible. Some individuals faced with horrific circumstances find a way to make a life, or try. Resilience is defined, in physics, as the capacity of some material to absorb energy and respond elastically so as to retain its integrity and not become deformed as a result of the forces it is subject to. The emotional equivalent is a person's ability to absorb stress and not be broken by it. Faith and hope foster resilience. Basic public health conditions and health and mental health services add to the likelihood of resilience. But resilience must be nurtured. People, not institutions, are what foster resilience. This is why individuals, families and communities, for their neighbors and those across the tracks, need to ask "what can I do?"

The continuing magnitude of distress in Haiti should not fail to respect Haitians' fortitude. The destructive conditions which have weighed upon the vast majority of the Haitian people continue. Yet, Haitians have returned to work and the rest of life. The necessity of these purposes remarkably asserts itself in the face of circumstances that shake the imagination.

* This post was co-authored with Cassis Henry, M.D., a Fellow in Public Psychiatry in the Department of Psychiatry at Columbia Physicians and Surgeons. She has been a member of Partners in Health in Haiti for many years.

HOW THE STRESS OF COMBAT AFFECTS FAMILY AND WORK AT HOME

LIS: over one-third of U.S. soldiers deployed to Iraq and Afghanistan are not active duty, they are members of the National Guard and Reserve*. One in five will develop a mental health disorder. Spouses and children are repeatedly separated from their loved one, as is the soldier from his or her family; families consequently live with more limited resources as a member is gone and under the constant anxiety about the possible injury or death of their soldier. This post reports on a conference convened by the Carter Center in Atlanta, Georgia, titled "A Veteran's Journey Home: Reintegrating Our National Guard and Reservists Into Family, Community and the Workplace." Take a read.

US VETERANS

We are at war. And over one-third of U.S. soldiers deployed to Iraq and Afghanistan are not active duty, they are members of the National Guard and Reserve*: these men and women are typically older, married and employed. They are soldiers who brave the perils of combat and separation from family, work and community. One in five will develop a mental health disorder. The stress of combat, repeated deployments under persistent threat of harm means that many are returning home with extraordinary rates of mental and substance use disorders; with evident or sometime subtle problems thinking clearly as a consequence of traumatic brain injury (TBI); and with rates of suicide that now result in more self-inflicted deaths than those sustained from the enemy.

Because of these stresses, family and work problems upon return are not uncommon and can sometimes be catastrophic. What is going on and what can be done that will place a type of psychological Kevlar into the minds of these men and women to prevent harm and what can be done if they are psychologically injured to minimize illness and maximize recovery?

Over 1 million men and women have served in the Guard and Reserve since 2001. When deployed they go more frequently (many times with three or four deployments), for longer stays in combat areas and with less advance notice than in the past. This means disruption. Disruption of their lives, their families' lives and their work lives. Spouses and children are repeatedly separated from their loved one, as is the soldier from his or her family; families consequently live with more limited resources as a member is gone and under the constant anxiety about the possible injury or death of their soldier.

Work is impacted when a soldier leaves for lengthy and repeated tours that effect job performance and productivity, and test even the most supportive of employers. Imagine a business with five employees where one is repeatedly gone. When the soldier returns with PTSD, TBI, depression or is abusing alcohol or drugs then the stresses of absence and disruption are complicated by the soldier's psychic pain—the invisible wound of war, and the impaired thinking and functioning that interfere with work and family relationships.

Twenty-six years ago, Former First Lady Rosalynn Carter began The Rosalynn Carter Symposium on Mental Health Policy. This year's meeting, held November 3 and 4 at the Carter Center in Atlanta, Georgia, was "A Veteran's Journey Home: Reintegrating Our National Guard and Reservists Into Family, Community and the Workplace." The challenge the conference presented to its invited attendees, according to Thomas Bornemann, Ed.D., Director of the Center's Mental Health Program, " ... is to meet our moral obligation to serve the men and women who served and suffer ... taking a public health approach, where we understand a population of people in need and develop solutions that advance national policy and practices." I love the mission statement of the Carter Center: Waging Peace. Fighting Disease. Building Hope.

We heard from Lieutenant Colonel Anthony Mohatt of the Kansas National Guard who established a command philosophy of wanting to know and has staffed his unit of 1,700 soldiers with mental health, family support and chaplaincy staff to ensure that emotional problems are identified and help is made available. He has also proven to his men and women, over a number of years, that promotions are not denied those with mental health problems if they continue to do their job well.

Liisa Hyvarinen Temple, a freelance multimedia producer and instructor at the University of South Florida, told us about her husband, U.S. Air Force SMSgt Rex Temple, who has had four deployments and 10 overseas tours. Together the couple created a blog for his yearlong deployment to Afghanistan to connect him with her, his parents and extended family and friends which has become one of the most popular social networking sites for deployed troops with 300,000 unique visitors to date.

We heard how JPMorgan Chase pays full benefits during deployments lasting up to a year, including a special benefit to assist with childcare. They recruit soldiers because of their decision making and leadership skills. Dr. Barbara Van Dahlen, a clinical psychologist, started Give an Hour where today over 5,000 psychiatrists, psychologists, social workers and other mental health professionals across the country provide an hour a week of free mental health services to veterans and their families to complement the work of the Veterans Administration and community mental health services. Colleges are creating special entry programs for veterans to help them transition from the culture of war to the culture of the campus—"Boots to Books" at Sierra College in California being one example. Veterans Courts are springing up around the country so that soldiers whose illnesses drive aberrant behavior are diverted to treatment instead of jail.

New York State (NYS), along with the Medical Society of the State of NY, the NYS Psychiatric Association and the National Association of Social Workers, developed and delivered basic training to 3,500 service providers on what to ask and how to recognize TBI, PTSD and other psychic injuries. Too few employers understand the value that veterans bring to the workplace, although the NYS Department of Labor and the NYS Division of Veterans Affairs have joined forces to provide returning vets with training and assistance in keeping or finding a job.

By law throughout the land since 2008 a set of reintegration services was instituted called the "Yellow Ribbon Program." Soldiers are now provided specific activities for them and their families at pre-deployment and after 30, 60 and 90 days after their return. They learn about the new normal that is their new life and are educated about the ways that trouble can emerge (including problems with anger, alcohol and drug abuse, and high risk behaviors) and how to get help. A comprehensive assessment of their health and mental health is done at 90 days. The VA, where soldiers can get medical and mental health services, has vastly expanded its programs and staffing to meet the needs of war returnees.

In other words, a lot is going on that focuses on prevention and intervention for those who have served. But not enough of those in need have workplace support and opportunities and the community services that can make a difference in enabling a successful reintegration. The numbers of veterans needing support and services are in the hundreds of thousands and growing each year. Fear of stigma or concerns about diminished career opportunities if you have a mental health or neurological problem (like TBI) keep so many soldiers from seeking care. Too few mental health professionals know the military culture or are experienced delivering effective treatments for the mental health disorders that war produces.

Our country has come to separate soldiers from the wars they are waging—to differentiate soldiers in the war zone from whatever our politics may be about the Iraq and Afghanistan wars. This is truly an advance from the antipathy that those who served in Vietnam faced. Last year a beer advertisement had soldiers arriving at a domestic airport terminal clearly returning from some place distant. Other travelers recognized their special role and stood and saluted. I choked up. But patriotism is not prevention and honoring the service of our soldiers is not the same as taking responsibility for their safe and successful return and reintegration. The Carter Center conference connected many across the country devoted to reintegrating veterans and challenged all of us to shape and institute effective policy and practices for the future.

I thought as I left the grounds of the Center that the fight we have to wage is not only for peace it is also for the peace of mind of those with the invisible wounds of war who served and are serving in Iraq and Afghanistan.

………………….

* Army Guard and Reserve, Coast Guard, Air National Guard, Air Force Reserve, Marine Corps Reserve and Navy Reserve.

Take a look at: http://www.milblogging.com; http://afghanistanmylasttour.com/; www.americasheroesatwork.com; http://www.rand.org/multi/military/veterans/

Webcasts of the Carter Center Reintegration Conference can be found at: http://cartercenter.org/health/mental_health/symposium.html

DISCUSSION AND CRITICAL THINKING QUESTIONS

What are the faces of trauma?

How does it produce its toxic and often enduring effects?

Are their preventative strategies to forestall its impact?

What are clinical approaches to its remediation?

What are the public health initiatives needed to respond to the presence of traumatic events in this country and around the globe?

IMAGE CREDITS

Fig 4.1: Copyright © Depositphotos/ambrozinio.

Fig 4.2: Copyright © Depositphotos/belchonock.

Fig 4.3: Copyright © Depositphotos/edesignua.

Fig 4.4: Copyright © Depositphotos/elswarro.

OPENING COMMENTS

Recovery is a term that had its behavioral health beginnings in the field of substance use disorders (of course, it's now used to describe even getting better from a cold). But the recovery concepts that now dominate the fields of both mental health and addictions are duly getting the attention and action they warrant.

It is well known that the fatalistic view of serious mental illness that prevailed when I was a young doctor should no longer be endorsed. Instead, a spirit of optimism, tempered by good treatment, a supportive community, and time, is what we owe patients and their families who come to us for help. We can offer optimism and hope, because people do recover from mental and substance use disorders. That does not mean they are like they were before they became ill, or that they are without symptoms. Recovery recognizes that a life can be lived with illness, whether that be diabetes or depression, coronary heart disease or bulimia, or arthritis or PTSD.

In this section, I offer reviews of a number of documentary films whose stories exemplify illness and recovery. These are films that can be watched by individuals affected by mental illness, by their families, and by their communities—including watching them together. I also offer a number of articles on resilience as it pertains to disasters, war, and mental and addictive disorders.

While being Pollyanna is naïve, being hopeful is not—it is informed, and helps support individuals and their families in the hard and ongoing work of recovering from mental and substance use disorders.

THE BUSINESS OF RECOVERY: A DOCUMENTARY FILM REVIEW

THE BUSINESS OF RECOVERY

LIS: The ads for recovery centers, especially the 'high end' ones (that is, expensive) often read and sound like hucksters, snake oil salesmen, ready to exploit a person or family's desperation about a life-threatening substance use disorder. Addiction treatment, alas, has become an industry, and one with few quality controls. Consumers, therefore, need to follow the dictum Caveat Emptor and know what to look for, what to ask, and what to insist upon. This powerful documentary looks behind the veils of this industry and shows why patients and families need to be prudent "buyers" and is a call for the addiction/substance use disorder treatment system to enter the 21st century in its treatments as well as to put patients, not profit, first.

Results guaranteed! 92 percent recover! Pool, personal chef, and equine therapy included!

A promotion for snake oil? For a destination resort? Not exactly. That's what families often read when they go online, frightened and desperate that a loved one with an addiction may die unless they are treated and get better. That's what those in the throes of an addiction read as well, and the seduction can be alluring.

The addiction treatment "industry" (not including public, state, city and county treatment programs) is principally for-profit, and it is big business. The private, not-for-profits are in the business as well, with their CEOs and medical directors making high six-figure incomes. Annually, industry revenues are $34 billion (2013), as we see in a screen shot and voice over in the riveting documentary, The Business of Recovery. Addiction is ubiquitous in our society, and its toll is grave (to read more, including about Robin Williams and Phillip Seymour Hoffman, please go here).

We know the mental health care system is flawed, and there is a great deal of press that reveals the consequences. The substance use treatment system is even more troubled, but it has largely escaped notice. That leaves patients and their families all the more subject to its false claims, inadequate treatments, and financial exploitation.

Perhaps the greatest fiction the addiction treatment industry propagates is that of the effectiveness of the 12-step (AA) method of recovery. "Ninety percent of recovery centers are based on AA ... " the documentary tells us and we go visiting some of the best known and most (financially) successful programs in this country. AA is synonymous with the 12 steps, a spiritual approach to recovery, developed by "Dr. Bob" (Smith) and Bill Wilson, who founded AA in the U.S. in 1935. Yet studies of AA, discussed in the film by Dr. Lance Dodes, estimate that AA works for 5–10 percent of those who use it. That means that one in 20, maybe one in 10, respond to AA—yet 90 percent of the treatment programs, including the most pre-eminent, not to mention the most expensive, are fundamentally based on a method with a very low response rate.

People with addiction and their families are not told about how small their chances of response are before they enter treatment or begin to pay tens of thousands of dollars every month for treatment. In the documentary, so ably done by director Adam Finberg and producer Greg Horvath, we meet patients and families who have spent vast sums of money for treatment, who have mortgaged their homes or spent their savings or money meant for the education of all their children. We see interviews with addiction program directors who, apparently in earnest, swear by AA as if it really worked a lot better than it does.

You want to see this documentary if you have an addiction, as nearly one in 10 American workers do, or if a loved one is abusing or becoming dependent on alcohol, narcotic pain pills (or heroin), amphetamines, marijuana and its even more toxic synthetic varieties (like K2 and Spice), tranquilizers, and other drugs of abuse. In fact, you probably want to see this documentary to be an informed consumer—to judge if you are being sold snake oil or a program that might do better than helping one in 20 treated.

The April 2015 issue of The Atlantic Magazine had a feature story by Gabrielle Glaser called The Irrationality of Alcoholics Anonymous. We read there, as well, about the limits of AA but also learn that over the past two decades other treatments have been developed that can significantly increase the likelihood of abstinence and recovery. "The Business of Recovery" does mention these treatments but its accent is on exposing an industry that has yet to enter modern times. The business of recovery doesn't need to abandon AA; it can include it as part of a comprehensive approach to managing addiction.

New and noteworthy treatments for addiction include motivational techniques (pioneered by Bill Miller, Ph.D.) and cognitive-behavioral therapies. There is also SMART RECOVERY, an alternative to AA that seeks to address problems, not accept being powerless as AA prescribes. Today we also have Medication Assisted Treatment (MAT), the use of medications that can reduce cravings and help prevent relapse, like naltrexone, acamprosate, buprenorphine, Antabuse, buprenorphine (to learn more about this office based treatment for addiction to narcotics, including the epidemic of pain pill abuse, please go here), and methadone—each prescribed on an individual basis according to the drug(s) involved and the particulars of each patient.

Furthermore, and this is critical, what few addiction programs actually do (though many claim they do) is to assess the patient for the presence of a co-existing psychiatric condition, like depression, bipolar disorder, PTSD, and anxiety disorders. Unless a co-existing mental disorder is properly diagnosed and effectively treated the likelihood of achieving sobriety is markedly diminished since a person's neurochemistry, emotional state, and motivation are not sufficiently stable to engage in the hard work, to meet the demands, of recovery.

The National Institute of Drug Abuse (NIDA) offers a helpful guide of questions by which patients and their families can assess an addiction program. These include is the treatment individualized to the patient; comprehensive (that is, not just AA); truly delivers evidence-based (scientifically proven) treatments; attends to co-existing mental disorders; and is of sufficient duration to work.

Toward the end of this film we hear that what is being sold by recovery programs is hope. Indeed, hope is at the heart of an effective path to recovery; it is the fuel that patients and families need when they enter and try to sustain treatment and rebuild a life. What is due them, and what they too often are not getting, is joining that hope with the most effective, comprehensive treatments we have to date. Extolling AA and blaming the patient when it does not work is not science, it is ideology—at best. The message of this documentary is clear: It's time that the addiction/substance use disorder treatment system enter the 21st century and put patients, not profit, first.

To find out more about this film, go to: http://thebusinessofrecovery.com/

VOICES: A DOCUMENTARY BY HIROSHI HARA AND GARY TSAI

LIS: We enter the lives of three people with serious mental disorders, psychotic illnesses, where they hear voices that others do not. They are hallucinating, one of the core "positive" symptoms of illnesses like schizophrenia, schizoaffective disorder, and acute mania. The stories depicted are tough, with much suffering. My one regret about this documentary is that it does not convey how many people with these illnesses go on to a life of relationships, work and contribution—even if they continue hearing voices. That said, we owe a genuine thank you to those who made this film and their subjects for giving us so humane and forthright a story.

Voices is a beautifully rendered documentary on the lives of three people with severe, persistent, psychotic illness. For 56 minutes we enter lives upended by an illness, schizophrenia, which for these three led to substantial disability, homelessness and catastrophe.

The film starts with the premise that the promise of community mental health was never realized. It proceeds to show how the failure of the enlightened policies of President John F. Kennedy and the 1960s legislation he signed to end institutional care (and instead provide care in neighborhoods proximate to where people lived) produced the " … emotional realities and consequences … " we see today.

We first view the stark lives of the street homeless, featuring a black man, Thomas. He is a tall, bearded, and wears a rumpled long overcoat with layers of clothing beneath and sleeps under a blue tarp in a park with the pathognomonic piled-high shopping cart nearby. Then there is Sharon, an older Asian woman living in a locked group home, her lips smacking as she speaks from a movement disorder known to be the result of long term use of the first generation of anti-psychotic medications. And then there is Aaron, a young white man, whom we see in photos recent and past as a bright eyed boy, laying the foundation for the heart breaking story his life became.

For Sharon and Aaron, their families portray how mental illness invades a family and forever changes it. For Thomas, who has no family to turn to, it was the kindness of strangers, shop owners and neighborhood workers that enabled him to survive 20 years on the streets. For me, the film was more about the impact of severe mental illness (that is not effectively treated) on family and community than about those with the illness, though their suffering is palpable (for more on families and mental illness please go to my TEDx talk on my website—when-mental-illness-enters-the-family). We witness how family and community care for the most vulnerable, at a great emotional cost that few can bear with grace.

Sharon had been a Vietnamese beauty from a prosperous family who was educated in Switzerland, married and had a son whom she raised in the USA, with the help of her brother, as a divorcee despite her illness. Her son, Tuan, a student in his 20's, shoulders the hurt of his experience yet loves and supports his mother without reservation while still yearning to have his mother understand his love for her. In a more lucid moment, with her hallucinations and delusions transiently receded, she speaks into the camera and says "I have a disability … there are a lot of people {who are} disabled that do things. Luckily my family {is} supportive."

Thomas is almost toothless, meanders in this thinking, and considers himself " … a lord." When asked what he would do if he won the lottery he remarks he would " … spend two days in a room with peace and quiet." I wondered if anyone had offered him just that with "first step housing" rather than giving him food and money so he could remain on the streets, aging and deteriorating from exposure and neglect (endhomelessness.org).

But it is Aaron's story that cuts through any effort to deny or minimize the stark problems of those with malignant forms of mental illness. He was a beautiful boy, a good student, popular, a leader and a fine athlete. Then in late adolescence he fell ill with schizophrenia and spiraled down into isolation, homelessness and ultimately to acts of brutal violence that were driven by his paranoia and access to guns. We hear his story from his father, a fisherman, as well as an aunt and a cousin. Their grief is as immense as it is inconsolable. What a compelling case for early intervention in schizophrenia (schizophrenia/raise/coordinated-specialty-care-for-first-episode-psychosis). It is also a call to have us open, again, the debate about how privacy laws and their interpretation can keep families from knowing and helping their loved ones, as well as the rigidity of liberty laws that allow people to "die with their rights on."

My one concern with this remarkable documentary is that we don't see the evidence that many people with schizophrenia do recover—with good treatment, consistent support, not losing hope, and the tincture of time. It would be as if a documentary about cancer only showed those who became gravely ill or died, when we know that so many others are blessed with far more sanguine outcomes.

While the film declares, in a full written screen shot at the outset, that "There are no answers here … {we mean to} illuminate … " the message is all too clear. The words of Aaron's father towards the end of our journey with these people and their families press the point better than any written message or voice over plea. He tells us that it is " … too unfair … like with a disabled person trying to get into a hospital with no ramp." We " … need to do something sooner … it is too late after he purchased guns … after the bullets started flying."

The film is dedicated to "all those touched by mental illness." That means all of us, since no one is spared—whether that be the person affected, family, friends, neighbors, communities, or by the social and economic burden of untreated mental disorders. It remains a tragedy that the stories of these three people and their loved ones and friends need to be told. Yet since it still does, we owe a genuine thank you to those who made this film and their subjects for giving us so humane and forthright a story.

For more information, please go to:
www.voicesdocumentary.com

BUCK: NO HORSING AROUND

LIS: This is a film not just about a horse whisperer but a human whisperer as well. It is also a film about violence and recovery. "Buck" is a documentary film about Buck Brannaman, nearing 50 and a legend as a "horse whisperer"—though that term hardly does him justice. He spends nine months of every year crisscrossing the USA doing four day clinics on how to be one with your horse. But the essence of what he does is to inspire the person who brings his or her horse by teaching confidence, skill and compassion. To paraphrase Buck, it is not a problem horse he sees but a horse with a problem owner. This is an inspiring and delightful movie.

"Buck," a film about Buck Brannaman, directed by Cindy Meehl, in its own seemingly effortless and totally endearing way is a film about violence.

Violence comes in a variety of forms: physical, sexual, and emotional—commonly in combination. Violence is visited upon fellow human beings—young and old, family and friends, and random strangers—and those creatures that fall under our control, be they dogs or cats and, case in point, in "Buck" it is horses.

Whole agencies are created, funded and staffed to protect against violence (e.g., child protection, elder abuse, cruelty to animals) and a vast criminal justice system of courts, jails, prisons, parole and probation exists to help contain it. Yet violence endures unmercifully.

The closer the perpetrator is to the victim the more corrosive the damage. Sadistic parents have a profoundly deleterious effect, as do siblings and other close relatives. The more persistent the abuse the greater its impact and without someone to step in to protect the deeper are the wounds. In the most chilling and counterintuitive of ways, people who are violent have been almost always themselves victims of violence, thus its transmission from generation to generation.

"Buck" is a documentary film about Buck Brannaman, nearing 50 and now a legend as a "horse whisperer"—though that term hardly does him justice. He spends nine months of every year criss-crossing the USA doing four day clinics on how to be one with your horse. As one narrator put it, " … some horsemen have a handful of tricks, Buck has an arsenal." Though that too does not convey the essence of what he does, which is to inspire the person who brings his or her horse by teaching confidence and skill and compassion. To paraphrase Buck, it is not a problem horse he sees but a horse with a problem owner.

Rewind Buck's life, as the film does, and we see him as a blond haired, blue eyed boy, the younger of two sons, who was a child cowboy star at the remarkable age of four who even did ads on TV for a cereal brand. But this all-American family was ravaged by violence which reached full force after his mother died and his father, then an alcoholic, began to beat him and his brother every night, for years, until a football coach discovered the welts and called the local sheriff. He was taken in by the Shirley family (his foster mother is a featured character in the film) and given a chance to live without abuse and to learn a life of ranching and responsibility as part of a caring family that had as many as 23 (!) foster children, all boys. So begins his exit from the cycle of violence.

Buck finds his calling when as a young man he comes upon Ray Hunt, his great predecessor as a horse trainer. He witnessed that "breaking" a horse could be done without aggression or violence, long a tradition among horsemen. Buck's path was fashioned at that moment as he tells us in one of his many reflections throughout the film. He spends years learning from Hunt, modeling himself after what was 'the good father'. He would not be his father inflicting pain and terror but rather a person who could be firm, attuned, disciplined, kind and show how that could be done through the vehicle of training horses. And when you see that done, I assure you, it is a sight to behold.

What makes this film so extraordinary is not just how amazing a figure Buck is but the way the narrative illustrates how violence can be mastered. We witness Buck who leaves the legacy of violence behind (but not forgotten as he remarks) and the countless horsemen and women whom he has helped discover that you can make a horse dance or herd cattle without pain because in the end that horse wants to take pride in its work just as much as you do. The examples in the film of his skill with horses and people are arresting, each one a heartbreaker, even when he fails, as happens with one horse and its owner. We are treated to Will Rogers's philosophy that is not only voiced but undeniably shown in horse corrals, stables and training clinics while drinking in gorgeous footage of the cowboy life and the American West.

I wish I had a horse so I could go to one of Buck Brannaman's clinics. I don't. But then again, it's really not about the horse.

'NO LETTING GO'

LIS: There is no letting go when you have a sick child. In this moving documentary, we meet the "Spencer" family, reflective of the true story of the producer and co-screenwriter Randi Silverman. They lived comfortably in a suburb north of NYC, with a businessman father, a stay at home mom, and three boys—until mental illness began. One son, Tim, was a sweet child; but over time that sense of him was being lost as his mental illness progressed. His parents tried but they could not control his behaviors, and nor could he. Through this film we go deep inside this family, a mark of great courage by the writer/producer who was telling her own story without sentimentality or evasion—and thus the story of every family with a child with a serious mental illness—and in this instance the boy's recovery. The film is one of the best primers I have seen for families, and they are legion in number, facing similar problems.

There is no letting go when you have a sick child. But the journey from illness onset to getting effective treatment and on to recovery (for the fortunate)—and the tribulations along the way—is different when the illness is a serious mental disorder.

One in five youth will develop a mental illness, half of them by the time they are fourteen and 75 percent by the age of 24. In the USA, that is 14 million youth, annually. But for the great predominance affected, and their families, typically many years are spent with the condition untreated or in seeking effective care that can make a difference.

So it was for the "Spencer" family in No Letting Go. Their experience reflects the true story of the producer and co-screenwriter Randi Silverman: they had lived comfortably in a suburb north of NYC, with a businessman father, a stay at home mom, and three boys until mental illness began. Their middle son, Tim, was ten (though even younger in the actual story) when he began to be unable to attend school, have friends, bear his anxious and dark moods, or tolerate being with his family. The family sought help from a psychologist and then a child psychiatrist. They tried therapy and medications. They moved their son from one school to another, hoping that would make a difference. The mother read everything she could but more so tried everything she could but nothing worked. The boy's illness grew worse, his functioning became ever more compromised, and his fits of rage were more than the family could manage.

With mental illness, especially when it is not recognized, understood or effectively treated (and as few as 20 percent of youth actually receive proper care), the impact on the child, family, school, and community have painful reverberations on each other. The film shows us how, unlike with physical illness, mental disorders can often pit family members against one another, profoundly disrupt the lives of all those close to the ill child, evoke condescending and gratuitous judgments from friends, relatives and educators, foster discrimination and bullying at school, and engender horrific doubt and guilt in all those intimately affected.

Tim was a sweet child; but over time that sense of him was at risk of being lost as his illness progressed and he descended into mental illness. His parents tried but they could not control his behaviors, and nor could he. Through this film we go deep inside this family, a mark of great courage by the writer/producer who was telling her own story—and thus the story of every family with a child with a serious mental illness—without sentimentality or evasion. The film is perhaps one of the best primers I have seen for families, and they are legion, facing similar problems.

As a psychiatrist and public health doctor who has worked in my field for over 40 years I struggle to explain mental illness to families (and to those who are ill). Countless books and articles are available and try. But nothing is as powerful in conveying information that touches the heart as is a story. And a story visually portrayed, with an arc that takes us on a painful ride from which we emerge with hope, is a beautiful thing.

The actors are a fine ensemble. Cheryl Allison plays the mother who not only faces mental illness in her child but then confronts serious physical illness herself. She brings us into her character and we realize how even the best of efforts can take a very long time to work, all the while testing confidence, stamina and belief. Noah Silverman, a real life son of the writer/producer and thus the actual brother of the boy who was ill, played the teenage Timothy and did remarkable justice to the experience of mental illness in an adolescent. Richard Burgi, as father Henry, illustrated with aplomb how a dad goes from not knowing and judging to knowing and making a difference. Jan Uczkowski, as the oldest son Kyle, I thought was the best among the crew: we felt his anger, his disappointment in the fallibility of his parents, his loss, and his love. Critically played roles were delivered by a number of child actors who portrayed the boys in the family and their friends from early ages until their adolescence. Fans of Orange Is The New Black will recognize Alysia Reiner as mom's friend who makes a difference and who, as well, faced mental illness in her family; this role is truly different from her as the warden in OITNB—she has range. The other actors harmonize well. They seem on a personal as well as a professional mission to enjoin us to enter this family's experience with mental illness, and to demonstrate the vital role that family has in a child's recovery.

My colleagues and I, as well as countless families, now have a terrific resource. No Letting Go is an alternative, a master class, to many fine books for parents, families and friends facing mental illness in a child and who need to appreciate how these conditions perplex, confound and cause pain. And its message of not letting go, never giving up, is one we all need to hear and see.

No Letting Go screens in New York City and Los Angeles, and then goes on Video on Demand at the end of March. Watch it and tell others about this film—for that may be the gift they need to help them face mental illness and find a path to recovery.

"GIRL ON THE EDGE"

LIS: In this film, we have a 15-year-old girl, divorced parents, an estranged and likely unstable mother, an exploitative 18 year old boyfriend, drugs and sex. In other words, a sadly far too common story familiar to and lived by countless families across this country. This is, however, a privileged family and they can find, pay for and receive the best of mental health care. But the principles of recovery, itemized in my review below, I believe are universal. What can work are a dedicated family and friends; a non-stigmatizing community; good treatment (counseling, medications for some, and expressive therapies like music, art, writing, or horses—or some of all of these); perseverance by the person affected and their loved ones; repeated exposure to others who are further along in their recovery; the tincture of time; and keeping hope alive—for all concerned, including the professional caregivers. Never give up. And don't go it alone because there are many others experiencing what you are, and who want to help. This film is a story well told that provides hope.

Take a 15-year-old girl and add in divorced parents, an estranged and likely unstable mother, an exploitative 18 year old boyfriend, drugs and sex and what do you have? A sadly far too common story familiar to and lived by countless families across this country.

This time the family was that of Jay Silverman, an accomplished film and TV producer, director and writer, and he has brought his keen skills to this semi-fictionalized movie. Silverman directed and co-wrote *Girl On The Edge*. His admiration for his traumatized daughter, (second) wife and the clinicians who helped them is palpable, lends pathos and provides hope for others traveling a similar path.

Hannah (Taylor Spreitler) is fifteen and looking for love in all the wrong places. She attaches herself to a self-absorbed eighteen year old, Tommy (well played as a villain by Shane Graham), who soon drugs her at a party. She becomes not just the victim of his sexual assault but a disgrace among her peers as her naked photos wind up on the smart phones of everyone she knows. The clouds of Hannah's life grow even darker and soon she is using drugs, cutting herself and at risk to give it all up to suicide.

Her father, Jake (Gil Bellows), and step-mother (Amy Price-Francis) try and try but the problems prove too intractable and the dangers too great. Collecting other members of the family they organize what is called an "intervention," a moment when the family says we love you too much to allow your life to be destroyed. They take necessary action. In their case, it was arranging for their daughter to be admitted to a rural, residential program for adolescent girls. The fictional ranch in this film is called Maheo and was modeled after the two programs the Silverman's daughter did attend, one in Utah and one in Hawaii. Led by an avuncular Hank (the iconic Peter Coyote) and staffed by psychologists and counselors, including an equine therapist, Maheo becomes the venue for Hannah's passage to a life of safety and trustworthy relationships. The horses, a former shelter horse in particular, mirror each girl's struggle and become an essential medium for their recovery.

The Silvermans are privileged people and did the right thing for their daughter, and that was very hard. But few families will be able to afford a private ranch for months of treatment; others may but only by having to mortgage their home or accrue large debt. However, the Silverman's story need not be for those of financial means alone: what the film illustrates are the necessary elements for any troubled teenager, or adult, to rebuild a life after trauma or with a mental or addictive disorder.

The principles of recovery I have seen work in settings as varied as ranches, wilderness settings, group homes, therapeutic schools and hospitals, day programs, or living with relatives committed to helping them are, I believe, universal. What can work are a dedicated family and friends; a non-stigmatizing community; good treatment (counseling, medications for some, and expressive therapies like music, art, writing, or horses—or some of all of these); perseverance by the person affected and their loved ones—for the course is always marked by ups and downs; repeated exposure to others who are further along in their recovery; the tincture of time; and keeping hope alive—for all concerned, including the professional caregivers. Never give up. And don't go it alone because there are many others experiencing what you are, and who want to help.

Recovery from trauma and mental and addictive disorders is built on trusting relationships, protecting people from their own shame and the shaming of others, and small but clear steps that can be observed and used as anchors and reassurance when the going gets rough. We see that portrayed with care in *Girl On The Edge*. That's a message so many families need to see, and this film offers them a story to believe in.

For more info, please go to www.girlontheedgethemovie.com

HELPING YOUNG PEOPLE SUCCEED

LIS: This HuffPost was written to describe the perhaps unexpected and certainly welcome and admirable public position taken by the Duchess of Cambridge (Kate Middleton)—through an initiative called Young Minds Matter. The Duchess is pointing the way for her country, and others like ours, to detect emotional problems in youth (ages 5–12) and take action to remedy them. In this post, I describe a number of ways, clinically, programmatically and from a public health perspective, to help distressed youth in our country.

THE DUCHESS OF CAMBRIDGE

Hats off to The Duchess of Cambridge for her remarkable vision in seeing that the future for all children, and thus our societies, lies in their having a strong foundation in emotional and mental health—and her determination to make that happen.

Did you know that 50% of all mental conditions appear before the age of 14? That 75% appear before the age of 24? We are talking about depression, eating disorders, ADHD, anxiety and PTSD (trauma) disorders, and more severe conditions like bipolar disorder (manic-depression) and schizophrenia. Unless properly detected and effectively treated these conditions handcuff a child's social, emotional and scholastic development and pirate away a more successful future.

As a public health doctor and psychiatrist, my job is to identify how we can enable more youth, in this case those with problems, be identified and receive effective services. In this post, I will focus on two ways this can be done: First, by detecting emotional troubles in youth 5–12 (the age group that Young Minds Matter is focused upon) in the principal sites where we find them and their families, namely in pediatricians'/GPs' offices and in schools. Second, by illustrating with examples what we can do, especially involving their families who are often the first to see troubles and best able to powerfully and positively impact their kids.

Pediatricians and GPs routinely monitor a child to ensure she or he is progressing along the normal development steps like walking, talking, and socializing with others; they also monitor blood sugar and weight (particularly body mass index or BMI, a measure of weight and height) to try to detect pre-diabetes and intervene before the illness sets in. As adults, we are familiar with this process—called screening—for example for high blood pressure and lipid (cholesterol) levels. There are very reliable and commonly used screening tests for emotional and behavior problems in youth as well.

One very good example of a screening tool is the Pediatric Symptom Checklist*. This checklist focuses on emotional and physical health and can be done in fewer than five minutes and scored in half that time; it is used with youth 4–16 and completed by a parent (or a youth for older adolescents). Either 17 or 35 questions ask that items be checked that "best describes your child", such as "Complains of aches and pains", "Less interested in school", "Worries a lot", "Feels hopeless", "Distracted easily", "Takes unnecessary risks", "Blames others for his or her troubles", and "Takes things that do not belong to him or her". Each item is marked "Never, Sometimes, Often" thereby offering a picture of severity and allowing for scoring along a frequency gradient.

Another good example is the Child Behavioral Check List (CBCL). This screening test has versions for children 1.5-5 and for those 6–18; it is completed by a parent or teacher (for the second version). It takes a bit longer to fill out because it covers more areas of a child's life. These include the youth's involvement in sports, hobbies, organizations; the child's friendships and academic performance; and a set of questions (not true, somewhat/sometimes true or very/often true) such as "argues a lot", "fears going to school", "refuses to talk", "headaches, nausea, stomachaches", "nightmares", "accident prone", "too shy or timid", "strange ideas", "vandalism", and "worries".

There are many other screens available to use for different age groups or settings, or that specifically focus on areas of concern, such as ADHD, depression, anxiety and eating disorders. What is most relevant is that we have tools that can help a family, doctor, teacher and even older youth reliably identify problems—the essential first step to their remediation. It is also critical that services be readily available since identifying a problem without providing access to good treatment adds to the suffering of all involved and is, in fact, clinically irresponsible. We would not detect diabetes, asthma or anemia and then not treat it. The same standard practices of screening and intervening also must exist for emotional and behavioral problems in youth.

A fine example of intervention in pediatric and general practices is Dr. David Kolko's work on behavioral problems in youth*. His work focused on ADHD, anxiety and behavior problems using a PSC-17 screen with 5–12 year olds and their caregivers. Kolko employed a team approach with a care manager and on-site behavioral health services (including therapy and medication) working together with the pediatrician and nursing staff for 6–12 sessions. Some US states (Massachusetts and New York, for example) have developed excellent teaching, consultation and referral programs in which child psychiatrists offer ongoing services to pediatricians, their practices, and the youth and their families they serve.

Starting even earlier with youth in schools in the USA is done by ParentCorps, developed by Dr. Laurie Miller Brotman. This evidence-based program is embedded into schools and has operated successfully in high poverty areas in NYC as part of early childhood education. ParentCorps seeks to " … strengthen home-school connections and help teachers and parents provide high-quality environments that are safe, predictable and nurturing—to ensure that all students develop the social, emotional and behavioral regulation skills that are the foundation for learning."

Other school interventions, especially for latency and early adolescent youth, involve providing mental health services in school-based health clinics. This arrangement not only offers convenience it helps lessen stigma.

The greatest gift we can give young people is the opportunity for a future. We all have so much to gain from investing in the social and emotional development of the next generation. The Duchess is pointing the way. We would be wise to follow her lead.

RECOVERY FROM SERIOUS MENTAL ILLNESS: SOMETIMES IT TAKES 'THE VILLAGE'

LIS: Recovery from serious mental illness is possible, and in fact common. But it does not happen without a coordinated, caring community and clinical services. In this post, I describe a visit to "The Village", in Long Beach, California, and with its heralded leader, Dr. Mark Ragins. No one enters a 'wrong door' at The Village since there is no wrong door: everybody is welcome and asked what do you want? Then the clinicians and consumers there go about trying to make that happen. Sometimes that can be done promptly, sometimes it can take a year or two. But they don't give up, and they often succeed—far more than many a community mental health service. Recovery from mental illness can work, but sometimes it takes 'The Village'.

Sam, as we will call him, was proudly wearing a luminescent football jersey and a big smile on his face. He had spent 25 years living on the streets and prisons of California when I met him in Long Beach as I toured "The Village." He had achieved four years of being successfully housed, out of prison and away from the brutality of the streets. At first, he told me, he would just show up at "The Village" asking nothing but taking a shower or a sandwich. When I asked him what got him engaged in the program and making a life after all the years on its margins he said, "they did what they said, for over a year, then I trusted them."

The Village, a comprehensive mental health center in Long Beach, California, under the aegis of The Mental Health America of Los Angeles (MHA-LA). It was started as a urban demonstration project 20 years ago as the state experimented with the question of what are the best services to provide those whose pained lives were beyond their communities' know-how about how to help. The program strained, even back then, the public treasuries that paid for their daunting medical, social service and correctional expenses. In a remarkably innovative financing design The Village was paid a flat annual fee per person to deliver what set of services it considered would make a real difference. Outcomes would be measured in terms of impact on quality of life, including gainful employment and being part of a community, as well as reductions in hospital, jail or prison stays.

Mark Ragins, MD, was one of a group of dedicated staff there to launch this experiment in quality care. He remains the medical director today. Initially they served anyone who was disabled by mental illness, but over time they took the Malcolm Gladwell approach (see Million Dollar Murray, The New Yorker, 13 February 2006) that focuses on the high users of services. That means seeking out and providing for the chronic homeless and those with histories of long term institutional care, including foster care, hospitals, jails and prisons. About 400 people are served today.

Ragins, referred to as Dr. Mark by consumers and colleagues alike, now spends his time on the Welcoming Team, where the most frightened and emotionally scarred of recipients begin. "I thought I could have the most impact on people in the first three to six months and help them move on. I focus on engagement, compassionate listening, relationship building, building hope and creating an expectation of participation in their own recovery." He is a bit of a guru in the world of public mental health and serious mental illness, traveling and teaching others the art of what I like to think about as meeting people where they are and taking them where they are afraid to go. When Steve Lopez of the LA Times was looking to help Nathaniel Ayers, the anchor for his Pulitzer Prize journalism and the character portrayed by Jamie Foxx in the critically received film, The Soloist (2009), and to study, as well, the street homeless of southern California, he contacted Ragins who guided him through his work.

No one enters a wrong door at The Village since there is no wrong door: everybody is welcome and asked what do you want? Answers range from a shower, day labor, medications, and getting on Medicaid. "You ask, we try" is their ethos. The Village takes in "refugees"—people who feel estranged from their community which has yet to find a way to house or feed or deliver anything but emergency medical services to these souls. At The Village they believe in charity and not making demands that their consumers are not yet ready to meet, including taking medications or getting off drugs and alcohol. Low demand, progressive expectation is the model where you begin low and slow then expect more as a person trusts you are acting in their interests to help them get what they want and need.

But the world has changed since 1990 when The Village began. They now depend on Medicaid and HUD (the Federal agency for Housing and Urban Development) funds for their overall program, including a drop-in center and housing designed for people with serious mental illness and addictions. But their efforts are often thwarted by lack of affordable and supportive housing (where services are located or linked with the tenants), absence of jail diversion programs, and California's budget woes that have eroded mental health services despite Proposition 63, the millionaire's tax to augment county paid mental health services. In California, as well, getting on Medical (Medicaid) has become an ever greater challenge. And even when someone has Medical it pays for traditional medical services but not for rehabilitation and housing, both essential to ending the merciless cycle of institutional and street life and becoming a contributing member of a community.

When you ask someone with a serious mental illness what they want they respond with the very things we all want: a home, a job, a car and a date on the weekend. The mental health field is slowly adopting a recovery model of care. Instead of seeing people with chronic illness as fated to a life without prospects recovery holds that people can rebuild their lives. That takes support by professionals, family and community. That means providing treatment as a person will take it, step by step, with increasing expectations for a life of safety, health and community. It means offering hope, respect and trust. Recovery can work, but sometimes it takes 'The Village'.

THE HUFFINGTON POST

THE PSYCHOLOGY OF RESILIENCE

LIS: Why is that two boys from the same desperate, impoverished and dangerous neighborhood—be it Watts, Bedford-Stuyvesant or downtown Detroit—can each have diametrically different lives? Why do some people recover from disaster or war, and others can't find their way out of the trauma? Some important answers lie in what we call resilience. Resilience is central to improving the public mental health, much like immunity has achieved that status in public health. This article identifies ways by which resilience, and thus recovery, can be fostered in those affected—and their families and communities.

RESILIENCE

Why is it that two boys from the same desperate, impoverished and dangerous neighborhood—be it Watts, Bedford-Stuyvesant or downtown Detroit—can turn out so differently? One is using drugs and committing petty crime by the age of 12, and in prison for a violent offense by 20; the other stays in school, attends college, gets married and finds employment?

Why is it that in wake disasters such as 9/11 and Katrina, some who were directly affected suffer terrible PTSD (post-traumatic stress disorder), depression, alcohol and drug abuse while others feel distress yet go about rebuilding their lives, families and communities? Why is it that some soldiers deployed, even for multiple tours, in Iraq and Afghanistan, develop severe psychological problems while others go about their lives and their missions and return home never forgetting but not impaired by the horrific exposure they have had?

Perhaps the best concept we have to explain such radically different responses to extraordinary, even life threatening, stress is called resilience. Resilience is a term that originates from physics and refers to the capacity of a substance to return to its original state after being subject to intense levels of pressure, heat or other external force. What a great term for human nature to adopt. It conveys a capacity to return to what was after experiencing trauma, tragedy, life threatening danger, persistent adversity or all of these profound and too often inescapable fates that humans encounter. Sometimes resilience is called adaptation, but resilience has a dynamic feeling to it, a sense that we all can tap into properties that enable us to rebound to where we were before misfortune, natural or manmade, strikes.

I had the privilege of recently participating in a small conference hosted by the Columbia University/Mailman School of Public Health, where Dr. Linda Fried is dean and Dr. Sandro Galea and Dr. Thomas D'Aunno are leaders in departments whose work focuses on the topic of the meeting, "Resilience in the Face of Adversity." (Disclosure: I hold my university faculty appointment at this school.) The Mailman School recognizes that a field of public mental health is emerging and that Columbia and its experts must aim to serve in a leadership position to advance public mental health. We all understand public health, with its honored traditions of reducing neonatal and maternal death and childhood infectious illnesses, containing diseases like tuberculosis, AIDS and avian flu, promoting nutrition and sanitation and in recent times focusing upon chronic illnesses like heart disease, diabetes and asthma.

But what too few people appreciate is that principles of public health apply to mental health: focus on a health problem with profound quality and/or duration of life consequences affecting large numbers of individuals; identify scientifically proven interventions that can be feasibly and effectively delivered to that population; mobilize a campaign to reduce the impact of that problem (which includes public education, community engagement and methods of prevention or treatment); and measure to see if what the campaign purports to be doing is being accomplished. The Columbia meeting was a needed step in establishing that resilience is central to improving the public mental health, much like immunity has achieved that status in public health.

We now have a sound scientific base about disaster and trauma. We know, for example, that in disasters the greater the degree of exposure to the horror and danger during and after an event the greater the risk of post-traumatic psychological disease. We know that supportive families and cohesive communities reduce the risk of developing mental disorders while fostering resilience.

Problem-solving help—not merely emotionally expressive therapies—that conveys a spirit of hope and belief that something can be done are what people need in the wake of catastrophe, acute or chronic. Belief in something bigger than oneself strengthens both individuals and families, and promotes recovery. Helping others helps. Seeking meaning, even in the darkest of moments (as documented by concentration and prisoner of war camp survivors), can be sustaining. And, very recently, we are discovering the neurobiological correlates of resilience.

A colleague, Dr. Glenn Saxe, discovered that children with severe burns given higher doses of morphine had fewer problems with post-traumatic symptoms, like low mood, anxiety and flashbacks. This finding that we can mitigate how brain neurotransmitters process and encode traumatic experiences has led the military to explore a similar approach in wounded soldiers and may be applicable in emergency rooms for victims of trauma, assault and rape.

Troubled and threatening communities are pervasive throughout the world. Natural disasters strike without regard to who will be affected or when. Man-made trauma such as war, domestic abuse, crime and violence, genocide and terrorism, are our contemporary demons. We are not on the cusp of eliminating these modern day plagues as we have with polio and smallpox. But we have a growing body of science and practice that informs us about how to prepare for disaster and trauma, how we must respond in its immediate aftermath, and how we can promote recovery in impacted individuals and communities. The core concept for policy and practice is resilience and its field of study is public mental health.

DISCUSSION AND CRITICAL THINKING QUESTIONS

How do you define recovery? How do you define resilience?

Are these "soft" concepts, or are they strong and necessary for people with chronic illness of any sort?

Why does knowing—and believing—about these concepts matter? And to whom?

Who have you seen recover from a mental or substance use disorder? How did they do that?

What are examples of compelling stories you have about individual or group resilience?

How can you help spread the word about recovery and resilience? How can it make a difference in your life?

IMAGE CREDITS

Fig 5.1: "The Business of Recovery." Copyright © by Greg Horvath Productions, LLC. Reprinted with permission.
Fig 5.2: Copyright © US Mission Canada (CC by 2.0) at https://commons.wikimedia.org/wiki/File%3AThe_Duchess_of_Cambridge_Visits_Calgary.jpg.
Fig 5.3: Copyright © Depositphotos/vaeenma.

OPENING COMMENTS

In this section, I present a set of articles on six prominent celebrities in music, film, and in one case, professional sports. The people I write about are Brian Wilson (The Beach Boys), Amy Winehouse, Prince, Robin Williams, Philip Seymour Hoffman, and Chris Herren. All suffered from either mental or substance disorders—or both. The toll of these illnesses was catastrophic in all of their lives. The stories of celebrities are critical to being able to communicate about these conditions widely, to the general public. Doing so opens doors and minds that can destigmatize not just the individuals affected, but the illnesses themselves. It is also when we can use the power of the moment to advocate for the better detection and treatment of these deadly disorders.

NOT SO GOOD VIBRATIONS: LOVE AND MERCY

LIS: Many consider Brian Wilson of the Beach Boys to have been one of the most talented R&R composers of the last century. This film, dramatized, tells his story, particularly his problems with drugs and with an exploitative sham of a therapist. The movie's cast is comprised of superstars: Paul Dano (singing his own vocals); John Cusack; Paul Giamatti; and Elizabeth Banks. The director and producer is no minor character himself—Bill Pohlad—who gave us 12 Years a Slave, Into the Wild, and Brokeback Mountain. Brian Wilson suffered a whole lot of not so good vibrations in his lifetime. But at the end of the film we get an actual glimpse of him, today, crooning "Love and Mercy," and we see how these sweet words make for very good vibrations.

Do you need to have been a Beach Boys fan to go on the ride this film offers? It helps, but it's not at all necessary. Hardly anyone will not be familiar with the melody or lyrics of some of the Beach Boys'—and their lead composer and arranger Brian Wilson's—greatest hits: The "surfin" tunes (Surfin Safari, 1962; Surfin USA, 1963), California Girls (1965), Help Me, Rhonda (1965), Wouldn't It Be Nice (1966), Good Vibrations (1966), and many more. Dwarfed by the giants of the '60s (including The Beatles, The Rolling Stones, Bob Dylan, The Grateful Dead, Peter, Paul and Mary, and others) Brian Wilson's musical accomplishments, especially arrangements, are not well known outside the industry—an historical omission this film aims to correct.

We witness creativity in motion as Brian Wilson, his brothers and cousin (Mike Love) struggle to get past the simplicity of their early work ("sunshine pop") to the more complex musical compositions and unique blend of sounds that Wilson labored, successfully, to produce. But we see a lot more, and that is what's unique and gripping in this movie, even though it is formulaic in its narrative of torment and triumph.

Wilson was not formally trained but was a relentless musical innovator. He was driven by his abusive father, Murray Wilson (played despicably by Bill Camp, chewing on his pipe and spewing narcissistic venom), as well as by his own intense competitiveness. But it was Brian's personal ambition to not settle for the pop sounds that made the group rich and famous, despite the resistance of his father, whom he fired as their manager, and the fellow Beach Boys.

But early on he started to develop a set of mental symptoms (we see depicted his obsessiveness, hallucinations, and paranoia) but cannot be clear whether these were drug-induced, or from a psychotic illness like schizophrenia or from severe trauma, or all of the above. Young Brian is played by Paul Dano, singing his own vocals and rendering the youthful artist's downward and inward spiral with extraordinary deft. But it is older Brain played by John Cusack who steals the film and our hearts. Rivaling Brian's father for the most hate-able person in the film was the deeply unethical and totalitarian psychologist, Eugene Landy, who ran Brian's life for years, played with gusto by Paul Giamatti. Rounding out the cast, and easy on the eyes, is Elizabeth Banks who rescues Brian from the controlling and exploitative hell that Landy fashioned in the name of treatment for his patient.

The director and producer is no minor character himself. Bill Pohlad gave us 12 Years a Slave, Into the Wild, and Brokeback Mountain. Incidentally, he also casts his son as Brian Wilson the young boy in the film.

At 121 minutes, the film could have used a bit more editing to compress it to perhaps 90 minutes, with less time spent in pools and recording studios. But all the time needed to deliver us music, madness and recovery is wonderfully spent. The chemistry between Cusack and Banks jumps from the screen; the story of how love saved Brian Wilson may be Hollywood but I was moved by it. You can see it coming but who cares as long as the bad guys are defeated, recovery from the torment of mental illness (and oppression) is realized, and love prevails.

Brian Wilson suffered a whole lot of not so good vibrations in his lifetime. But at the end of the film we get an actual glimpse of him, today, crooning "Love and Mercy," and we see how these sweet words make for very good vibrations.

AMY: A FILM REVIEW OF THE AMY WINEHOUSE STORY

LIS: Amy Winehouse was one of the most accomplished jazz vocalists of this millennium. She died of an alcohol overdose on July 23, 2011, at the age of 27. This two hour documentary shows her as a comet crashing to earth; it is hard to watch, sort of like watching a train crash. Her great song, Rehab, seemed to me to be more a cry for help, and sadly how her life was more about relapse, not recovery. The music is great and the story painful, but the character analysis too shallow.

AMY WINEHOUSE

Amy Winehouse died of an alcohol overdose on July 23, 2011, at the age of 27. Like a comet she ascended brightly in the night sky and then rocketed into a rapid and terminal descent.

Her extraordinary songwriting, vocals and jazzy-blues style surprisingly emerged from the chrysalis of a north London, middle class Jewish family. Her gifts blazed by the time she was a teenager, catapulting her to fame before she had the capacity to bear it. Among fellow, accomplished musicians she was likened to greats like Billie Holiday, Ella Fitzgerald, Sarah Vaughan and Tony Bennett for the mood, melody and phrasing she delivered in her songs.

AMY is a two hour documentary bio-pic directed by the British writer/director/producer Asif Kapadia, known for his films that examine characters set in timeless landscapes under troubled circumstances. Seems like he applied those skills to his approach to AMY and her life. This film is a chronology of news clips (though there was a lot of her memorable music). But it was all surface. Papparazzi like clips and images, endlessly and agonizingly shown—especially as she began to enter her death spiral of despicable men, drugs and alcohol.

Her maturation as an artist began well before the film takes off. Yet we don't get a sufficient sense of a family with professional jazz musicians, a grandmother who was a singer and who enrolled Amy in theatre school, or how she became a featured vocalist with the National Youth Jazz Orchestra. And Amy's emotional troubles appeared before her fame, fortune and addictions. We see a chubby teenager who learned to manage her bingeing and weight with bulimic behaviors. Instead, family life is presented in a series of photos and home movies, with an occasional voice-over—a patina not a portrait of a life that was already headed for disaster.

Despite the extraordinary footage of Amy the artist at work (until she couldn't—and we see a lot of that as well) the film dwells on the painful and catastrophic. Her great song, Rehab, was more a cry for help and an ongoing fiction for she was famous for relapse, not recovery. AMY was like watching a train crash: it was hard not to be riveted. But then I was left to wonder, how did that all happen? There was little getting to know her and what drove or destroyed her.

Where were interviews with family, friends, Amy herself, men who were not just narcissists and sociopaths (like Blake Fiedler), enemies, business agents, etc. Even experts in music or medicine who could make sense of her gifts and her demons. Where was getting past the performances and into the soul of such a soulful young person? Perhaps that was not possible, but that would have made the movie something beyond a dystopic experience for me.

Amy Winehouse was one of the most accomplished jazz vocalists of this millennium. Her tragedy was of equal proportions. I think not just shrinks like me would have appreciated more of a textured study of this gifted artist. I wanted more than to just witness her protracted explosion from a great distance, like from the back of a concert hall where I could see too little and understand even less.

UNGUARDED: THE HIGH LIFE OF CHRIS HERREN

LIS: Watching Chris Herren play basketball is like watching beautiful, modern dance. He was an artist on the court, and addicted to drugs when not. But the drugs got the better of him, too many times, and his professional sports career was destroyed. Herren was blessed with resilience and a loving and enduringly supportive family—those were the conditions he needed to rebuild his life, and devote it to others suffering from the disease of drug addiction.

After the movie screening in the Tribeca Cinema in Lower Manhattan as he settled into a stool, microphone in hand for the Q and A, Chris Herren rubbed his left knee—the knee that hurt too much to continue to play for the Boston Celtics and accelerated his dependence on drugs and alcohol.

The occasion was a preview of an ESPN documentary ("Unguarded"—Nov. 1, 2011, ESPN, directed by Jonathan Hock) on the high life of this gifted athlete from Fall River, Mass., who wowed them at Durfee High School and onto a pro career that was as brilliant and transient as a comet in the autumnal sky.

You will want to see this film if only to marvel at the moves this basketball guard displayed from his days in the playgrounds of Fall River, to Boston College, to Fresno State under the wing of the legendary gnome—like Coach Jerry Tarkanian. Drafted by the Denver Nuggets in 1999, he was traded to the Boston Celtics in 2000. Man, could this handsome, beaming, arm-pumping athlete drive, pass and shoot. Even under the influence.

But ultimately, his arms were where he stuck a needle loaded with heroin. He traded a shelf of trophies for a rap sheet of felony convictions. His fans booed him. His family cried from the pain he brought upon himself and them. He converted "nothing but net" into nothing but a life compulsively driven by dope. As painful as that is to watch, imagine what it must have been to live.

Chris Herren went from drinking and grass to his first line of cocaine when he was 18. But it was narcotic pain pills that took him to the major league of drug addiction. First it was Percodan™, then Vicodin™, but not until Ocycontin™ did he become a pro. Life centered no longer on basketball: it centered on scoring this pill that has become a nationwide killer of people, not just pain.

There is an expression in the world of addictions: "The man takes the drug, the drug takes the drug, the drug takes the man." Soon Herren was taking Oxycontin™ not to get high, but to manage the withdrawal, the "dope sickness," that comes when the body is denied a substance upon which it has become dependent—the drug takes the drug. When his wife took the car keys so he couldn't drive to his drug dealer 12 miles away, he got on his 10 speed bicycle and pedaled, on the highway, to get his fix. When he went to play basketball abroad—no longer U.S.A. material—first in Italy, then China, Turkey, even Iran, he upped his game to heroin when pills were not readily available. The drug had taken the man.

He had been at rehab a few times—in college and the pros. I have learned no one ever knows when the life-long process of recovery will "take"—when the repetitive relapses will transform into days, weeks, months and years of sobriety. For addicts, families and my fellow clinicians, the message is never give up. You may not be able to predict when that will happen, but it sure does, more often than we imagine.

As it did happen with Chris Herren. He was blessed with a loving and enduringly supportive family. He had not only the gift of being a great ball player, but he had (has) the gift of being amiable—the kind of person you want to succeed, almost no matter how much he has hurt you and others. He was given really good treatment. It was Daytop, a drug treatment program in the New York area begun in the 1960s and the unbending demands of its counselors, that helped Herren find his heart and soul once again. The man has emerged from the drug.

Chris Herren is the father of three children and still married to his childhood sweetheart. He is now more than three years into his sobriety and coaching youth basketball. His smile warms your heart. You want him to win. He tells his story with humility and with the hope that someone, some youth or aging addict, or person at risk for a life too full of ruin, will find hope, treatment and the road to recovery. One day at a time.

PHILIP SEYMOUR HOFFMAN AND AMERICA'S MOST NEGLECTED DISEASE

LIS: Philip Seymour Hoffman was found with a syringe in his arm and packets of presumably what was heroin scattered about his West Village apartment. Addiction is a disease, from which he succumbed. In this article, I report on a major policy paper released by CASAColumbia, a renowned policy center focused on the addictions. I detail prevalence figures, the gap between treatment need and its provision, and the social and economic costs of addiction. The numbers are staggering, the individual and family pain incalculable.

Life is short, and tragically shorter if you lose your battle with addiction. As did Philip Seymour Hoffman—an actor whose stunning portrayals of a wide range of troubled characters vividly lingers in the minds of countless movie goers. He reportedly was found with a syringe in his arm and packets of presumably what is heroin scattered about his West Village apartment.

Addiction is a disease. Addiction is not recreational drug use. It is characterized by compulsive drug and/or alcohol use despite clear harm to relationships, work and physical health. When addiction advances we see physical dependence on the substance where the body experiences withdrawal when blood levels drop. Like other diseases, addiction makes no distinctions between gender, race, ethnicity or socioeconomic status.

Addiction is the leading cause of preventable death in the USA. CASAColumbia, a renowned policy center on addiction, reports that of the approximately 2.5 million deaths (2009) in the U.S., nearly 600,000 deaths were attributable to tobacco, alcohol or other drugs. The costs of addiction to government (not to mention families, businesses and communities) exceed $468 billion annually.

Addiction in this country remarkably escapes our attention despite its huge prevalence. According to CASAColumbia:

Forty million Americans age 12 and over meet the clinical criteria for addiction involving nicotine, alcohol or other drugs. That is more than the number of people with heart conditions, diabetes or cancer. Meanwhile, another 80 million Americans fall into the category of risky substance users, defined as those who are not addicted, but use tobacco, alcohol and other drugs in ways that threaten public health and safety.

Yet, and this may be even more difficult to believe, only one in 10 people with any form of addiction report receiving any treatment—at all. Past-year illicit drug use treatment (age 12 or older) was 15 percent, and past-year alcohol use treatment (also age 12 or older) was 8 percent.

Mr. Hoffman's loss to his family, his friends, his professional community and his admirers cannot be expressed with statistics. Instead, his loss tells us story of a life abruptly cut short by addiction during his peak of creativity. It is a reminder to us all how lethal a substance use disorder can be.

There are many paths for recovery from addiction. Help is available: 1-800-662-HELP (4357) or 1-800-273-TALK (8255).

No one size fits all. For some, 12-step programs are lifesaving. Some people may be suited for a program calling for abstinence, while others may benefit from what is called "harm reduction," a path that starts with reducing use (and danger) and can build from there. Recent years have seen the introduction of medications that aid people in remaining substance free (called medication-assisted treatment, or MAT). These are often best coupled with 12-step or counseling programs. We all, not just addicts, need to surround ourselves with people who support our well-being while assiduously avoiding people who want to exploit and otherwise take advantage of us. A variety of non-Western activities (like yoga and meditation), as well as nutrition and exercise aid in recovery.

Addiction is America's most neglected disease. Every day we lose people to its lethal outcomes. May Mr. Hoffman's epitaph include a reminder of how far we have yet to go to save others from so tragic a fate.

DISCUSSION AND CRITICAL THINKING QUESTIONS

What do you remember from when the media reported on these celebrities?

What did you think? What did you say? To whom?

Why are celebrity stories about mental and substance disorders so powerful? What do they convey? What are the opportunities they create?

Why is addiction called "America's Most Neglected Illness"? Do you agree? Why or why not? Why does it matter?

OPENING COMMENTS

The Diagnostic and Statistical Manual of Mental Disorders (DSM) is the American Psychiatric Association's (APA) "bible" of the diagnosis of mental disorders. In 2013, after 20 years with the 4th edition, The APA released its 5th edition, under a great cloud of controversy and criticism. I wrote two *HuffPosts* on the development and content of DSM-5, which are below. And with two friends, I wrote a short book (74 pages) that parodied the DSM, called the *Diagnostic Manual of Mishegas* (The DMOM); mishegas is a kind Yiddish word for craziness. There is also below a *HuffPost* that describes a faux interview by Charlie Rose(nberg) with the authors of The DMOM, a less than august, but funny, book.

CHAPTER 7

EVERYTHING YOU ALWAYS WANTED TO KNOW ABOUT *THE DIAGNOSTIC MANUAL OF MISHEGAS*, (DMOM): AN INTERVIEW WITH THE AUTHORS

THE DIAGNOSTIC MANUAL OF MISHEGAS

LIS: The DSM (The Diagnostic & Statistical Manual of Mental Disorders, now in its 5th Edition) is The American Psychiatric Association's bible of diagnosis of mental disorders. Its reach is far beyond American psychiatry as well. The 5th Edition was released in 2013 and preceded by great controversy and dissension—in the field of mental health and in the general press as well. With two friends (one a writer, the other a mental health policy expert) we wrote a parody of the DSM, called The Diagnostic Manual of Mishegas (DMOM), and released it two weeks before the actual DSM came out. Mishegas is a loving Yiddish word for craziness. The DMOM was a far smaller book but with a cover design that simulated the DSM. It was full of stories, anecdotes and jokes, taken from Yiddish lore (but you don't have to be Jewish to love it!). Friends warned me it could ruin my career. But instead, levity was welcome in my field and this little book was a big success. This HuffPost pretends that Charlie Rose, the storied interviewer of Presidents, Kings and celebrities, sits down to interview the 3 authors of this book. I hope you find it funny!

Now that The Diagnostic Manual of Mishegas (The DMOM) has been released, we authors have graciously provided what we consider to be a Charlie Rose(nberg)-type interview about the genesis of their manual.

Why? Because the American Psychiatric Association's Diagnostic and Statistical Manual of Mental Disorders 5—the "Bible of Psychiatry"—at 1,000 pages and retailing for $160, will appear on May 18. We thought the public would want a lighter version, in more ways than one.

So, unhindered by any reputable scientific advisory group or professional review process, we produced The Diagnostic Manual of Mishegas. At 74 pages and selling for a mere $10, how can you go wrong with this alternative to the DSM-5?

The DMOM is based upon a newly-discovered document by the brilliant if frequently farmisht Dr. Sol Farblondget, M.D., Ph.D., PTA).

We imagined sitting down across the table at Katz's Delicatessen with Charlie Rose(nberg), from the Lower East Side of New York and known for his unsparing command of a conversation, asking the questions you want answered:

CR: What is "mishegas"?

Mishegas is the Yiddish word for crazy, but much kinder and gentler. We're all a little mishugah. As Gershem Orwell wrote in his book Funny Farm, "All men and women are mishugah, but some men and women are more mishugah than others."

CR: Why bother having a manual that uses Yiddish diagnostic terms?

To your probing question, we answer a question with a question, as psychiatrists are known to do: Why not a manual using Yiddish diagnostic terms? Who can understand the hundreds of diagnostic categories in the DSM, 'phenomenological subgroups and course specifiers, notwithstanding numerical codes and factitious and dissociative disorders' that not even the people who devote their lives to can agree upon? But Yiddish, ah Yiddish! Yiddish is a time-honored source of wisdom into the vicissitudes of human emotion. Just as an Inuit has 40 words for snow, so Yiddish has even more words for the forms of mishegas, as you will see in the DMOM.

For each category of mishegas, having learned from Leo Rosten (The Joys of Yiddish), what makes for a bestselling book, we include an anecdote or joke that can be used, generally, in mixed company.

For instance: Farmisht means a little confused, or befuddled.

An elderly man walking along Collins Avenue in Miami Beach stops another elderly man. "Listen," he asks, "Was it you or your brother who died last week?"

CR: You say your book was based on a document discovered by a man named Farblondget. But isn't farblondget a nervous condition in your manual?

Yes, and with a name like Farblonget, our Dr. Sol was destined to become the inventor of a Yiddish system of diagnosis, much as a doctor we once knew—by the name of Goldfinger—was destined to become a proctologist.

CR: Does your manual have diagnostic categories like those in the DSM?

We use the thoroughly-comprehensible distinction that Dr. Farblondget made. We simply divide all mental disorders into two categories—mishegas major and mishegas minor.

CR: Can you give us examples?

With pleasure, though not with as much pleasure as a good hot pastrami sandwich delivers. A person who has conversations with God without permission from his rabbi, priest, or health insurance provider probably has mishegas major.

CR: And mishegas minor?

All of human life comes under the heading of mishegas minor.

Take tsuris addicts, who are lifetime adherents to suffering about everything and anything. They know that life is tragic—in fact, that even every silver lining has a cloud. For example, four women are sitting on a park bench in Miami Beach. The first one says, "Oy." The second one says, "Oy vay." The third one says, "Oy vay iz mir." And the fourth one says, "Ladies, I thought we promised not to talk about our children today."

CR: So does that mean there is only one condition under mishegas minor: mishegas minor?

Are you mishugah? Of course not. We provide readers with the crucial distinctions among many common human forms of suffering such as, farmisht, ferdrayt, fartootzed, and farblondget. Because we are comprehensive (and needed to fill more pages to charge $10) we also have a list of conditions we call "Cockamamy Conditions of Character."

CR: Such as?

Schmuck. Everyone knows what a schmuck is, especially if you live in New York City or Hollywood. But do you know the difference between a schmuck and a putz? How about schlemiel, schlimazel, or schmuck-with-earlaps. Our DMOM contains an exhaustive, but not exhausting, overview of shades-of-schmuck (not to be confused with the forthcoming 50 Shades of Schmuck), inspired by a schmuck we once knew who kept asking:

"Why am I a schmuck? Why am I a schmuck?"—What a schmuck, right?

And we also have descriptions and tell-all anecdotes of a wide range of mishegas including yentas, momzers, chalariahs, shnorrers, and nogoodniks.

CR: Does the DMOM have anything to offer to those of us who are concerned about aging?

Are you kidding? Of course! Alter kockers, for example, and alter kockerdom, receive major attention. "The truth," Sol Farblondget has often said, "is that being an alter kocker ain't such a bad thing, especially if you compare it to being a teenager."

CR: And where can I get your book?

We brought you a copy but we sold it to someone in the cafeteria when we were looking for a bagel. But it's online at Amazon.com and is guaranteed to make you plotz with laughter, to turn your guilt into gelt, and your kvetching into kvelling.

IMAGE CREDITS

Fig 6.1: Copyright © Fionn Kidney (CC by 2.0) at https://commons.wikimedia.org/wiki/File%3AAmy_Winehouse_Kidney_2008.jpg.

THE DSM-5: THE CHANGES AHEAD (PART 2)

LIS: This is the second in a 2 part series on the 5th Edition of the American Psychiatric Association's "Bible," the Diagnostic and Statistical Manual of Mental Disorders (DSM), after more than 20 years of DSM-IV. I cover some of the actual changes in how diagnoses will be made for the DSM-5. In theory, the DSM-5's new and revised diagnostic conditions will reflect the additional scientific information gathered since the last edition, as well as efforts to better cluster and recognize the varied levels of severity of conditions. It will also provide measures for patients, families and doctors to determine if treatment is working. The introduction of a new diagnostic manual has implications for patients, families, doctors, health systems, and payers, to name a few. Was the public's interest served by this 5th edition? It was time for a new edition but not a whole lot had changed.

THE DSM 5

Part I of this series described the process underway to reconstruct the American Psychiatric Association's "Bible," the Diagnostic and Statistical Manual of Mental Disorders (DSM), creating a 5th edition after more than 20 years of DSM-IV. Time for a new model.

The DSM is a hefty tome that specifies 283 mental illnesses, categorized by disorders, including mood, anxiety, eating, sleep, personality, impulse control, adjustment, substance-related, schizophrenia and other psychoses, delirium and dementia, developmental impairments and other diverse conditions.

In Part I of this series, I described how the APA is trying to ensure public transparency, continuous input and ongoing improvements into the drafting of the DSM-5. In this second part, I will cover some of the actual changes in how diagnoses will be made for the DSM-5. In theory, the DSM-5's new and revised diagnostic conditions will reflect the additional scientific information gathered since the last edition, as well as efforts to better cluster and recognize the varied levels of severity of conditions. It will also provide measures for patients, families and doctors to determine if treatment is working. Let's look at some examples.

I will start with substance abuse and addictive disorders, since they are ubiquitous throughout the world—and as controversial as they are universal. The current draft of DSM-5 proposes that "substance use disorder" replace what we now think of as abuse (seen by behaviors) and dependence (evidenced by withdrawal when the body is denied its drug). Each intoxicant would have its own section, such as alcohol use or inhalant use disorder.

The website identifies the primary reason for this revision as the view that the term "dependence" is misleading: We are urged to not confuse the fact that tolerance and withdrawal are normal responses to some prescribed (read: medically necessary) medications that affect the central nervous system, and thus these physical states should not be seen as an illness. A substance disorder, instead, is a distinct syndrome that includes compulsive drug-seeking behavior, loss of control, craving and marked decrements in social and occupational functioning. Maybe we can reduce stigma with this revision? A good question that time will answer.

But the addiction soup gets thicker when it comes to wondering what, indeed, is an addiction? Is gambling (yes, probably)? Is sex? How about the Internet (without porn)? The votes are not in.

Another critical—and very controversial—diagnostic grouping is autism spectrum disorders. Is there an epidemic going on? You would think so, if you listen to the news. The workgroup's recommendation for a new category of autism spectrum disorders reflects its view that autism and Asperger's syndrome (think Dustin Hoffman and "The Rain Man") are a continuum from mild to severe. Many families and advocacy groups are a bit agitated about ending the distinction, which would have effects (likely good and bad) on policy, clinical programs and funding.

In the world of developmental disabilities, the DSM revisionists want to do some wordsmithing on intellectual developmental disorders. "Mental retardation," the experts urge, should be changed to "intellectual developmental disorders" (which would bring the DSM in line with the International Classification of Diseases proposal for its 11th edition—see Part I for insight into the international scene). But importantly, and realistically, severity of an intellectual disability would not be based only on IQ but by impairment in adaptive functioning as well. That is really overdue.

Another critical cluster of disorders is called "Schizophrenia Spectrum and Other Psychotic Disorders." These are serious and often persistent mental illnesses where a person has profound impairments in being able to appreciate the reality about him or her and diminished functioning in education, work and social relations. The revisions for these conditions, which affect about 1 percent of the population but are among the most costly in terms of loss of quality of life and social cost, are less controversial but allow for an extensive assessment of severity that includes hallucinations, delusions, disorganized thinking and behavior, loss of mental capacity (cognitive impairment) and diminution of feelings, expression and even the ability to act (called avolition, or loss of the ability to start an action). This detailed assessment is a very good idea but is raising questions about the paperwork burden of completing severity measurement scales.

Premenstrual dysphoric disorder (PDD) is a serious mood problem in women that occurs during the premenstrual period. It will appear in the appendix to the main body of the DSM-5 text. The evidence is that this is distinct from premenstrual syndrome (PMS). The addition of this condition could help promote its recognition and promote more research (and better treatment) on this common and disturbing condition. Is this pathologizing monthly lunar-menstrual mood swings, some wonder?

Another debated condition is what is called mild neurocognitive disorder. The aim of this brand new disorder is to identify people at risk for developing dementia, including both Alzheimer's disease and vascular dementia (caused by loss of blood supply to a region of the brain). Symptoms include memory and language loss as well as attentional and reasoning impairments. Do you want to know if you have dementia?

There is a lot more—including eating disorders, personality disorders (a huge and evocative topic since we all have personalities), and traumatic stress disorders (all the more critical in light of our soldiers, domestic violence, sexual abuse and disaster victims). You can see all of this, and more, on the DSM-5 website. The design of each section on a disorder is very well done, since there are tabs for the proposed revision, the rationale for the revision, severity scales and the current DSM-IV to compare to.

Perhaps one of the most important changes in the DSM is called dimensional assessments (noted above in the discussion of schizophrenic disorders). DSM-IV has had the problem of fitting neatly into the complexity of human symptoms: People with schizophrenia have problems with depression, anxiety even insomnia. There has been, to date, no means to account for these problems, their severity—and, perhaps most importantly—to determine if a person is improving in treatment. Dimensional assessments will enable clinicians to record the presence of a variety of problems as well as their severity (very severe, severe, moderate and mild) and thereby be able to track how a person is doing over time and in response to different treatments. This is as needed as it is complicated and demanding.

No wonder the APA constructed 13 work groups, more than 160 people, to revise the DSM—even before it has to go through the gauntlet of its internal committees, councils and the APA Board of Trustees. Some will say, have said, a fool's errand. After all, how many angels can dance on the head of a pin? I say, however, medicine is a science. Psychiatry is a branch of medicine, a huge limb, in fact, in need of continuous pruning, watering and shaping. Science is not perfect. But the quest for the perfect, in progressive approximations, is what separates science from fiction, opinion from evidence and guesswork from clinical medicine.

For more information see the DSM-5 website.

* Disclosure: I am an APA member. I have held numerous elected state and national positions at the APA, actually worked there from 2000–2002.

THE AMERICAN PSYCHIATRIC ASSOCIATION'S NEW BIBLE *PART 1 OF 2*

LIS: This first of two articles describes the process to reconstruct the American Psychiatric Association's "Bible," the Diagnostic and Statistical Manual of Mental Disorders (DSM), creating a 5th edition after more than 20 years of DSM-IV. I discuss four reasons (at least) why diagnosis, and thus the DSM, matters. The production of this new edition experienced endless criticism, especially about delays and public perception. The DSM-5 development process has been less than perfect—but it has been more transparent than many claim and engaged many, independent experts. The criticisms, in part, I think derive from the enormous complexity of this task, its ambitions, as well as its "democratic" process, and we know what Churchill said about democracy.

PART I OF A TWO PART SERIES

For the fourth time since 1952, when the first edition appeared, the American Psychiatric Association (APA)* is again revising its diagnostic manual. Who cares, some may ask? Seems like a lot of people do care—and should. Is there dispute about what is being drafted, and how it is being done, by this organization of 38,000 member psychiatrists? Indeed.

The DSM-5 is shorthand for the Diagnostic and Statistical Manual of Mental Disorders, 5th Edition. The APA began revising the 4th Edition (which had undergone some minor revisions and thus was called DSM-IV-TR) in 2000 with the goal of releasing the 5th Edition in 2011 (when the international coding system for billing was due to change—see below). Estimates now are that it will appear in 2013. It has been 20 years since the last full revision and one is overdue. The DSM is a hefty tome that specifies 283 mental illnesses, categorized by disorders, including mood, anxiety, eating, sleep, personality, impulse control, adjustment, substance-related, schizophrenia and other psychoses, delirium and dementia, developmental impairments and others. It also provides a system for adding the presence of general medical illnesses as well as ratings of functioning and stress.

Were you to open the book to a particular illness, say depression, you would see a list of symptoms (for depression these include sleep and appetite problems, difficulty concentrating, sadness and guilt) whose presence must be met for a specific duration of time for a person to warrant that diagnosis. You would be instructed to ensure that the condition you are observing is not due to something like thyroid disease or a drug that depresses the central nervous system—both of which can cause depression and would require different treatments. You would learn something about the course and prognosis of the illness but would read nothing about what causes the illness, nor would you find information about specific treatments. The DSM has eschewed, to date, delivering information about the causes and therapeutics of mental disorders. Instead, its goal for decades has been to characterize the signs and symptoms of an illness with enough clarity and specificity that mental health professionals around the world observing the same condition would arrive at the same conclusion about what they are seeing; this is called reliability and has been the DSM's grail.

With a common descriptive language for making a diagnosis, psychiatry would ensure that treatments were properly matched to a condition (for example, for depression and not bipolar disorder, just like you wouldn't want to be treated for asthma if you had pneumonia). Plus it would be possible for researchers to compare treatments, over time, to better know what worked for what condition. Clinicians in Europe, South and North America, Africa, Asia, wherever, would be talking about the same conditions with a common language that would also reveal rates of the condition, wherever it appeared. Over time, the hope was that the DSM's diagnostic precision would uncover the risks, protective factors and causes of different mental illnesses.

There are four reasons (at least) why diagnosis, and thus the DSM, matters:

1. Most public and private payers in the U.S. healthcare system only reimburse for treatment of psychiatric diagnoses formally recognized in DSM (though having a diagnosis does not ensure insurance coverage or payment). Our medical care system, be it for psychiatric conditions or any illness, is based on diagnosis. You can only be admitted for care in a clinic, doctor's office or hospital if you have an illness, which means you have a diagnosis. In short, no diagnosis, then no treatment and no payment. In fact, FDA approval for the treatment of a medication for a psychiatric disorder requires that it be listed in the DSM: no diagnosis, no drug approval.
2. There would be no way to judge the quality of medical care were there no diagnoses. Neither patients nor medical teams could know whether a treatment is effective for a particular condition without a diagnosis, nor would they be able to customize treatments by dose, duration,

safety and side effects, age, race and ethnicity, acute or chronic care, and the like. Quality is the appropriate provision of the right treatment for a specific diagnosis—sometimes described as doing the right thing right.

3. Diagnoses can provide socially acceptable reasons for not functioning as normally expected. To wit: he has had a myocardial infarction and will be out of work for a month; she has influenza and cannot attend classes; she has a serious depression complicating her diabetes and cannot attend to her family and work because she must enter the hospital for care for both conditions. Moreover, disability and entitlement programs (like Medicaid and Medicare) require a diagnosis for a person to be eligible for support a person might not otherwise receive.
4. There are those who say diagnosis makes a difference in reducing the stigma that people with mental illness experience. Maybe, for some, having an understandable medical condition does help reduce harsh judgments by others; depression may have achieved that standing, as perhaps has PTSD. For other disorders, like schizophrenia and bipolar disorder, as some of my colleagues have said, it will be their effective treatment, especially reductions in frightening or socially disruptive behaviors, which will actually reduce stigma.

In sum, diagnosis makes a big difference. So, we better get it right. Enter the APA and their effort to get the DSM more right after 20 years of stasis. The APA constructed 13 work groups, over 160 people, to revise the DSM, along with review and critique by the APA's internal committees, councils and board of trustees.

In an effort to publicly share progress in DSM-5 development and solicit feedback from the manual's users, the APA posted online their draft material and twice invited comments; their website has received over 7 million visitors, 40 million hits, and 10,000 comments. Potential members of the drafting teams were required to fully reveal and divest themselves of any potential conflicts of interest (e.g., industry consultations, stock ownership, or helping to market a medication) before being appointed. This set the process back by some time, but created an unprecedented level of transparency. Now, field trials have begun at 11 academic medical centers throughout the country with a variety of mental health professionals. In addition, real-world office practice sites will soon begin trials by psychiatrists, psychologists, social workers, nurses and counselors. The APA is working with the World Health Organization (WHO) to set up field trials in primary care settings.

In short, a great many experts are creating the latest DSM while being subject to professional and public scrutiny of their motives and their product, and it is about to be test-driven in hospitals and offices to see how it works. The iterative and open DSM-5 development process has and will permit continuous improvements along the way. Yet none of this guarantees excellence, though it fosters it and allows for a more trustworthy process.

Criticism has especially collected about delays and public perception. The already two-year deadline extension has taken a lot of attack—despite explanations about the workgroup membership vetting and need for sophisticated field trials. Yet the really critical deadline lies ahead (October 1, 2013) in time for the DSM-5 to be linked to the ICD-10-CM (the International Classification of Diseases, 10th edition—U.S. Clinical Modification). The ICD is a disease coding (billing) system produced by the WHO, modified by the U.S. Federal Government, and required for all Medicare, Medicaid, and private insurance claims. In other words, the DSM provides diagnostic criteria and the ICD provides billing codes: both are actually needed for medical business to be done. Ironically, if the DSM-5 had been published in 2011 (using current ICD-9-CM codes) it would have to be republished with the new ICD-10-CM codes in 2013! Unintended delays, in fact, have resulted in a synchrony that will enable clinicians and administrators to have the new diagnostic system and the updated billing codes arrive at the same time. And they would not have had to buy a DSM in 2011 and an updated one in 2013.

The APA was also trumped for a while in communications about the DSM by experienced experts, Dr. Allen Frances, the editor of DSM-IV in particular, who has been critical of virtually all aspects of the DSM-5 development process. His initial critique left the APA looking flat-footed about what it was doing to make things right.

These are serious issues. But they are not being ignored. Time will tell if they will be properly corrected. The DSM-5 development process has been less than perfect. The final DSM-5 product could be at risk for not being as clinically meaningful and usable as it needs to be. As for the former, I am reminded about what Churchill said about democracy: " ... the worst form of government except {for} all the others that have been tried"

As for the latter, more about the product in Part II of this series where I will discuss the actual diagnostic and content changes proposed for the DSM-5. These include a new category of behavioral addictions; revisions in disorders of development previously described as mental retardation; far more about mental disorders affecting children, including considering introducing what is now called 'risk syndromes' to foster early identification and intervention; a focus on the co-occurrence of disorders, which is often more the rule than the exception; and 'dimensional assessments' which are basically means by which clinicians can evaluate the severity of a person's condition and monitor if treatment is working—to name a few. Will the 5th Edition exonerate itself from its critics? The world of mental health needs that to happen.

For more information see the DSM-5 website: www.dsm5.org

* Disclosure: I am an APA member. I have held numerous elected state and national positions at the APA, actually worked there from 2000–2002, and currently sit on its Council on Communications.

DISCUSSION AND CRITICAL THINKING QUESTIONS

Why does the DSM hold such hegemony in the field of psychiatry?

What are its strengths and weaknesses? What are its societal implications? What are its financial implications for patients, families, doctors, hospitals and medical insurers?

Do you use the DSM? Can you avoid using it? What do you think of its utility? It dangers?

What do you know about the DSM and other international diagnostic schemas, like the International Classification of Diseases (ICD)?

Do you think the DSM could be better? How?

Do you think the system of diagnosis, based on Yiddish terms, offered in The Diagnostic Manual of Mishegas (The DMOM) is better than the DSM? If so, why? It certainly has fewer diagnostic labels, fewer pages, and costs a fraction of what the DSM costs!

IMAGE CREDITS

Fig 7.1: Jay Neugeboren, Michael B. Friedman, and Lloyd I. Sederer, "The Diagnostic Manual of Mishegas." Copyright © 2013 by The Authors. Reprinted with permission.
Fig 7.2: Copyright © Yoshikia2001 (CC BY-SA 3.0) at https://commons.wikimedia.org/wiki/File%3ADsm-5-released-big-changes-dsm5.jpg.

OPENING COMMENTS

This section includes a number of my op-eds from *The Wall Street Journal*, *The Washington Post*, *U.S. News & World Report*, and *The Huffington Post* that take on highly controversial topics including violence, the "tragedy" of mental health law in this country, and increasing taxes on alcohol to reduce its use by underage youth. There are also commentaries on the "social determinants" of health and mental health, federal legislation to ensure that people with mental and substance disorders are not discriminated upon by insurance companies, and a link to a *YouTube* video of a debate I had with a major policy "expert" on whether we should revitalize the old and dangerous practice of putting people in long-term mental asylums. These are meant to provide you examples of using the media to assert critical issues, and to advocate on behalf of people with mental and substance use problems.

CHAPTER 8

VIOLENCE: WHAT WE KNOW AND WHAT WE NEED TO KNOW

LIS: Violence in our communities has dominated the media and our psyches. Mass murders occur with an annual frequency that exceeds the number of days in the year. In this post, I characterize four prototypes of people who perpetrate violence: psychopaths; those who are enraged and aggrieved; people with acute psychotic illnesses; and those actively using psychoactive substances (including alcohol and legal and illicit drugs). Of course, these are not mutually exclusive but understanding these four types can reduce stigma towards those who do not warrant discrimination as well as more specifically inform interventions meant to reduce the risk of violence.

VIOLENCE

Violence is painfully once again in the headlines in this county. Orlando tragically adds to the list of mass shootings this year that demonstrates that the U.S., with 5 percent of the population of the globe, had 31 percent of its public mass shootings. The number of mass murders in this country in 2016 to date exceeds the days passed this year, which is to say at least one mass murder occurs, on average, every day.

How can we understand the types of individuals who perpetrate acts of violence? There are at least four prototypes of people who seek to harm other people. I described them in a video podcast recently (Mental illness and Violence—4 minutes) and write them here to help mitigate stigma about mental illness and violence. Each prototype is not exclusive of the others; in fact, the more categories a person conforms to the greater the risk of violence.

The four prototypes are:

1. PSYCHOPATHS—they don't care about other people.
2. THOSE WHO ARE ENRAGED AND AGGRIEVED—they want to settle a score.
3. THOSE WHO ARE ACTIVELY PSYCHOTIC PEOPLE—their risk for violence is greater than the general public, but treatment reduces the risk they pose and improves the public safety.
4. THOSE WHO ARE ACTIVELY USING ALCOHOL AND DRUGS—these substances disinhibit individuals; they remove the brakes we have that prevent a thought from becoming an action. Active substance use and abuse creates the greatest risk of violence of all these groups.

Psychopaths are sometimes referred to as sociopaths or anti-social personalities. They lack empathy for others. Their principal, if not exclusive, concern is for themselves. Other people are a means toward their self-absorbed ends. By no means are all psychopaths violent, but some are, especially if another person represents a threat or a significant impediment to what they want. Think of the mafia or people from adolescence who hurt animals and people and who often do not leave their teenage years without a criminal record. So-called "white collar" criminals who exploit, extort and manipulate are often psychopaths but are not generally violent. If we can prevent youth from pursuing a psychopathic lifestyle we stand a chance, but once incarcerated they are often further socialized into a life of crime.

People who are enraged and aggrieved can escalate to violence. Their anger and wounded pride are powerful fuels for hateful action. These are people whose aim is to settle a score. But perhaps more importantly they need to restore their damaged self-esteem by destroying those whom they believe are responsible for their troubled station in life. Individuals who return to avenge where they lost a job or had a girl friend or spouse turn them away are examples of those who hurt or kill the people they blame. It is likely that some people who are radicalized have a foundation in these feelings. Murder coupled with suicide is yet another way these aggrieved and shamed souls take their revenge against others and themselves.

People with psychotic mental disorders, like schizophrenia, schizoaffective disorder and bipolar disorder, can be violent when under the sway of active delusions (e.g., fixed, false ideas especially paranoid delusions that cause them to be intensely fearful of others) and/or experience hallucinations (especially persecutory or command hallucinations that demean them or demand they take action against others). We can understand these people as responding to psychotic ideas that are responsive to good psychiatric treatment. When their illness is under control they are more or less at no greater risk for violence than the general public. But when actively psychotic they do present a risk—both to people they know and strangers. The public safety is best served when their conditions are detected, properly diagnosed and effectively treated.

Individuals using and abusing substances like alcohol and drugs (of various sorts including synthetic marijuana—Spice, K2, etc; crystal meth; PCP; and a host of other manufactured chemicals available today or en route for tomorrow's ingestion are especially at risk for impulsive, suicidal and homicidal behaviors. Here too prevention starting in early adolescence, detection of individuals using in schools, primary care practices and work settings, and effective, comprehensive treatments offer communities the best chance of reducing self-destructive actions and behaviors dangerous to others.

Violence is ubiquitous, and has been so for millennia. But the rates of violence, including suicide, in the USA now far exceed other countries. To make a difference and reduce the epidemic of violence we need to start by not alleging that all violent acts are the result of mental illness. Then we need to serve each of these archetypes differently according to what will reduce their risks of harm and thereby improve the safety of communities.

More of the same exhortations, blaming and erroneous mixing of motives and prototypes has not been effective. We need to find a better course, what other choice do we have?

CHAPTER 8

THE SOCIAL DETERMINANTS OF MENTAL HEALTH

February 2016
Psychiatric Services, Volume 67, pp. 234–235

LIS: Ninety percent of the determinants of our health (and mental health) derive from our lifetime social and physical environment—not from the medical care we receive. Americans have been said to " ... confound health care with health." In this psychiatric journal commentary, I identify the environmental, behavioral and epigenetic (how our DNA is turned on and off by our environment and how we lead our lives) factors that shape our wellbeing and longevity. Examples of social determinants of mental disorders include adverse childhood experiences (ACEs), poor and unequal education, food insecurity, poor housing quality and housing instability, unemployment and underemployment, limited access to health care, poverty, and discrimination. The commentary concludes with the program and policy implications from knowing what predominantly drives our health.

THE SOCIAL DETERMINANTS OF HEALTH

Sederer, LI. The Social Determinants of Mental Health, Psychiatric Services, Psychiatric Services 67:234–235 February 2016, online at http://ps.psychiatryonline.org/doi/10.1176/appi.ps.201500232

BRING BACK ASYLUMS DEBATE—EZEKIEL EMANUEL V. LLOYD SEDERER

April 22, 2015
https://www.youtube.com/watch?v=_efFSi1jfcI

LIS: Dr. Zeke Emanuel was the principal medical advisor in the Obama White House when the Affordable Care Act (Obamacare) was fashioned and legislated. He also happens to have been the brother of Rahm Emanuel, then the President's Chief of Staff (now Mayor of Chicago). Zeke now heads the BioEthics Department at the University of Pennsylvania and in that role, with colleagues there, he published an editorial in a prominent medical journal calling for the "return of (mental) asylums", the types of facilities known to have failed again and again. I was asked to debate him on this topic at a national mental health conference. This YouTube link will bring you to a video of the debate. You can decide who won!

OBAMA TASK FORCE ON PARITY CAN STOP INSURANCE DISCRIMINATION FOR MENTAL ILLNESS & ADDICTION

May 19, 2016
http://www.usnews.com/opinion/articles/2016-05-19/obamas-mental-health-task-force-can-stop-insurer-discrimination

LIS: A diverse group of impacted individuals and organizations testified before a "listening session," chaired by leaders from President Barack Obama's recently appointed Mental Health and Substance Use Disorder Parity Task Force, and hosted by the American Psychiatric Association. A federal mental health and addictions parity law, enacted in 2008, has yet to do its job of ensuring that those people affected with these conditions, and their families, receive proper care no different from the covered financial and treatment limits they would encounter with other chronic diseases such as diabetes, heart disease, Parkinson's and asthma. Present were champions of the initiative like former Rhode Island Democratic Congressional Representative Patrick Kennedy and former first lady Rosalynn Carter. People with mental and substance use disorders suffer the same discrimination as occurred with civil rights and HIV/AIDS. The task force I report on here is an Executive branch effort to end that discrimination.

DYING WITH YOUR RIGHTS ON: MENTAL ILLNESS, CIVIL RIGHTS AND SAVING LIVES

LIS: There was a time, 50 years ago, that psychiatrists and other physicians could involuntarily commit people to mental hospitals, where their freedoms were greatly compromised and treatments foisted upon them essentially without their permission. Since then the civil rights enforcement of people with mental illnesses has become exceptionally stringent, so that necessary actions to protect individuals from themselves and others have become very difficult to achieve. In this article, I detail examples of people "dying with their rights on" and point to solutions, many in place, which can save lives.

MENTAL ILLNESS

I am a psychiatrist who has treated patients for over 35 years, run all varieties of psychiatric services and worked in city and state government. But I still cannot bear to read or hear a story of a fatal outcome for a person with a serious mental illness who dies from neglect or some form of self-harm. I was especially distressed to read an article in The New Yorker (Rachel Aviv, May 30, 2011, Annals of Mental Health) called "God Knows Where I Am: What should happen when patients reject their diagnosis?" The article deeply troubled me because of the outcome for the person it profiled: Linda Bishop was found dead, presumably from starvation and hypothermia, in a home she had broken into in New Hampshire several months after she had a two-year psychiatric hospitalization. Her last journal notation was in January 2008, and her body was accidently discovered in May.

Neither Bishop's sister, a longtime advocate for her (who works in the justice system) whom a court years earlier declined to make Bishop's legal guardian, nor Bishop's daughter were informed of her condition during her extended stay in New Hampshire's state hospital—nor were they told when she was discharged. Instead, a fantasy relationship that Bishop had for years in her head, with no contact with the man, was her plan for support, even marriage, upon leaving the hospital.

The story of Linda Bishop's multiple psychiatric hospitalizations, her misdemeanor (non-violent) offenses and time in jail, her abandonment of her teenage daughter, her assertion that she was not mentally ill and her refusal to follow any treatment plan, the lack of evidence that she could care for herself, and the self-imposed distance from her family was all too familiar to me and my colleagues working in public mental health, even if the details of her situation may vary in some ways from others. Recognized experts (and longtime colleagues) Drs. Tom Gutheil and Paul Appelbaum in 1979 (!) aptly called this type of tragedy "rotting with their rights on."

Our laws stipulate that Bishop had to consent to provide information to her family, which she did not. Privacy violations would have been the consequence of the hospital contacting her family during the hospital stay or at the time of discharge. Bishop's "right" to live where (and how) she wanted derives from legal rulings that stipulate a person's right to live in what is called "the least restrictive setting."

The letter of the law had been met. And the patient died.

Arguments have been made on the polar extremes of this dilemma. On one side are patient rights advocates who are stalwart about privacy and self-determination. In fact, legal organizations are present to defend these rights in state hospitals throughout this country. Considerable legal rulings now protect individuals from involuntary hospitalization and involuntary treatment by requiring court action to achieve both, with the exception of emergency situations. On the other side are advocates calling for increasing commitments of people with serious mental illness, including outpatient commitment (and requiring that those committed take psychiatric medications for their disorders), and longer hospital stays.

Never having been one for extremes, except maybe when it came to my playing sports, I believe there are viable middle grounds—even if difficult to reach.

For example, nine years ago the first Mental Health Court was established in New York City, under the remarkable (and continued) leadership of Judge Matthew D'Emic. There are now seven such courts in NYC, about 25 in New York State and approximately 200 around the country (not counting drug and domestic violence courts). A mental health court accepts referrals from other courts where there appears to be a mental illness complicating the crime. Court mental health specialists evaluate the person for a mental illness, and if present, the defendant can plead guilty (in New York State) and be "sentenced" to court ordered treatment under the supervision of the judge; other states may divert the person from jail, have charges held in abeyance pending completion of the treatment program, or other procedures according to local statute. This form of supervised treatment is typically for a year (the maximum sentence for a misdemeanor). More recently, there are mental health courts working with felons where the court ordered treatment can go on for years.

For example, outpatient commitment already exists in almost every state (this has been the case in New York State for over 10 years, instituted after Kendra Webdale was pushed before an oncoming subway train by a man with a psychotic illness). The law, Kendra's Law, has been renewed twice, each time for five years. We don't need more outpatient commitment (though some state statutes warrant updating); we need more outpatient treatment that works.

Which brings me to my main point: outpatient mental health services in this country don't work very well, despite the dedicated people who work for them. The result is that early intervention and the provision of comprehensive, continuous, proven (evidence-based) treatments is being delivered to less than 20 percent (!) of people who need it. That means more than four out of five people are not getting what they need for their illness and recovery. Lack of good care coupled with lack of housing are the principal drivers for the clinical deterioration, chronic homelessness, use of jails and prisons as institutions to contain people with mental disorders, and suicidal and violent behaviors among those who are mentally ill. This country is in need of a mental health overhaul, as candidly portrayed in the President's New Freedom Commission on Mental Health (December 2002; disclosure: the Commission's chair was Michael Hogan, Ph.D., now Mental Health Commissioner for the state of New York, and my boss).

Mental health has treatments that work. It has mission-oriented professionals and provider organizations. But it lacks organization, accountability and financing that pays for what is accomplished rather than what is simply done. Sounds familiar? That's because mental health care is part of health care, where the same issues apply in capital letters.

As this country grinds its way to a more responsive, and hopefully affordable, health care system, what can be done now? For one, mental health clinics can be held to specific standards of care and their licenses made dependent on delivering those standards. Measurement-based care can be introduced (and required) where improvement from mental illness is tracked just like we track blood pressure, blood sugar and lipids. Incremental financing reforms can better support evidence-based practices as well as outreach and engagement of those hardest to reach and retain in care. People in recovery from mental illness (called peers or consumers) can be made a part of the public mental health system so they serve as navigators and trusted persons for those wary of mental health care. And no one stands a decent chance of getting better from a serious mental illness without safe and reliable housing with access to quality health and mental health services.

Indifference is cruel and costly. We can make a difference. People can have their rights and their lives—and their families, too. That's what health care, including mental health care, is really all about.

THE TRAGEDY OF MENTAL HEALTH LAW

The Wall Street Journal Op-Ed
January, 12, 2013, p. A13

LIS: In an almost full page Op-Ed in a Saturday Wall Street Journal I argued that the pendulum of mental health law has swung too far—in two areas, namely privacy and liberty. Privacy requirements now too often impede the provision or exchange of critical medical and mental health information from (and to) families and others who could be essential to a patient's or a community's wellbeing and safety. Liberty refers to the extraordinarily high bar that exists today to hospitalizing someone involuntarily or treating a person with a mental illness who is refusing care. The personal, family and social costs of these high requirements for privacy and safety have become too great to allow their enduring.

SCALES

PAY FOR HEALTH REFORM WITH AN ALCOHOL TAX

LIS: Americans like their beer, wine and spirits. Sales are good, even in bad times. Turns out that twenty percent of spirits consumed in America are by underage youth, which is illegal and associated with accidents, suicide and poor school performance. From a public health perspective we know that use (sales) of alcohol to underage youth is highly price sensitive, which is to say that the more a substance costs the less it is purchased. This controversial Op-Ed proposed raising taxes on alcoholic beverages (which are actually quite low and have not seen increases in a very long time) in order to reduce consumption, and its consequences, by our country's youth. I was unable to appear on FOX business news on this topic but my co-author did. But the *New York Post* (a right leaning tabloid) had a ½ page story calling me a "quack" for this idea, which I framed and have hanging proudly in my office.

DISCUSSION AND CRITICAL THINKING QUESTIONS

The Press (media) has been called the '4th Estate' of democracy, and especially refers to print journalism. Dating back to the French Revolution, the first three estates have been considered the clergy (first estate), the nobility (second estate), and "commoners" (third estate). Today the press has extraordinary power in a democracy, heightened by the 24 hour news cycle, social media and the presence of web based devices in about everyone's hand. I have offered above examples of some of my efforts to use the press for social change.

What do you think are the major social issues involving mental disorders? Involving substance use disorders?

Are you highly libertarian and hold that government should stay out of people's lives or do you hold to the importance of laws and regulations to help ensure the public health?

Do you think people with mental disorders should be able to "die with their rights on"?

What actually influences our health? Is it access to good health care, or other factors? Are we confounding "health care with health"?

Are people with mental disorders violent?

Are there public health approaches to reducing underage consumption of alcohol, and the health and safety consequences of this illegal activity? What are they? Do you 'buy' them?

IMAGE CREDITS

Fig 8.1: Copyright © Depositphotos/leolintang.
Fig 8.2: U.S. Department of Health & Human Services, "The Social Determinants of Health," http://www.cdc.gov/socialdeterminants/. Copyright in the Public Domain.
Fig 8.3: Copyright © Depositphotos/dgmata.
Fig 8.4: Copyright © Depositphotos/gabylya89.

CHAPTER 9

OPENING COMMENTS

This section has but one article, a book review I wrote after meeting a mother who lost her daughter to the complications of a medication prescribed for Borderline Personality Disorder. I include this review in this compilation because of how deeply troubling this condition can be, how often people with this condition are avoided by many clinicians, and because of the role a family can have in helping someone with this disorder, often despite their protestations.

REMNANTS OF A LIFE ON PAPER: A MOTHER AND DAUGHTER'S STRUGGLE WITH BORDERLINE PERSONALITY DISORDER

LIS: This book, a memoir, is the story of Pamela Tusiani and her family. We read about their labors and love for each other in alternating prose by Bea, the mother, and "remnants" from Pamela's journals, which she faithfully kept and are given to us in spare and thoughtful segments as time goes by. The book follows their story for 2.5 years, a nightmarish struggle from the time Pamela at age 20 became manifestly ill with this common mental disorder—about which we know far too little about its pathogenesis and even less about how to master its destructive symptoms and debilitating psychic confusion. Never did they lose hope. And even after this tragic outcome the family continues to devote itself to helping individuals and families impacted by mental illness.

If you are looking for reasons to believe in God, they abound in this book.

If you are looking for reasons not to believe in God, they abound in this book.

I knew the outcome of the Remnants of a Life on Paper, having heard it from the mother, Bea Tusiani, whom I met recently for the first time at a psychiatric meeting in NYC. Yet this book was still a page-turner of a memoir—written, compiled and told with utter candor and generosity by a mother who lost her 23-year-old daughter. We accompany, for 2.5 years, a family's nightmarish struggle from the time their 20-year-old child became acutely ill with a common mental disorder—about which we know far too little about its pathogenesis and even less about how to master its destructive symptoms and debilitating psychic confusion.

Personality disorders, by definition, are disturbances of character that begin in adolescence and form the ongoing basis of how a person feels, thinks and behaves. These disorders are not transient: They are enduring and exceedingly difficult to change. Borderline personality disorder (BPD) is one of these character disturbances: people affected show a myriad of often changing symptoms (which can make diagnosis difficult, at first) including intense mood swings; impulsivity leading to often horrific judgment and self-destructive behaviors; chaotic relationships driven by urgent needs for attachment, yet an inability to tolerate closeness and dread of abandonment; episodes of loss-of-reality testing (where psychotic symptoms transiently appear); profound difficulties maintaining a sense of identity (who am I?); and commensurate problems in tolerating living in one's own skin. Frequently, alcohol and drug use and abuse, and anorexia and bulimia accompany BPD and add to a person's turmoil and treatment challenges. Here is how Pamela Tusiani put it (p. 144):

> The demon nests inside me.
> When it wakes, I fall into a trance of violent paranoia.
> Blue and yellow pills line up at full attention.
> Tempted by distaste,
> My heart pumps with thick muddy rage.

BPD is twice as common as schizophrenia and bipolar illnesses (combined), with likely more than 10 million people in the USA impacted (2 to 6 percent of the adult population). Women are more frequently diagnosed with this condition, but they are not alone in experiencing it. BPD disproportionately represents psychiatric inpatient and outpatient statistics, perhaps because of how the internal turmoil of the condition generates external chaotic and destructive behaviors.

Pamela was the third child of native New Yorkers and an honors college student at Loyola College when she was first hospitalized at the Johns Hopkins Medical Center psychiatric unit in 1998. Experienced doctors then said she was depressed and that treatment would help her in a matter of weeks. But the depression was the tip of the iceberg, or maybe an indication of the hell brewing inside. She did not promptly recover. She left school, returned to NYC, had multiple hospital stays and 12 ECT treatments before the diagnosis of BPD was made. She was often suicidal, took overdoses of pills and cut herself frequently and deeply. After five months and five hospitalizations she seemed to be doing worse, not better.

Her parents, Bea and Mike, are impressively resourceful people. With their unrelenting support and advocacy Pamela was admitted to Austen Riggs, a long-term, open psychiatric treatment center that focuses on providing intensive psychotherapy. It is set on a small campus of residential buildings located in the semi-rural New England town of Stockbridge, Massachusetts. She spent 19 non-consecutive months there, as her parents paid out of pocket the tens of thousands of dollars it cost each month. Riggs proved that it "has more freedom than she can handle." (p. 94). The clinical leadership at Riggs said she had to leave and recommended (what evidently they believed) to be an accredited program for people with "dual diagnoses," i.e., psychiatric and substance-use disorders, in Malibu, California, called Road to Recovery. This program was equally financially demanding and 3,000 miles away from family and home.

Pamela's course at Road to Recovery was labile, with times of sobriety and rebuilding her life and times of falling into states of impulsivity and self-abuse. She developed seizures, which proved to be "psychogenic," meaning that it was her psychology, not her neurology that produced them. Such is the power of the mind.

People with BPD have limited responses to psychiatric medications, and many drugs (of a variety of classes) were tried on Pamela—but her depression, anxiety, distortions of reality and impulsivity prevailed. The side effects of these drugs, alone or in combination, can be unbearable, especially if benefits are minimal: weight increases, fatigue is constant, libido evaporates, concentration is very hard, and dizziness an ever-present threat. Over two years after her first episode of illness, her mother read about a medication called Parnate, a drug that I used a great deal until the serotonin drugs (like Prozac and Paxil) came along in the 1990s. Parnate is in the class of anti-depressants called monoamine oxidase inhibitors (as is Nardil), and has been shown to be helpful in "atypical depressions," the type of mood states that people with BPD can have. Pamela spoke with her prescribing psychiatrist affiliated with the California program about Parnate and she began to take it. That the medication, however, left her vulnerable to a known, serious adverse effect, to which she succumbed—likely unnecessarily so.

I believe all behaviors serve a purpose. They may not make sense at first, but they are "solutions" (p. 219) to severe psychic states that demand response or relief. Cutting is a good example, where the act can seem senseless but instead it quiets (transiently) emotional pain and self-loathing. Compulsive sexuality or drug intoxication also serve purposes, which are vital to understand if a person is to find other, less destructive, answers to their compelling distress. The long-term treatment of mental disorders (including BPD), when done well, involves helping a person understand their experience and find alternate methods of mastery. Pamela was well into her journey of recovery when a series of treatment program and medical errors conspired to kill her. The awful irony was that she did not take her life, but irresponsible, stigmatizing and poor residential and medical care did.

One of the moments, and there are many in the closing pages of this book, that gives me shame about how professionals and administrators do not meet their responsibilities, was in the Emergency Room at UCLA medical center. Pamela had been brought there after experiencing a known hypertensive drug reaction induced by eating certain types of cheese while taking Parnate. The reaction is characterized by very high blood pressure with confusion, headache and restlessness. But instead of those serious symptoms being recognized, her clinical state was attributed to her being a drug user, a "mental patient," and she was put on suicide watch. The result was that she did not receive the proper medical evaluation and care that might have spared her life. This is disturbingly common today, over 10 years later, as reported in medical reports of psychiatric patients being segregated and not getting proper attention for heart, lung or other problems that prompted their emergency visit. Many don't say they have a psychiatric condition to prevent this from happening.

Other moments that made me cringe were told with clarity and intelligence throughout the book.

Among the most disturbing are examples of demonizing parents of a person with a mental illness or blaming the victim (of rape, for example) because she has a psychiatric condition. Reading about what appears to have been a coverup of wrong doing in the California residential program was enraging for me. Imagine what that was like for her parents and siblings. Having been the medical director of McLean Hospital, a Harvard psychiatric teaching hospital, and a government official for more than 12 years, I believe everything depicted in this profound book is not only possible, but happens more than we want to think.

The story of Pamela and her family's labors and love for each other is told in alternating prose by Bea, the mother, and "remnants" from Pamela's journals, which she appears to have faithfully kept and are given to us in spare and thoughtful segments as time goes by. There are also vivid paintings and drawings by Pamela at various stages of her short life from the time she became acutely ill. These are emblematic of her demons as well as illustrative of her creative talents.

Paula Tusiani-Eng, another daughter in their family, is also listed as author. She was instrumental in the legal work and in giving the story its first-person voice. This book is a family affair—surely one way they have worked to recover and to help others similarly affected.

But I am most admiring of Bea. As has been said, no parent, no mother, should see a child die. And to lose a child who may have recovered is all the more agonizing. Bea Tusiani only tells us at the end of the book that she is a writer—though it is plain enough how powerful a writer she is as she lets the story, the events she chronicles, show us so much about her daughter, her family, and our flawed mental health and medical systems. What is also so inspiring about the book Bea Tusiani has given us, which is why I found hope (reason to believe), is how she gives us a front-row seat, so we witness the courage, love, determination and stamina of the Tusiani family. I am sure that Pamela would be proud to see how her pain, spirit and resilience—and that of her loved ones—have been so sensitively and cogently captured in these "remnants ... on paper."

DISCUSSION AND CRITICAL THINKING QUESTION

What do you know about Borderline Personality Disorder? What are its psychological and biological determinants? Do you think of it as a mental illness?

Why do so many clinicians eschew working with people with this condition?

What are the treatment approaches that can help, even if only partially?

How can families support a loved one with Borderline Personality Disorder, even when they are often in the angry cross-hairs of their loved one?

CHAPTER 10

OPENING COMMENTS

Levity, or humor, is not only entertaining; it can be highly instructive as well. Humor also can be helpful to people suffering from a variety of physical and mental disorders. Over the years, I have written only a few humor pieces, two of which I include here (though there is also an earlier in this volume *HuffPost* "interview" and a book—a parody, below). I hope they amuse you, evoke a smile from time to time, and perhaps deliver their lessons with a spoonful of sugar.

A FOWL FABLE

LIS: My wife and I were at dinner in a friend's home in rural France. The main course was a rooster, raised on their land and cooked to perfection. But what happens to the body of a male (rooster in this case) when it has been dominated by another male, when its role among the females (chickens) has been eliminated? And what is the message for the rest of us, male and female, when it comes to how we will lead our lives?

ROOSTERS

My wife and I recently had a holiday dinner at the home of friends living in rural south central France. It was a *repas extraordinaire* of six courses, complementary wines and with just about every item grown or raised by our hosts in their garden or livestock collection. They are hoteliers during the summer season and artisans when the tourists evaporate from the Aveyron, the least populated Département in France.

After appetizers, soup and salad with marinated salmon came the plat principal, an oven-baked fowl. It was a rooster, weighing in at 4.4 kilograms, which had been free-ranging on their property the day before. The hostess, an American who had lived in France many years, had delivered the bird back to its maker, and then baked it a honey brown. She treated us to its story as it cooled from the oven to be served at the proper temperature.

There had been two roosters and a dozen hens in a large pen to protect them from predators. But within the birds' haven the battle of the cocks had been decided early on. One rooster, with a plumage of burnt orange and thighs to beat the band, had quickly established his dominance. This rooster survived, at least for now. The second rooster had spent months cowering, hardly lifting its adorned head. If needed, for reasons not clear, it could be found in some remote recess of the sanctuary, seeking the same from its fellow male. Instead of mating with the hens and cock-a-doodling it ate voraciously, I suppose an alimentary substitute to satisfy its instinctual urges of sex and aggression. It was soon copiously plump and clearly not the keeper when it came to Darwinian considerations of the chicken species kept by our French friends.

Our hostess added, not at all sheepishly, that when preparing the bird she noticed that many of its glands had severely shrunken: dried out, in French. She thought some of these internal organs were what conferred masculinity on the rooster. Since I had no evidence, no samples to inspect, I imagined they were what distinguished males from females or delivered the adrenalin and cortisol needed for fight, not flight. This story could deter a man from enjoying this course but the rooster's fragrant aroma and soft sheen, from basting and baking with wild champignons, did not seem to prompt any hesitation in the four of our gender at the table.

The rooster was fantastic. His sacrifice was our culinary heaven. Only his bones were left after a couple of generous helpings taken by the festive diners.

The cheese followed, and then the desert and coffee. But no further mention of the doomed yet delicious bird. But I could not put the story or an image of desiccated innards to rest in my mind. We were delivered a story as much biblical as bird. To wit, witness what happens when we shrink from life, when we live in the shadow of another: not only is our being, our self-regard, diminished but we literally shrink inside, the substance of our literal being is also eaten away.

Tomorrow is another day, another chance for a feathered friend or member of our species. What will it be? Bounty for the reaper, be she a Frenchwoman or a figure more mythic? Or the one who raises its head high, who seizes the day, and burnishes life with zest outside and in? In the end, perhaps the message is don't be chicken.

THE HUFFINGTON POST

LES GRANDS HAMSTERS D'ALSACE

LIS: An adorable photo at the bottom of the front page of the New York Times caught my attention some years ago. It was of one member of a species of hamsters indigenous to eastern France. It seemed to me, while true (it was in the NYT!), the story also was a fable in disguise. I subsequently had occasion (a wedding) to travel to the region. Sitting in a Strasbourg café drinking coffee and eating ice cream on a warm afternoon this story came to mind. What message do you take from it?

HAMSTER

You might recall the scandalous behavior that led to the 18 million € ($25 million) in reparations ruled earlier this year by the European Union's highest court (The Court of Justice) to be paid by the government of France. No, it was not related to Dominique Strauss-Kahn (DSK). It was for the unconscionable treatment of a rare species of hamsters—les grands hamsters d'Alsace.

Page 1 of the *New York Times* (10 June 2011) featured a photo of an adorable and seemingly perplexed hamster and guided the reader to the story within. The population of this already endangered species had dwindled dramatically leaving them on the precipice of extinction. Why, you ask? The indifference of civilization is the answer: after hibernating for the winter, les grands hamsters awake ready to eat and procreate, in that order; but instead of finding fields of spring alfalfa and grass as they peer out of their winter burrows there are now autobahns and towering buildings. What fields are left were given over to corn as farmers saw greater profits from this crop, not considering for a moment that corn would yield nothing edible for the ravenous hamsters until late summer—if they had managed to escape fatality from passing high speed Peugeots and BMWs. Their libido stood little chance in the face of starvation, vehicular menace and urban sprawl.

Banding together with French nature conservationists, les grands hamsters retained lawyers and sued. They won big: eighteen million Euros is not hay.

Protected environments for the victims were established, hamster châteaux if you will, where they returned to fine dining and romance and have begun to repopulate the Alsatian countryside.

I recently had occasion to visit Alsace and while there I checked in on those impacted by this suit, including our furry, and now rich, hamster friends.

First I spoke with some farmers. While suitably contrite about the devastation they almost brought down upon the animal kingdom, they lamented the sudden emergence of a powerful farming cooperative for which many of them now worked. After receiving the rather large award from the government, the victorious legal team began buying land on behalf of their clients and taking control of regional crops through a hamster owned and operated agribusiness.

No more corn was its first mandate. Local farmers told me that their future may be as precarious as had been that of les grands hamsters.

Dusty from my time in the countryside I headed to local towns. I arranged appointments with a number of government officials who were eager to speak, but only under the condition of anonymity. They told me that the nouveau riche rodents were unbridled in the way they used their newly won power. One longstanding mayor reported his poll numbers plummeting and his political opponent, a prominent grand hamster, pulling ahead as election day approached. One Town Hall was being retrofitted with tiny tables and chairs to accommodate the rodent denizens of Alsace.

My trip ended with an audience before the leadership council of Grands Hamsters. I arrived anxious to get their side of the story. I was ushered into a huge salon where the floor was covered with straw and the tables bountiful with nuts and dried fruits flown in that day from North Africa. Some of their chiefs were puffing on cigars and the ladies wore handmade lace. Hamster pups were running wild everywhere I looked. Their abundance was a sight to behold.

I began by sympathizing with their plight, even if no longer apparent. I think I won their amitié. But they were no longer looking back, only ahead. They sought my counsel about leveraged buy-outs and genetically engineered alfalfa. They wanted to know about windmills and other forms of alternative energy. They even asked about PACs (political action committees). My questions about the plight of the farmers and the demise of the former ruling class of Alsatians were dismissed with a Darwinian scoff.

When they realized that as a psychiatrist and journalist, I had nothing tangible to offer they made quick work of me, though they did oblige a photo-op.

As I headed back to my hotel I thought about how all our destinies can precipitously change, especially in a market economy. I called my broker and asked if there were any futures to be bought in Grand Hamster enterprises.

He said he would look into it.

GORNISH HELFIN: NOTHING WILL HELP

LIS: Yiddish humor may not be well known but it can be universal in its ability to cut through matters and get to the heart of things. In this humor piece, I ask "when is it right to do nothing"? We start with a legendary (fabricated) story about the great Jewish actor, Mendel Kupietzky. That fable takes us to a prescription for care that just may be underutilized, captured so well by the Yiddish phrase Gornish Helfin (nothing will help). This is not cynicism or fatalism, this is perhaps a form of wisdom hidden in humor.

When is it the right time to not do something?

When, according to a report in the recently published *Diagnostic Manual of Mishegas* (DMOM), the great Jewish actor, Mendel Kupietzky, fell down in the middle of a Yiddish-language performance of King Lear. A doctor rushed to the stage and began examining him. A man in the balcony started yelling, "Give him an enema! … Give him an enema!" And when, a moment later, the doctor threw out his hands in a gesture of helplessness and announced that Mendel was dead—still the man from the balcony kept yelling "Give him an enema! … Give him an enema!" and would not stop despite pleas from other actors and members of the audience. Only when the theater manager appeared alongside the doctor and looked up at the man in the balcony and said, "He's dead, sir. An enema can't help. *Gornish Helfin. Gornish Helfin.* (Nothing will help.)" Only then did the man in the balcony remit but not without a final comment. "Give him an enema!" he cried one last time. "It can't hurt … "

But it can hurt. Sometimes doing something when someone else is trying to do something on his (or her) own or when a person may be ill (more likely attempted than when dead, as in this apocryphal

Yiddish story) can add insult to injury, or be an unwelcome intrusion or an unnecessary medical "procedure" when nothing is needed or called for.

The wisdom of *Gornish Helfin* is that sometimes we need to accept that it is better, at least for the moment, to do nothing since doing something will produce nothing of use, and may make matters worse. While some Yiddish scholars may insist that *Gornish Helfin* is fatalistic, that it means truly nothing can help, a more sanguine view is that sometimes doing nothing is a fine idea indeed.

Parents, in particular, want nothing more than to have their children free of pain and suffering. Happiness is even better. But pain and suffering, well, they need to go when it comes to our children, right? Yet, I recall as clear as day the time my son, then in his late adolescence, said, "I don't want you to try to fix this, only to listen."

As a psychiatrist, I have seen young adults with mental illness screw up their courage and tell their parents to let them try—even if they fail; they are saying that part of growing more independent is being able to bump your nose into the walls of everyday life. People of all ages with disabilities learn adaptation; how to live in the world despite their limitations, not by being protected but by learning to protect themselves.

Gornish Helfin is not indifference or callous disregard. It is recognizing when doing something will not help, at least not then, and could get in the way of a person standing on his or her own, or daring to try.

Gornish Helfin may, as well, offer a path out of the wildly expensive habits of many doctors and patients! *Gornish Helfin* might prove a means of encouraging more watchful waiting (as has been learned with prostate cancer). It could help dampen the false (and costly) promises suggested by a rash of new genetic and other biomarker tests as well as imaging studies for mental disorders that just are not ready for prime time (Biomarkers for depression: Promise or prime time?). It could prove an antidote to the prescribing zeal that has 10% of this country on antidepressants when there are many fine alternatives to pills, especially for conditions of mild to moderate severity.

Who knows? Maybe *Gornish Helfin* could spawn a movement of self-care—of better nutrition, exercise, stress management, yoga and meditation, proper sleep and moderate use of intoxicants—behaviors that actually could make a difference. Maybe it's not an enema that's needed but ways of purging our culture of its romance with everything medicinal when sometimes a stroll in the park, moments with a loved one, and tincture of time may prove to be the best medicine.

DISCUSSION AND CRITICAL THINKING QUESTIONS

Are you a fan of Jon Stewart, Stephen Colbert, Chris Rock, SNL (or others)? What is it about their delivery that captures your attention and gets under your skin? Why is humor such a powerful—and memorable—form of communication?

Have you ever come across Yiddish humor? Or just funny Jews?

What in the world is Gornish Helfin? Is it meritless drivel or maybe not?

MY (RELATED) BOOKS

OPENING COMMENTS

I have now written, including this volume, twelve books, some of the earlier ones through multiple editions. I have selected five for your information, which focus on mental and substance use problems, one a parody. They are:

—Improving Mental Health: Four Secrets in Plain Sight

—The Family Guide to Mental Health Care

—The Diagnostic Manual of Mishegas

—Treatment choices for alcoholism and substance abuse

—Psychoactive Drugs: How To Better The Pied Piper

Each is briefly described below, and of course this material complements and supplements the many individual articles described above—but none of them (except this volume) is a compilation or duplication of what I have published in articles and commentaries.

IMPROVING MENTAL HEALTH: FOUR SECRETS IN PLAIN SIGHT

American Psychiatric Association Publishing, 2017 (released in November 2016)

IMPROVING MENTAL HEALTH: FOUR SECRETS IN PLAIN SIGHT

THE FAMILY GUIDE TO MENTAL HEALTH CARE

Improving Mental Health: Four Secrets in Plain Sight is a short book, 109 pages including photos and images, is meant for professional, student and general audiences. The Foreword is written by Patrick Kennedy, who has suffered from bipolar disorder and substance use, who served 15 years in Congress and is the son of former Senator Ted Kennedy. The "secrets", which I stress are hidden in plain sight, are: 1) Behavior serves a purpose; 2) The power of attachment; 3) As a rule, less is more; and 4) Chronic stress is the enemy. Each is actionable by clinicians, families and patients, and in rather immediate ways. Siddhartha Mukherjee, MD, the Pulitzer Prize winner for The Emperor of All Maladies (and more recently The Gene) had this to say about this book:

"Sederer's thoughtful and provocative book could not be timelier. It arises out of a seemingly confusing moment in mental health and poses an immense creative challenge: to draw out the rules, or laws, that govern the psyche as it adapts to an ever-changing world. His "laws" or "secrets"—often counterintuitive, yet full of clinical utility—illuminate his profound understanding of patients and their particular predicaments. There's a powerful thread of wisdom that runs through Sederer's writing like a bright red line, reminding us that by identifying the driving tenets of clinical care we refresh and deepen our engagement with it in the future. I read this book in a single setting, and felt so much wiser at the end."

THE FAMILY GUIDE TO MENTAL HEALTH CARE

WW Norton, 2013

LIS: In this book I try to answer two of the most vexing questions that families have asked me, again and again, when they have a loved one with a mental illness. The first is a composite—how do I trust what I see, where do I turn and whom do I trust if I think my loved one has a mental illness? The second is how do I help my loved one get the treatment needed to recover when they adamantly refuse to do so. I offer examples, scripts for families to use, and Q & As. Common sense principles of good care are described to help families assess if the treatment offered is quality care. The "Faces" of mental illness, namely its categories of illnesses, are portrayed as a family member, not a clinician, would see them. Medications are summarized and recovery-oriented care made clear. The Appendices include: "virtual" visits (in text) to an emergency room, an inpatient unit, and an outpatient clinic; and a set of measurement instruments for detecting and monitoring mental disorders, which can be tracked in a way analogous to diabetes, hypertension, asthma and lipids. The Foreword is beautifully written by Glenn Close, whose sister has long-standing bipolar illness and her family has experienced generations of mood disorders.

THE DIAGNOSTIC MANUAL OF MISHEGAS

A Parody of the DSM5
Jay Neugeboren, Michael Friedman & Lloyd Sederer
Create Space, 2013

LIS: Mishegas is a loving term for craziness. With two friends, also Jewish New Yorkers, we decided to offer an alternative to the DSM5, which was due for release in May of 2013. Two weeks before the DSM5 was released we self-published this book—which was both a tiny fraction of pages and price compared to the actual DSM. Moreover, we offered an alternative nosology to the hundreds of DSM disorders, ours with a mere handful of conditions that are recognizable to everyone, including your friends, enemies, family and in-laws. The three categories of disorders we detail are 1) Nervous Conditions (like tsuris, spilkes, plotz and fartoots); 2) Cockamamy Conditions of Character (like schmuck, noodj, kvetch and yenta); and 3) Categories of Mishegas related to Food, Sex and Age (like alter kocker, mishugener eating disorders and dementia with benefits). This really short book, 74 pages and cheap (!), uses Yiddish phrases, anecdotes and jokes to describe the varieties of mishegas to which humans are prey. I was cautioned that this book could ruin my would-be career, but its levity carried the day and it has been widely distributed among psychiatrists and mental health clinicians. It is a great birthday, holiday or anniversary gift!

TREATMENT CHOICES FOR ALCOHOLISM AND SUBSTANCE ABUSE

Harvey B Milkman & Lloyd I Sederer (Editors)
Lexington Press, 1990

LIS: When I glance at this book today (26 years after its publication), an edited collection of writings by experts in substance use disorders, I am struck how timely it remains. Back then, addictions were very poorly understood, their treatments often disdained and those with them too often blamed and discriminated against. In this book, we aimed to help change those troubling societal views and reactions. The field has matured immensely since that time, especially with the sophistication of brain and cognitive neurosciences. I am proud to have been an early contributor, with my great friend and colleague Dr. Harvey Milkman, who has gone on to a career of distinction in this field, especially for youth.

PSYCHOACTIVE DRUGS: HOW TO BETTER THE PIED PIPER (*WORKING TITLE*)

For release in 2017

LIS: Every culture on the earth has used intoxicants, except for the Eskimos where the weather precluded their propagation. But when white men came they brought intoxicants, especially alcohol, and now there are no exceptions to the rule that human beings, over time and continents, will grow, manufacture, distribute and use intoxicants, drugs that change the way we feel, think and behave. I believe that drug use, abuse and dependence (legal and illicit) are among the principal societal issues of the 21st Century, along with climate change, immigration, poverty and social disparities, and terrorism. This book begins with the premise that drugs serve a purpose, which is why people use them and why they continue to endure. Efforts to control drug production and distribution ("the war on drugs") have failed miserably for hundreds of years. Efforts to exhort people to not use drugs by proclaiming their deleterious effects have been similarly ineffective. In this book, I focus both on why our policies have failed and what can be done now to make a difference—including prevention, alternatives, treatment and stigma.

DISCUSSION AND CRITICAL THINKING QUESTIONS

Mercifully, three of these books are fewer than 200 pages—one is a mere 109 pages and another a shocking 74 pages. Two of them have pictures! As a reader, I have come to appreciate short books, which can be read and not put into a pile of good intentions. My writing for the general public, amply illustrated in this volume, has taught me to be concise, clear and (hopefully) meaningful.

Several of the books described here are meant to be 'cross-over', namely they can be read by clinicians, students and the general public. I hope I have accomplished that goal.

The books themselves focus on mental and substance use disorders and families impacted by mental illness and what they can do. One is a parody of the DSM5.

Do you still read books? Non-fiction I mean?

Do you ever read non-fiction books because you want to, not because they assigned or references you must use? If so, which ones, especially in the areas of mental and substance use disorders?

What is the role of families in improving mental health care?

How does humor serve a purpose?

What lies ahead for our fields?

IMAGE CREDITS

Fig 10.1: Copyright © Depositphotos/jetFoto.

Fig 10.2: Copyright © Depositphotos/Martina_L.

Fig 10.3a: Dr. Lloyd I. Sederer, Improving Mental Health: Four Secrets in Plain Sight. Copyright © 2017 by American Psychiatric Association Publishing. Reprinted with permission.

Fig 10.3b: Lloyd I. Sederer, The Family Guide to Mental Health Care. Copyright © 2013 by W. W. Norton & Company, Inc. Reprinted with permission.

CHAPTER 11

OPENING COMMENTS

The written word is now frequently eclipsed by audio and video commentaries. In this section, I offer three samples of my work: two on video and one on audio. The topics include violence, the family and mental illness, and mental health and cinema.

HOW TO STOP THE MENTALLY ILL FROM BECOMING VIOLENT

Mental Health Channel TV
March 7, 2016
http://www.mentalhealthchannel.tv/episode/how-to-stop-the-mentally-ill-from-becoming-violent

LIS: In this four minute, professionally filmed video I discuss four prototypes of individuals at risk for violence: psychopaths, those who are aggrieved and enraged, people in the throes of acute psychosis (especially paranoid in nature), and people actively using alcohol and drugs. The aims of the video are to diminish the inaccurate view that people with mental illness are more dangerous and to illustrate how an understanding of the four prototypes informs intervention to reduce the risk of violence (to individuals, families and communities).

PSYCHIATRY AND CINEMA PODCAST—(*AUDIO ONLY*)

Lancet Psychiatry May 24, 2016
(My 4 minutes cinema section begins at the 42 minute 39 second mark)
http://www.thelancet.com/pb/assets/raw/Lancet/stories/audio/lanpsy/2016/24may.mp3

LIS: Cinema has been a major medium for the expression of human drives and character, for portraying our foibles and heroic moments, and for telling stories that span the vast range of human emotions and events. In the short audio podcast I discuss psychiatry and the cinema with Dr. Niall Boyce, Editor-in-Chief of the journal Lancet Psychiatry. As they say, have a listen.

WHEN MENTAL ILLNESS ENTERS THE FAMILY—TEDX

January 6, 2015
https://www.youtube.com/watch?v=NRO0-JXuFMY

LIS: TED talks have become legendary around the world. In my TEDx 17 minute video I discuss mental illness and the family, which is directly related to my book The Family Guide to Mental Health Care. I illustrate how various conditions—like psychosis, depression and chronic medical illnesses with their frequent co-occurring mental disorders—can appear to family members. I discuss how a family can tell if a loved one is suffering a mental illness. And I offer four principal messages (and solutions) for families affected: don't go it alone; don't get into fights; learn the rules of how mental health care works and how to bend those rules; and appreciate that you are on more of a marathon than a sprint. If you find this TED talk valuable please provide the link to others who might want and need the information it contains.

FAMILIES

DISCUSSION AND CRITICAL THINKING QUESTIONS

Are people with mental illnesses more likely than the general population to harm others (not just themselves)? If so, when?

What behavioral condition is associated with the greatest risk of violence towards others?

What can we do to reduce the risk of family and community violence?

What films stand out for you as portraying compelling human dramas? What films stand out for you that illustrate mental and substance use disorders, their challenge and how recovery can occur?

Families are often the first to see the emergence of a mental or substance use disorder. How can they have confidence in what they are seeing? Where can they turn? Whom can they trust? How do they keep hope alive?

What are some principal strategies families can use to effectively cope with mental illness in a loved one, and do what they want more than anything—namely to help their family member recover and have a life of relationships, work, dignity and contribution?

IMAGE CREDITS

Fig 11.1: Copyright © Depositphotos/leremy.

www.ingramcontent.com/pod-product-compliance
Lightning Source LLC
LaVergne TN
LVHW062126200926
848484LV00007B/1775
* 9 7 8 1 5 1 6 5 5 6 9 3 9 *